Exploring Strateg... ...ge

The Exploring Corporate Strategy Series

Exploring Corporate Strategy (Text and Cases)
Gerry Johnson and Kevan Scholes

Exploring Corporate Strategy (Text only)
Gerry Johnson and Kevan Scholes

Exploring Public Sector Strategy
Gerry Johnson and Kevan Scholes

Exploring Strategic Change
Julia Balogun and Veronica Hope Hailey

Exploring Techniques of Analysis and Evaluation in Strategic Management
Véronique Ambrosini (editor)

Exploring Strategic Financial Management
Tony Grundy

Exploring Strategic Change

Second Edition

Julia Balogun
Cass Business School, City University

Veronica Hope Hailey
Cranfield School of Management

Series editors

Gerry Johnson
University of Strathclyde
Graduate School of Business

Kevan Scholes
Sheffield Hallam University

 Prentice Hall
FINANCIAL TIMES

An imprint of **Pearson Education**
Harlow, England • London • New York • Boston • San Francisco • Toronto
Sydney • Tokyo • Singapore • Hong Kong • Seoul • Taipei • New Delhi
Cape Town • Madrid • Mexico City • Amsterdam • Munich • Paris • Milan

Pearson Education Limited
Edinburgh Gate
Harlow
Essex CM20 2JE
England

and Associated Companies throughout the world

Visit us on the World Wide Web at:
www.pearsoned.co.uk

First published under the Prentice Hall imprint in 1999
Second edition published 2004

ISBN 0 273 68327 6

British Library Cataloguing-in-Publication Data
A catalogue record for this book is available from the British Library

10 9 8 7 6 5 4 3 2
08 07 06 05 04

Typeset in Garamond 10/13 pt by 3
Printed and bound by Ashford Colour Press Ltd., Gosport

The publisher's policy is to use paper manufactured from sustainable forests.

Contents

List of figures and tables

Figures

Tables

List of illustrations

Preface

Exploring Corporate Strategy by Gerry Johnson and Kevan Scholes is now established as the leading text in its field in Europe and beyond with worldwide sales exceeding 300,000. It is a text provided for students and practising managers which aims to develop their conceptual understanding of why and how organisations of many different types develop and change their strategies. It does so within a practical context whilst drawing on best strategic management practice as researchers, writers and practitioners understand it.

With so many managers and students now familiar with *Exploring Corporate Strategy*, we have responded to the requests for material which takes the themes and concepts of strategic management further in a way which is not possible within the confines of a broad textbook on the subject. This series of short, practical books therefore builds on the basic framework of *Exploring Corporate Strategy*.

Exploring Corporate Strategy has always placed great emphasis on the processes of strategic management and the problems and importance of managing strategic change. *Exploring Strategic Change* is the third of the books to be published in this series. The others are *Exploring Techniques of Analysis and Evaluation in Strategic Management* edited by Véronique Ambrosini and *Exploring Strategic Financial Management* by Tony Grundy. All of these books are developed under the editorial guidance of Gerry Johnson and Kevan Scholes and have the following aims:

- to provide further depth on aspects of strategic management which should already be familiar to readers of *Exploring Corporate Strategy*;
- to do this in a practical and applied way whilst drawing on best practice from researchers, writers and practitioners.

This second edition of *Exploring Strategic Change* addresses four main themes:

- that the task of managing change is context-specific and therefore an understanding of the organisation's change context is essential;
- that analysing the change context allows change agents to make design choices on the basis of 'best fit' for the organisation;
- that once the change process has been designed the next task is to both design and manage the transition;
- that there are established levers and mechanisms for managing transition.

The first half of the book focuses on the design of the change process and the analysis of the change context within an organisation. Chapter 2 addresses the subject of design choices by providing a menu of design options which are discussed within six overall groupings: change paths, change styles, change startpoints, change targets, change levers, and change roles. These are discussed at this point in the book in order that the reader is aware of the range of choices that are available to a change agent. Chapters 3 and 4 then examine the importance of determining contextual fit when selecting appropriate design choices. A diagnostic framework, the change kaleidoscope, is presented in Chapter 3 which helps to identify the key contextual features in an organisation. The kaleidoscope features are: time, scope, preservation, diversity, capability, capacity, readiness and power. Not only does analysis of these features allow the reader to make appropriate design choices, it prevents these features becoming barriers to change during the transition process itself. Both Chapters 3 and 4 illustrate how different features impact on different design choices. Chapter 4 demonstrates this through the use of three case studies of companies experiencing change and transition.

The second half of the book examines the transition process in depth. Chapter 5 explains the role of visioning in change and also introduces the idea of different stages of transition: mobilise, move and sustain. Both Chapters 5 and 6 examine the various mechanisms that can be used for each stage of transition. These include both symbolic levers and human resource management processes. The importance of fit with context is highlighted throughout the discussion on change levers and interventions. Chapter 7 explores the actual management of the transition process and puts forward ideas for evaluating change. The first and final chapters use a change flow chart to pull together the various stages of the change process that are detailed within all the chapters. These chapters also put forward thoughts about the centrality of change capability as a competence for managers in the twenty-first century and the personal skills and attributes required of effective change agents. The appendices contain information on various diagnostic tools that can be used by a change agent when analysing organisational contexts and making change judgements.

This second edition also includes two teaching cases with assignment questions. At the end of the first half of the book there is a case on Glaxo Wellcome, the international pharmaceuticals company, which decribes the changes undertaken by Glaxo throughout the 1990s, that then set the scene for the merger with SmithKlineBeecham to create Glaxo SmithKline. This case can be used to deepen understanding of how to apply the change kaleidoscope in practice, and how to develop change judgement. The second case at the end of the second half of the book describes the transformation undertaken by Clerical Medical Investment Group, part of the Halifax Bank of Scotland (HBOS) banking group. This case can be used to develop a more complete understanding of the issues involved in designing the transition process.

The website at **www.booksites.net/balogun** provides resource material to aid in lecture and seminar preparation.

Julia Balogun and Veronica Hope Hailey

Acknowledgements

Many people have helped us in the process of writing the second edition of this book. We would like to thank Nardine Collier, Margaret Hamer, Dee Donovan, Paul Arnold, Sarah Bolton and Milla Shah for their diligent, sympathetic and thorough approach in helping us to construct a manuscript fit for the publishers. Thanks also go to the many MBA students at Cranfield School of Management, both full-time and part-time, who offered important comments on the ideas presented in this book. Finally, we must thank our patient and understanding families who put up with our long periods at the computer. This book is dedicated to all of them.

To Paul, Guy and Annys
and John, Helen, Mary, Frances, Joanna and Sarah Jane

Publisher's acknowledgements

We are grateful to the following for permission to reproduce copyright material:

Illustration 2.4 'A new angle to an old story', Simon Caulkin, *The Observer*, 10 March 2002, p. 8, © Simon Caulkin; Illustration 2.5 'The UNHCR case – achieving the impossible', I. Sayers and G. Johnson (1999) in *Exploring Corporate Strategy*, 5th edition, Prentice Hall, by permission of Pearson Education Limited; Illustration 2.6 from 'KPMG (A): strategic change in the 1990s', Gerry Johnson (1999) in *Exploring Corporate Strategy*, 5th edition, Financial Times Prentice Hall; Illustration 2.7 'Voyage of discovery', G. Golzen, *People Management*, 11 January 2001, pp. 32–6, © Godfrey Golzen; Figures 2.6, A1.1 and A1.2 and Illustration 5.1 from G. Johnson, 'Mapping and re-mapping organisational culture' in V. Ambrosini, G. Johnson and K. Scholes (1998) *Exploring Techniques of Analysis and Evaluation in Strategic Management*, Prentice Hall, by permission of Pearson Education Limited; Illustration 3.4 from Littlefield, D. 'The big push', *People Management*, 6 July 2000, pp. 38–40; Illustration 3.5 'Canon: hard to copy' from *The Economist*, 2 November 2002, p. 79, © The Economist Newspaper Limited, London; Illustration 4.2 from Gratton, L., Hope Hailey, V., Stiles, P. and Truss, C. (1999) *Strategic Human Resource Management* reproduced by permission of Oxford University Press; Figure 5.4 from Adams, J., Hayes, J. and Hopson, C. (1976) *Transition: Understanding and Managing Personal Change*, reproduced by permission of Martin Robertson & Company. Illustrations 5.2 and 5.3 from Roger Stuart (1995) 'Experiencing organisational change: triggers, processes and outcomes of change journeys', *Personnel Review*, 24(2); Illustration 5.5 from 'Real change dealer', David Littlefield, *People Management*, 29 July 1999, © David Littlefield; Illustration 5.6 from D. Riordan, 'Working through trouble at mill', *The Sunday Star-Times* (Auckland), 4 May 1997; Illustration 5.7 Vas, A., 'Top management skills in a context of endemic organisational change: the case of Belgacom', *Journal of General Management*, 27 January 2001, pp. 71–89; Illustration 5.9 and Figure A3.1 reprinted from *International Journal of Project Management*, Vol. 16(1), Tony Grundy, 'Strategy implementation and project management', pp. 34–50, Copyright 1998, with permission from Elsevier Science; Figure 5.6 from *Organizational Transitions: Managing Complex Change* by Beckhard/Harris, © Reprinted by permission of Pearson Education, Inc., Upper Saddle River, NJ; Figure 6.4 reprinted with permission of Academy of Management, P.O. Box 3020, Briar Cliff Manor, NY 10510–8020. R.H. Lengel and R.L. Daft, 'The selection of communication media as an effective skill' (1988), *Academy of Management Executive*, vol. 2, no. 3, Exhibit 2, p. 227, reproduced by permission of the publisher via

Copyright Clearance Center, Inc.; Table 6.1 from G. Johnson and K. Scholes (1999) *Exploring Corporate Strategy*, 5th edition, Prentice Hall, by permission of Pearson Education Limited; Illustration 6.3 from Brooks, I. (1996) 'Leadership of a cultural change process', *Leadership and Organization Development Journal,* 17(5), pp. 31-7; Illustration 6.4 from Veronica Hope Hailey (2001) 'Breaking the mould? Innovation as a strategy for corporate renewal' in *International Journal of Human Resource Management*, Vol 12(7), pp. 1126-40, by permission of Taylor & Francis Ltd, website: http://www.tandf.co.uk; Figure 6.5 from 'Communicating change', Bill Quirke, McGraw-Hill Publishing Company, 1995, p. 119, Copyright Bill Quirke, Synopsis Communication Consulting, 113 Farringdon Road, London, EC1R 3BX; Illustration 7.2 from Noeleen Doherty (1997) 'Downsizing in Tysons Ltd' in S. Tyson (ed.) *The Practice of Human Resource Management,* London: Pitman Publishing by permission of Pearson Education Limited; Figure 7.4 from Balogun, J. (2003) 'From blaming the middle to harnessing its potential: creating change intermediaries', *British Journal of Management*, 14(1), pp. 69-84, © Blackwell Publishing; and Sophie Bindloss, Clerical Medical Investment Group, for Case 2.

We are grateful to the Financial Times Limited for permission to reprint the following material:

Illustration 2.1 'Multiple skills in a tough market', © *Financial Times*, 8 March 2002, Illustration 3.1 'Tough talk at the Boston tea party', © *Financial Times*, 2 May 2002, Illustration 3.2 'Motorola answers a wake-up call', © *Financial Times*, 24 October 2002, Illustration 3.6 'A new arrangement for a trou ed orchestra', © *Financial Times*, 31 October 2002, and Illustration 3.7 'The battle is over - the struggle begins', © *Financial Times*, 1 May 2002.

While every effort has been made to trace the owners of copyright material, in a few cases this has proved impossible and we take this opportunity to offer our apologies to any copyright holders whose rights we may have unwittingly infringed.

1

Exploring strategic change: an introduction

1.1 INTRODUCTION

For many years now it has been said that the pace of change experienced by organisations and those who work in them is getting greater. Change has become a way of life, in part because organisations are experiencing many different types of change. As industries consolidate, there are increasing numbers of mergers and acquisitions. The pressures on organisations to compete in a more global arena are leading to different competitive pressures and more strategic alliances. Rapid technological change is forcing organisations to adopt new technologies and change the way they both work and interface with their suppliers and customers. There has also been a series of management fads over the last two decades such as culture change programmes, total quality management, and business process re-engineering. In addition, many organisations need to change their strategy just to remain competitive. Yet the sad fact is that the success rate for most of the change programmes launched within organisations is poor. Figures quoted vary, but many commentators put the failure rate at around 70 per cent.

As a result, change management is becoming a highly sought-after managerial competence. It is increasingly recognised that implementation skills are required throughout the organisation, and not just within the senior management ranks. Large organisations, in particular, need to rely on their middle managers to push through, and in many cases lead, change initiatives. Change management is part of the generic managerial toolkit. This book aims to help managers and students alike to understand more about change management and to extend their competence in this area, by building on the concepts presented in its sister text, *Exploring Corporate Strategy* by Gerry Johnson and Kevan Scholes. We start where most other strategic texts end – with frameworks that can help managers put their strategic plans into practice.

Exploring Corporate Strategy and *Exploring Strategic Change* share compatible perspectives on change. *Exploring Corporate Strategy* presents three views of the process of strategic management. One view is that strategy can, and indeed should be, designed. As such, strategy is the outcome of careful, objective analysis and planning by top management, and is implemented down through the organisation. The second view is that strategic management is not so much about formal planning, but more of a negotiated process, subject to both managerial and cultural influences. Organisations can, and some would argue inevitably do, become captives of their own cultural heritage. The collective experience of the individuals within an organisation, and their taken-for-granted assumptions about their organisation, and their competitors, customers and marketplace, lead to strategies which are adaptations of the past. From this perspective change is about breaking out of the strategic inertia that has accumulated from previous years of success and is embedded within the organisation's culture. The third view emphasises how new ideas can originate from within organisations due to the diversity of the individuals within, and how these new ideas can lead to the emergence of new strategies. This suggests that the potential for organisational change and renewal is a struggle between this diversity and cultural inertia. The role of the proactive manager is to find ways of ensuring that the outcome is positive change rather than damaging inertia.

In *Exploring Strategic Change,* at one level we view change management as a task that requires the explicit development of clear plans. However, we also take organisational culture to be of central importance. A cultural perspective on organisations provides insight into barriers to change, and how these barriers can be overcome. We draw on this perspective in this text to help managers understand the complexity of the change task they are undertaking, and the range of interventions that need to be deployed to help effect change. We emphasise that change is about people – changing people and the way they behave – which requires more than a plan and some changes to organisational structures and systems. As a result, change often requires significant investment in terms of managerial time and energy, as well as financial investment. This text also emphasises the complexity of change implementation. Successful change requires the development of a context-sensitive approach. There are no formulae or ready-made prescriptions that can be rolled out. This is the key message of this book – the need for context sensitivity. We present a framework, the change kaleidoscope, which can be used to help achieve this.

The text is aimed at both business students and practising managers. However, throughout the book, reference is made to the *change agent.* We use this term for the person responsible for 'making the change happen' in any organisation. Many different people can fulfil this role. In some organisations it may be the Chief Executive, in others the Human Resources Director, or even a selected team of people, who have responsibility for managing the change process.

There are two main sections to the book: the first section, Chapters 2 to 4, explores the role of context in developing appropriate approaches to change; the second section, Chapters 5 to 7, examines how to turn the chosen change approach into a reality and make change actually happen. However, in this introduction we start by explaining some of the assumptions underpinning this text. Consideration is given to:

- The nature of organisational change and the philosophy behind this text.
- The need to develop a change approach which is suitable for the organisation's specific context.
- The managerial and personal skills required by successful change agents.
- The difference between the design of recipe driven or formulaic approaches to implementation and more context-specific approaches.

The chapter concludes with a flow chart that explains the structure and content of the book.

1.2 THE NATURE OF ORGANISATIONAL CHANGE

There are two schools of thought about how change occurs in organisations. The first sees change as continuous, with organisations transforming on an on-going basis to keep pace with their changing environment.[1] The second sees change as a process of punctuated equilibrium.[2] (See Figure 1.1.)

From this latter perspective, periods of adaptative and convergent change are interspersed by shorter periods of revolutionary change. Convergent change is adaptation within the existing way of doing things – it leads to extension and continuity of the past, whereas revolutionary change is a simultaneous change in the

Figure 1.1 A punctuated equilibrium model of change

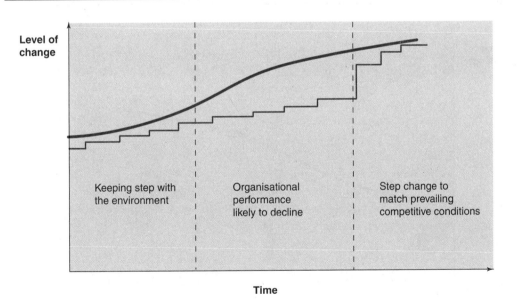

strategy, structure, systems and culture of an organisation leading to a radically different way of operating. Convergent adaptation through time leads to considerable inertia and resistance to new ways of doing things, which means that revolutionary change is likely to be reactive and forced by an impending crisis. An organisation becomes a victim of its own success as past ways of competing become embedded and taken for granted. A good example of this pattern of change has been seen at the British retailer, Marks and Spencer (M&S), over recent years. M&S had a particular way of doing things. It offered customers a selective range of quality merchandise at reasonable prices under the St Michael brand, focusing on classic wearable basics and essentials rather than fashions. It worked with British suppliers to ensure quality control. Specialist buyers operated (on the assumption that they knew what M&S customers wanted) from a central buying office which then allocated goods to stores. Central policies on store layout and management were followed to ensure consistency of image and standards. Since the stores had no changing rooms, M&S provided a no-quibble refund on all items purchased. Credit cards were not accepted – only the M&S store card. This formula worked for years, until changes in the retail industry in the 1990s rendered it uncompetitive forcing change upon M&S from 1998 onwards.[3]

Proponents of the more continuous models of change argue that it is possible to transform an organisation incrementally through time, leading to the same outcome as revolutionary change, but in a less dramatic fashion. Models of continu-

| Figure 1.2 | A continuous model of change |

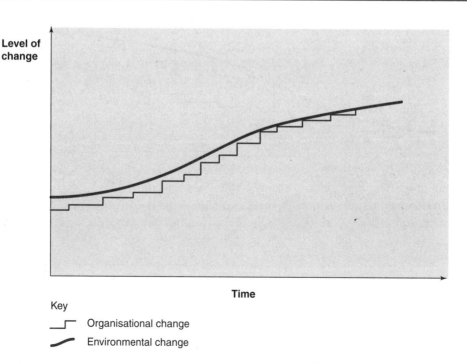

Key

⌐ Organisational change

╱ Environmental change

ous change argue for a higher and more consistent level of on-going change. (See Figure 1.2.)

In reality, there is little empirical evidence to support either view. Both these models of change could be right, but apply to different types of organisations, and maybe different stages of an organisation's life-cycle.[4] More continuous change models may be appropriate for organisations operating in industries where the pace of change in the competitive environment and new technologies is rapid, such as hi-tech industries, where constant organisational change is necessary for survival. However, it is not clear what form continuous transformation takes. It may be that on-going change occurs, but only around certain organisational features, such as products and structure. Other aspects may remain more static. Punctuated equilibrium models are more likely to apply to industries where changes to the competitive conditions occur less frequently and it is possible to remain competitive for a period of time without making any significant changes to the way an organisation operates.

In this book we are most concerned with organisations undertaking a step change, either in a proactive manner in recognition of the need for pre-emptive change given potential threats that may arise in the future, or in a reactive manner in response to an immediate need, such as a direct competitive threat. We are concerned with intentional, planned change: change circumstances in which the leaders of an organisation (or maybe even a division or a department) have examined their strategic position and deliberately formulated a new strategy which requires the organisation, and the people within it, to operate differently in some way. This could be, for example, a decision to enter a new market with existing products, requiring minimal changes within the organisation. Alternatively, it could involve a radical shift in strategy, and therefore the structures, systems and culture of the organisation. For example, in 1999 Hewlett-Packard split into two and launched a separate company called Agilent Technologies, composed of old HP businesses such as Test and Measurement and Semiconductor Products. The businesses within Agilent had to be reorganised to establish an independent operation. The transformation objectives also included a cultural shift. The aim was to bring forward the existing HP values, and introduce new values of speed, focus and accountability. Meanwhile, the streamlined HP, under the leadership of Carly Fiorino, has also been undergoing transformation, involving reorganisation, new systems and processes, and culture change. More recently the company has merged with Compaq, requiring more changes to integrate the two organisations.

Our position is that despite the rhetoric frequently heard today about the need for organisations to be more flexible, and to be capable of reinventing themselves through on-going continuous and emergent change, there are still many organisations who, for a variety of reasons, such as new forms of competition, find themselves in the situation where they need to undertake a step change in their strategy, like HP and Agilent. Both authors frequently encounter such organisations in the course of their work. However, such step change does not have to occur in a revolutionary manner. It can take many different forms. We discuss this in Chapter 2. Furthermore, this does not mean we believe that more continuous models of change are not viable. Indeed, the incremental change processes advocated by some continuous models of change can occur on a planned basis. In addition, the end goal of a planned change process may be to create a more flexible 'learning organisation' capable of on-going adaptation and self-reinvention. However, the change practices embedded within models of continuous change and learning are different. We briefly review these in the final chapter.

In addition, we view change as an on-going process. In today's more dynamic competitive environment, no organisation can stand still. As we have already stressed, change cannot be reduced to prescriptive recipes and neat linear processes. The content of change (what is actually changed), and the process or the way change is implemented, needs to be determined by the context of change, both the internal organisational context which includes the culture, capabilities, resources and politics of an organisation, and the broader external competitive context.[5] The changes made will in turn alter the context, leading to a different set of change needs (see Figure 1.3).

Finally, as we have already stressed, when we talk about 'organisations' changing, what we really mean is that people must change. Of course buildings, technology and products can all be changed, but if an organisation is to really change, then the people within that organisation also need to change the way they behave. This makes managing and achieving change a challenging undertaking for any manager. One extension of this line of argument is that the nature of organisations and organisational change is so complex that it is virtually impossible to manage change. Whilst we accept that people are unpredictable and can react to change in many different ways, we take the view that the process of change can

Figure 1.3 **Change as a process through time**

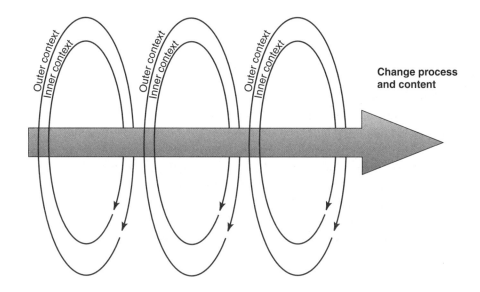

be facilitated if not controlled. Furthermore, we believe that the management of change is a competence that can be developed by practitioners, as well as being an exciting area for research. In this book we aim to give practitioners practical advice they can implement within their workplace. At the same time, we aim to add some new concepts to the broad range of academic literature on the management of change.

1.3 CONTEXT-SPECIFIC CHANGE

This book, unlike other texts, does not advocate 'one best way to change'. Change needs to be *context-specific*. In other words, the design and management of any change process should be dependent on the specific situation or context of each organisation. It is dangerous to apply change formulae that worked in one context directly into another.[6] Description should not be turned into prescription. All too often the lessons obtained from a few case studies of organisational change, by researchers, consultants or practitioners, are turned into best practice. Cases can be very important for illustrating what is possible. However, a limited number of cases, particularly when repeatedly cited, may imply that the formula that works for these organisations is generally applicable[7] when this is not the case. This is particularly true when the cases represent certain contexts, such as companies starting afresh at greenfield sites, or high-technology companies.

An alternative is to develop a contingency approach in which different contextual configurations are associated with a particular set of change design choices. Again, this is something this book avoids. To be feasible, such an approach typically requires a focus on a limited set of implementation options and a restricted range of contextual features.[8] For change agents this means that instead of identifying 'best practice' solutions or 'recipes', they need to start looking for 'best questions'. Even exhortations from 'best practice' models that sound like common sense, for example, 'you must get senior management support before attempting to manage change', may not be generally applicable. If the senior management are themselves major blocks to the implementation of change, the change agent may need to start with some other intervention and hope to gain senior support later on in the change process. Yet how can this be determined without analysing the context of each organisation? This book argues, therefore, that the internal and external context of the organisation should be examined as the starting point to determine the appropriate change process. Change agents should not automatically refer to best practice solutions or contingency approaches without understanding the applicability of these models to their context and what is feasible and what is not. However, understanding an organisation's change context requires the change agent to develop certain managerial and personal skills. These are discussed next.

1.4 MANAGERIAL SKILLS FOR THE CHANGE AGENT – ANALYSIS, JUDGEMENT AND ACTION

Change agents need to develop their *analytical, judgmental* and *implementation* skills. All three of these are important. Without analysis the temptation is to draw upon readymade change recipes; without judgement, after contextual analysis, change agents can miss the most critical aspect of the change context; and without action, the process can remain a planning exercise which never tackles the reality of change within the organisation.

Therefore, change agents need to possess *analytical* abilities, rather than to know the '10 best ways to run a change programme'. They need to be able to dig deep into an organisation, to understand its culture and the motivations of its staff, to develop a full and holistic picture of the organisation concerned. This is discussed in Chapter 3.

However, equally, the practitioner needs to be wary of 'paralysis by analysis'. It is easy to become overwhelmed by a detailed analysis. An additional skill is being able to *judge* which are the most critical features of the context. To give a medical analogy, a doctor giving a patient an examination following an accident might reveal that the patient has cracked ribs, but also lymphatic cancer. The ribs can be treated immediately, but clearly the most critical condition, requiring longer-term and more intensive care, is the cancer. Similarly, the change agent has to prioritise or weight the organisational features he or she uncovers in terms of how critical they are to the change process. The key skill for a change agent is to be able to recognise what is critical in the particular change context. This idea is examined further in Chapter 4 through a series of change case studies.

Finally, a change agent needs to develop the ability to manage the *implementation* of change. Management is practice not just analysis – it is about making things happen. Two key aspects of implementation that have to be addressed are which interventions to make in a change situation, and in what order to apply them. The change agent may recognise that a reward system must be changed within an organisation along with changes to production systems and job roles and responsibilities. Yet to avoid confusing the employees with too many simultaneous change initiatives, the agent has to decide which initiative should be carried out first and which one can wait until later. Choosing and sequencing change interventions are discussed in Chapters 5 and 6 of this book.

1.5 PERSONAL COMPETENCIES FOR THE CHANGE AGENT – SELF-AWARENESS

In addition to the managerial skills of judgement, analysis and action, change agents also need to possess *self-awareness*. This is not the only competence – others, such as the ability to deal with complexity, and to be good at influencing those around them to sell change, are widely recognised change agent competencies. Yet *self-awareness*, the capacity to understand one's own prejudices, preferences and experience, is equally important. Individuals view organisations in fundamentally different ways. Without realising it, change agents often allow their personal philosophy to influence the change approach and interventions they choose. As a result, they may give limited consideration, if any, to the actual change context and its needs. Change agents should be driven by the needs of the organisation, rather than by their own perceptions or prejudices of what has constituted 'good' change management in the past. It may also be easier for change agents to understand, and if necessary argue against, other people's prejudices or biases if they are armed with a certain degree of self-awareness.

A simple way to illustrate our point is to look at an individual's subjective/objective orientation. We often make the following distinctions between subjective and objective:

- *Objective*: rational, logical, analytical, facts, data, hard, quantitative.
- *Subjective*: intuitive, experience, moral, feelings, emotions, soft, qualitative.

Objective assessments are seen as hard and measurable. Decisions are made on the basis of tangible facts and figures. Subjective assessments are seen to be based on something less tangible, more intuitive than data driven.

Illustration 1.1

change in action

An objective versus a subjective world view

An objective perspective

'Organisations are physical and tangible. Things are done according to rules and regulations which are written down . . . there is something tangible and measurable about organisations . . . I'm very tool oriented . . . my inclination is to state very clearly what the objective is, to chart the process and assume that others working with me have sufficient rationality to see it similarly to myself.'

A subjective perspective

'Organisations should not be thought of as physical entities which can be controlled and modelled . . . An organisation is a social entity, something that is socially constructed by the people within it. I see an organisation in terms of its meaning systems rather than its physical aspects . . . This concept of organisation does have implications for the way I view change. For a start we have to be careful not to impose an objective mindset on what we see as an organisation and assume it is something we can control . . . An organisation includes peoples' attitudes and views, and for change to occur these have to change too. This is not to say that if you force people to change their behaviour by imposing new control systems and ways of behaving on them, they will not also change their attitudes. But you have no guarantee that they will change their attitudes in the way you want or anticipated, you cannot control the type of meaning change that occurs . . . If you take my view of organisations to an extreme, it in fact suggests you cannot control or manage change at all. As such all you can do is to facilitate change.'

Managers with a preference for either objectivity or subjectivity might describe organisations and their approach to change in a similar way to the respondents in Illustration 1.1. A manager taking an objective view of organisations may conceive of change in terms of reconstruction not necessarily perceiving a need to tackle underlying beliefs and assumptions. This sort of change agent may feel more comfortable with a directive change approach which involves little participation: they may not see a need to understand a wide variety of views at different levels of the organisation.

In contrast, managers with a more subjective orientation may rely on a more participative approach, which allows for greater involvement from all levels of the organisation. Such managers are more likely to assume that any change approach will need to allow for the existence of differing perspectives within the organisation, and will therefore want to work hard at fostering consensus. There is likely to be a greater emphasis on softer interventions such as communication.

Whilst subjective and objective perspectives are not opposite ends of a spectrum, for any change agent, an awareness of which perspective predominates within their own mind will make them aware of how they will view change. Their perspective must not become a prejudice or a formula. If an organisation is not in crisis and there is little readiness for change, a more objective manager should not automatically dismiss the option of extensive communication to generate some degree of readiness, even if it is not his or her preferred way of working. Likewise, if an organisation is in real crisis, a more subjective manager may have to accept that there is insufficient time for extensive consultation with all staff members, however much it goes against their personal philosophy.

1.6 THE TRANSITION STATE: DESIGNING CONTEXT-SENSITIVE APPROACHES TO CHANGE

There are many different ways of conceiving of the overall change process. Some use more colourful language than others, such as 'awakening', 'mobilising' and 'institutionalising'.[7] However, it is commonly accepted that during change it is necessary to consider three states – the current, the future and the transition.[9] (See Figure 1.4.)

Essential inputs to the diagnosis of the current organisational state are an understanding of the organisation's competitive position and the need for change, and an understanding of the internal organisational context. It is also necessary to develop some sort of vision of the desired future organisational state. The transition state, the process of changing the organisation from what it is now into the desired future organisation, can only be designed once the current organisational state is understood, and the desired future organisational state has been specified, at least in outline. Since we are assuming that readers of this text already have an understanding of how to diagnose the current organisational state, and how to develop an outline of the desired future state from, for example, *Exploring Corporate Strategy*, our main concern here is the transition state.

Figure 1.4   **Change as three states**

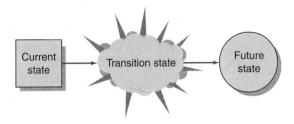

The transition state, the process of actually making the desired changes happen, often receives less attention than it merits. Implementation is conceived of in terms of the up-front planning for change, with scant attention to managing the transition process itself. Yet the transition state is not like either the current or future states. It is not possible to move from the current to the future state overnight. It might be possible to redeploy and relocate people in terms of named job roles and locations over a weekend, but to change the behaviour of those people, and particularly to change the organisation's shared beliefs, will take much longer. Specific attention is required to both the design and management of the transition state.

Typically lengthy consideration is given to the why and what of strategy development. The internal and external *context* of the organisation is analysed in order to gain an understanding of *why* change is necessary and the current state. In addition the strategists decide on the *content* of change – *what* actually has to change and the nature of the future state. However, what many change agents do at this stage (see Figure 1.5) is to turn to a number of existing change solutions – possibly the sorts of solutions suggested by Figure 1.6. They then derive the design of the change process from these predetermined change formulae often,

Figure 1.5   **A formulaic approach to change design**

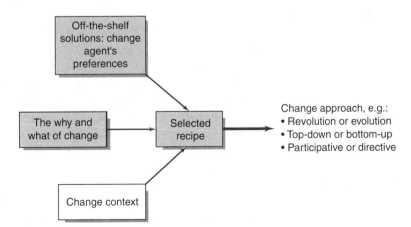

Figure 1.6	Source of existing change approaches

Change agents can choose from a range of existing formulaic approaches to change:

- The past experience of the change agent within previous organisations ('In XKX Tea Manufacturers we did it this way and it worked really well')

- Previous experiences of change within the organisation ('Well in 1998 we had to change to launch a new division and the way we did it then was like this – it worked really well')

- Organisational consultants ('Buy our proven approach to change. Twenty other companies have followed our 10-point plan and it has worked for them!')

- Books or articles on change ('Follow the rules for change set out in this book and you will achieve organisational breakthrough and beat the competition!')

- Dominant CEOs or other senior directors ('Bruce – I'm delegating the design of the whole of the change process to you. You have complete autonomy but I'd like to see it done this way! Change always happens when you follow these procedures – trust me . . .')

unfortunately, selecting a solution that is not appropriate to the current organisation's change context, although it might suit their personal preferences. As we stress above, this is not to denigrate the value of past experience or previous learning. However, the past must also be analysed with reference to the current context. A change agent needs to ask themselves questions such as 'Why did that work well for that organisation at that point in time?' 'What are the differences between that organisation's context then, and this organisation now?' and 'How might that affect the approach to change?'

A context-sensitive approach to change sees the stages in the design process as shown in Figure 1.7. As above, the *why* and *what* of change is analysed. The change agent then carries out an *analysis* of the *change context*, which examines the organisational features pertinent to the change situation. These include aspects such as the scope of change required, the time frame, the power of the change agent to effect change, the diversity within the workforce and the capability for change within the organisation.

Using the contextual analysis, the change agent *judges* which are the most *critical* features of the current change situation. For example, in some organisations the existence of strong professional groups may create diversity among the workforce. Professionals, such as hospital consultants, will often identify more readily with the values and aims of their professional association rather than with their employing organisation. It would be difficult to design a successful change process within a hospital without taking this into account. In organisations which employ few professionals this feature may not be so critical. Finally the change agent considers the appropriate *design choices*. Information derived from the contextual analysis will start to make some design options seem unworkable and

| **Figure 1.7** | **A context-sensitive approach to change design** |

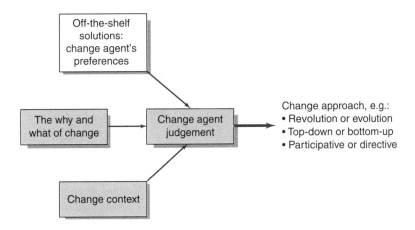

others either possible or essential. For instance, if the organisation has only a small amount of money to invest in change, some of the more expensive, educative styles of change, using expensive management development options, may not be feasible.

This text uses a diagnostic framework, the *change kaleidoscope*, shown in Figure 1.8, to help with this process. The kaleidoscope contains an outer ring concerned with the organisational strategic context, a middle ring concerned with the features of the change context, and an inner ring which contains the menu of design choices open to change agents:

● The *organisational strategic change context* refers to the broader strategic analysis conducted to determine why the organisation should change and what it should change to. This analysis is the focus of *Exploring Corporate Strategy*.

● The *change contextual features* are aspects of the organisation to do with its culture, competences and current situation, which change agents should consider before selecting the change approach. These features can be extracted from the broader organisational strategic context, and can be used by change agents to help determine the appropriateness of any change approach for a particular context. It is these features that are examined as part of the contextual analysis and they are explored in depth in Chapter 3.

● The *design choices* are the range of options a change agent needs to choose from when selecting an appropriate change approach. For example, what type of change path is best here? Do we need to do something radical and fast? Or would it be more effective in the long term if it were a staged change process, planned over time? Where should the change start point be? Should the change be organised so that it cascades down from the senior management, or would it be better if it was piloted on the edges of the organisation first? This range of choices is explored in detail in Chapter 2.

Figure 1.8   **The change kaleidoscope**

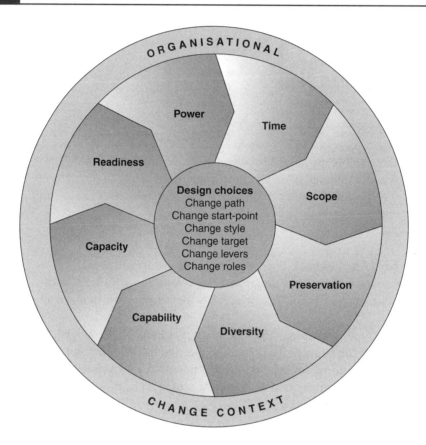

As explained above, the contextual features in the change kaleidoscope do not carry equal weight in all organisations – some will be more important than others in different organisational change contexts. This is why the diagnostic framework is called a kaleidoscope as its configurations of features will constantly shift according to the organisation being analysed. The kaleidoscope for an organisation will also change through time in response to earlier change interventions put in place. It is not static. The aspect of judging the relative criticality of organisational features is examined in more depth in Chapter 4.

1.7 THE TRANSITION STATE: DESIGN AND MANAGEMENT

Once the change agent has selected a change approach, this is not the end of the story. One of the key managerial skills is *action*. The change agent now has to design the change interventions or levers that will deliver the selected approach, and also manage the process of implementation.

The issues that need to be considered in *designing the transition* fall out of the design choices made. For instance, as a result of the design choice phase it may have been decided to focus on realigning employee behaviours as a means of achieving change. In order to achieve that behavioural change, the change agent will need to deploy a series of levers and mechanisms, such as new reward systems and training. However, the identification of the primary levers and mechanisms is only the beginning. If the new reward system is to be effective, other things may need to be changed, such as the appraisal mechanism. Existing practices that could obstruct the new required behaviours also need to be identified and removed. As pointed out above, there are also issues about timing. Are new rewards and training to be introduced simultaneously, or are new rewards introduced to reinforce the training? There are also likely to be many other changes which have to be scheduled. All these different interventions need to be sequenced during the transition along with other change interventions such as communication of the need for change, and the form of the changes. Effecting transitions is therefore a complex business.

Chapter 5 addresses this issue. It introduces the idea that transitions have three phases, *mobilise, move and sustain*, and considers the various activities that are necessary to take an organisation through all three phases. It also explains how any organisational change process is underpinned by the personal transitions of individuals within that organisation. Chapters 6 and 7 discuss transition management techniques such as communication and resistance management that can make transition through the change process more effective for the organisation and more acceptable to employees.

1.8 PUTTING THE JIGSAW TOGETHER – A CHANGE FLOW CHART

For change to be successful, managers charged with the responsibility of managing this activity need to address the complexities of both context and process. However, the very complexity can be offputting. Figure 1.9 presents a flow chart of the steps this text is advocating to inject some clarity into the process. It shows which questions have to be addressed at different stages of the change process.

Stages 1 and 2 are addressed within strategy texts such as *Exploring Corporate Strategy*, although this text will revisit the development of the desired current and future states in more detail in Chapter 5. Stage 3, analysing the change context and identifying the critical change features, are presented via a fuller account of the *change kaleidoscope* in Chapters 3 and 4. Stage 4, determining the design choices, follows on from stage 3, but this text discusses the design choices in Chapter 2, before the contextual features are described, since it is easier to appreciate how the contextual features impact on the design choices once the range of design choices is understood. Chapters 5 and 6 consider stage 5, the design of the transition, by exploring the different stages of transition, the use of

---

Figure 1.9   **The change flow chart**

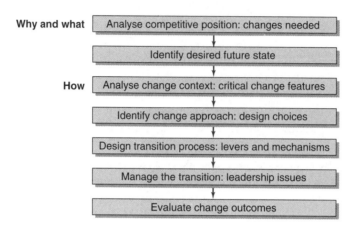

different change levers and mechanisms and the overriding importance of appropriate communication at all stages. Chapter 7 discusses how to manage and monitor the success of the change process and resourcing issues for the transition.

1.9 SUMMARY

This opening chapter has established the links that exist between this book and its sister text *Exploring Corporate Strategy*. It has also introduced the role of the *change agent*. In particular the chapter has introduced several central concepts that underpin the philosophy of the whole book:

- The view that change can be facilitated if not controlled.
- That all change design must be context-specific, which requires change agents to possess managerial skills of analysis, judgement and implementation; and personal competencies such as self-awareness.
- The difference between formulaic and context-specific approaches to change implementation.
- Transition as a stage in change which demands that attention is given to both its design and management
- A general change flow chart, which identifies different decision-making points in the strategic change process and sets out the overall way this text recommends a change agent should approach the management of strategic change.

These central concepts underpin the rest of the chapters of the book.

Exploring Strategic Change aims to provide an intelligent guide to managing change in today's complex organisational environments. It is hoped that readers will gain worthwhile insight into the challenging subject of change.

REFERENCES

1. For a discussion of how organisations undertake continuous change, see Brown, S.L. and Eisenhardt, K.M. (1998) *Competing on the Edge: Strategy as Structured Chaos*, Boston, MA: Harvard Business School.

2. This model of change is explained in more detail in several articles and books. See Romanelli, E. and Tushman, M.L. (1994) 'Organizational transformation as punctuated equilibrium: an empirical test', *Academy of Management Journal*, 37 (5), pp. 1141–66; Tushman, M.L. and Romanelli, E. (1985) 'Organizational evolution: a metamorphosis model of convergence and reorientation', in Cummings, L. and Staw, B. (eds) *Research in Organizational Behavior 7*, Greenwich, CT: JAI Press; Miller, D. and Friesen, P.H. (1984) *Organizations: A Quantum View*. Englewood Cliffs, NJ: Prentice Hall.

3. Collier, N. (2002) 'Marks and Spencer', in *Exploring Corporate Strategy*, 6th edn, Johnson, G. and Scholes, K. Harlow: Financial Times Prentice Hall.

4. A good review of the competing perspectives can be found in Burnes, B. (2000) *Managing Change: A Strategic Approach to Organisational Dynamics*, 3rd edn, Harlow: Prentice Hall.

5. For a fuller discussion of a processual view of change see Pettigrew, A. and Whipp, R. (1991) *Managing Change for Competitive Success*, Oxford: Blackwell.

6. Many authors make this point. See, for example, Pettigrew, A. and Whipp, R. (reference 5 above); Jick, T. (1993) *Managing Change: Cases and concepts*, Homewood, IL: Richard D. Irwin; Nadler, D.A. and Tushman, M.L. (1989) 'Organizational frame bending: principles for managing reorientation', *The Academy of Management Executive*, 3, pp. 194–204.

7. This is discussed by Guest, D. (1990) 'Human resource management and the American dream', *Journal of Management Studies*, 27 (2), pp. 377–97. Also see Storey, J. (ed.) (1989) *New Perspectives on Human Resource Management*, London: Routledge; and Blyton, P. and Turnbull, P. (eds) (1992) *Reassessing Human Resource Management*, London: Sage.

8. For a fuller review of change contingency models and the dangers of applying our learning from these models prescriptively, see Hope Hailey, V. and Balogun, J. (2002) 'Devising context sensitive approaches to change: the example of Glaxo Wellcome', *Long Range Planning*, 35 (2), pp. 153–17.

9. The concept of change as three states, the present, the future and the transition, is advanced by Beckhard, R. and Harris, R.T. (1987) *Organizational Transitions: Managing Complex Change,* 2nd edn, Reading, MA: Addison-Wesley.

WORK ASSIGNMENTS

1.1   There are a number of books by renowned senior executives who have managed change in their organisations. Why should these texts be read with caution?

1.2   Suggest why different approaches to change management might be appropriate in different organisations, such as a university, a high street bank, or a multinational enterprise.

1.3   Explore your personal perspectives on organisations (drawing on Illustration 1.1) and how this might limit the way you approach change.

1.4   What are the factors that can cause change initiatives to fail in organisations?

Understanding implementation choices: the options to consider

2.1 INTRODUCTION

Chapter 1 introduces the concept of the change kaleidoscope (see Figure 2.1). It shows that a change agent faces a bewildering array of implementation decisions – the *design choices* – that need to be made about how change should be

Figure 2.1 The change kaleidoscope

implemented within his or her particular context. This chapter explains these different design choices, and the options within each choice. The design choices from the change kaleidoscope are explained in detail before the contextual features. It is then simpler to explain the contextual features and how they link to the choices that need to be made.

The change kaleidoscope separates the array of choices that need to be made on any implementation approach into six categories, within which there are a range of alternatives. The six categories are:

- *Change path*: the type of change to be undertaken in terms of the nature of the change and the desired end result. This category is referred to as *change path* as distinct from *change type,* as in some circumstances it is necessary to undertake an enabling phase of change before it is possible to undertake the actual changes required.

- *Change start-point*: where the change is initiated and developed, which could be summarised simplistically as top-down or bottom-up, but there are other choices.

- *Change style*: the management style of the implementation, such as highly collaborative or more directive.

- *Change target*: the target of the change interventions, in terms of people's attitudes and values, behaviours or outputs.

- *Change levers*: the range of levers and interventions to be deployed across four subsystems – technical, political, cultural and interpersonal.

- *Change roles*: who is to take responsibility for leading and implementing the changes.

This chapter discusses each one of these choices in more detail.

2.2 CHANGE PATH

There are four main types of change illustrated in Figure 2.2. These four types are defined in terms of two dimensions – the *end result of change*, and the *nature of change.* The *end result* is about the extent of change desired. Change can involve a *transformation* of the organisation or a *realignment. Transformation* is '*change which cannot be handled within the existing paradigm and organisational routines; it entails a change in the taken-for-granted assumptions and "the way of doing things around here"*'.[1] It is a fundamental change within the organisation requiring a shift in strategy, structures, systems, processes and culture.

In the UK, many of the old nationalised industries have undergone transformational change as part of the privatisation process. From BT, to the electricity companies, the water companies, and more recently, British Rail, the culture of these organisations at privatisation could be described as job for life, bureaucratic,

Figure 2.2	Types of change

End result

	Transformation	Realignment
Incremental	**Evolution**	**Adaptation**
Big bang	**Revolution**	**Reconstruction**

Nature

risk averse, and command and control with an emphasis on hierarchy. Responsibilities were often unclear with little accountability at most levels of the organisation. Costs, and other criteria of commercial performance such as profit margins and customer service, were not the main priority. The focus was often more about technical expertise and engineering. Most of these organisations have subsequently tried to develop more of a private sector culture with greater commercial awareness and a focus on customer service.

Realignment is a change to the way of doing things that does not involve a fundamental reappraisal of the central assumptions and beliefs within the organisation, although it may still involve substantial change like a major restructuring. BHP, an international resources company based in Australia, underwent a major realignment as part of a turnaround in 1999. Eight business units were consolidated into three, the hierarchy was reduced with old managers leaving and new ones joining. Managerial rewards were refocused on performance-based compensation. The labour force was greatly reduced, offices were closed, operations streamlined, manufacturing capacity reduced, and projects lacking future potential were eliminated. In addition, non-core and underperforming businesses were sold off. The company was then in a position to build and develop the remaining healthy assets.[2]

The *nature of change* is the way change is implemented, either in an all-at-once, big-bang fashion over a period of, say, a year to 18 months, or in a more step-by-step, stage-by-stage incremental fashion. These two dimensions, the *end result of change* and the *nature of change,* provide the explanation for the four different types of change.

2.2.1 Adaptation and reconstruction

Adaptation is non-paradigmatic change implemented slowly through staged initiatives. Toyota's CCC21 programme, Construction of Cost Competitiveness for the twenty-first century, started in 2001, is an example of this. The aim is to reduce costs by $8 billion by 2005 through a review of design, manufacturing, procurement and fixed costs.[3] *Reconstruction* is also non-paradigmatic change undertaken to realign the way the organisation operates, but in a more dramatic and faster manner. A large number of change attempts fit within this latter category, for example many turnarounds, such as the one at BHP. Many such change programmes are significant and important to the longer-term survival of an organisation. The new CEO of Philips, Gerard Kleisterlee, in the first nine months of his appointment up to March 2002, replaced the senior executives of the consumer-electronics US division (a key market for Philips), outsourced production of mobile phone handsets and VCRs, closed factories (268 to 160), sold low-growth businesses, reduced overheads, and cut costs through use of shared services between divisions.[4]

Reconstructions such as that at BHP do sometimes lead into more fundamental transformational changes. Furthermore, the divide between a realignment and a transformation is not always clear-cut. The changes carried out as part of the turnaround may have already challenged old assumptions and beliefs, such as a job for life. Similarly, the reconstruction at Philips is set to move into adaptation, if not transformation, as Kleisterlee intends to sell more businesses between March 2002 and the end of 2003, and ultimately transform the bureaucratic infrastructure of Philips to create a high-growth, high-tech company. As the history of Philips shows, however, not all such initiatives do lead to longer-term change. This is the third major restructuring since 1990 for Philips.

2.2.2 Evolution

Evolution is transformational change implemented gradually through different stages and interrelated initiatives. It is likely to be planned, proactive transformation, in which change is undertaken by managers in response to their anticipation of the need for future change. Illustration 2.1 describes the evolution undertaken at the Birmingham factory of Yuasa, the Japanese battery maker. It shows how a series of integrated and phased initiatives and investments have created a shift from a traditional manufacturing culture to one of flexibility and customer focus.

Evolution can also occur in a more emergent manner. The British supermarket, Tesco, is a good example of this. In the 1970s and early 1980s, Tesco was primarily seen as serving the lower end of the market, with stores offering little to differentiate the chain from other supermarkets. Over the last 20 years Tesco has transformed itself into the leading supermarket in the UK, overtaking the

Illustration 2.1

change in action

Evolutionary change at Yuasa

Yuasa is a large Japanese battery manufacturer. It took full control of a battery-making factory in Birmingham in 1997, following a decade-long joint venture with Lucas. It is their only European manufacturing plant, and it has existed since 1920. The site produces 2 million batteries per year, of which about 90 per cent is for the UK market. Tough competition from rivals and pressures from the large car makers means that companies like Yuasa receive 30 per cent less for their products than they did in the early 1990s. Competition requires increased quality and manufacturing efficiencies.

As a result, starting in 1998, Yuasa initiated a change programme that over the last four years has seen productivity increase by 40–60 per cent, an increase in flexibility of production workers who now do a range of jobs rather than concentrating on a particular assembly or machine task, and an increase in the skills capability of the workers. There are now only 320 workers at the factory, compared with 550 in 1997. The changes have also required the employees to move to a service culture in which employees are willing to take on a series of tasks to meet customer requirements, as opposed to working only on fixed jobs. If a carmaker wants to change the specification of a particular batch of batteries, the factory needs to be able to react quickly which in turn requires workforce versatility. The plant should be profitable for the first time this year since 1997 on a turnover likely to be in the region of £30 million.

These changes have been achieved through a series of initiatives. There has been a £30 million investment programme, including investment in new machinery to speed up the production process. The production processes have been reorganised and bottlenecks have been removed, partly through increasing the flexibility of the workers. However, the skills of the workers at the factory have also been increased to aid their flexibility. Training has been important here. Some has been provided by the Japanese owners, based on working practices established in their other plants. Plant workers also received lessons on improving efficiency from external groups who specialise in this area. A key part of the change process was to examine the detail of problems in the production process, to enable the identification of design faults and new items of manufacturing equipment required, and therefore eliminate wasted effort and improve delivery times.

Source: Adapted from Marsh, P., 'Multiple skills in a tough market: UK Manufacturing Part I', *Financial Times,* 8 March 2002, Inside Track, p. 14.

historical holder of this position, Sainsbury's, in the mid-1990s. This has been achieved through a series of integrated initiatives, with each change programme building on previous changes.

2.2.3 Revolution

Revolution is fundamental, transformational change, such as that at Yuasa, but it occurs via simultaneous initiatives on many fronts, and often in a relatively short space of time, such as 18 months. It is more likely to be a forced, reactive trans-formation, due to the changing competitive conditions the organisation is facing. If an organisation's strategy is still rooted in the ways of behaving that used to lead to success, then the mismatch between the strategy being pursued and the new strategies required may be great enough to force fundamental change in a short space of time if the organisation is to survive. An organisation may also need to implement planned transformation rapidly, because, for example, the organis-ation sees the need to pre-empt fast competitor response, or realises that rapid change is necessary to meet changing customer needs.

A point we will return to later in the book, however, is that it takes people time to change their behaviours, and even longer to change their attitudes and the way they think about their work. Furthermore, not all individuals within an organis-ation are willing or able to undertake the changes asked of them. Change is there-fore facilitated by a process of natural attrition as those less able or willing to change leave the organisation and are replaced by individuals more suited to the new ways of working required. This can take some time.

Therefore, one way to achieve a revolution may be to literally (physically) change the people. Degussa, a German conglomerate with businesses in heavy chemicals, healthcare and precious metals, has done just this. Following a rapid series of mergers and acquisitions and a simultaneous divestment programme for non-core businesses between 2001 and 2002, it now focuses on speciality chem-icals.[5] For most businesses, such a radical approach is simply not feasible. Therefore, in reality, revolutions are few and far between. Most transformational change occurs through a more evolutionary path. Furthermore, whilst it may be possible to transform a corporate portfolio in terms of the range of businesses within a short space of time, longer-term change is often needed to weld the new corporate entities into a cohesive whole. Degussa now needs to deliver promised cost savings and synergy effects, and if it wants to lead the consolidation in the speciality chemicals industry, it may need to merge with a competitor.

2.2.4 Paths of change

The last point of the above paragraph is important as it emphasises why this book talks about *paths of change* as opposed to *types of change*. The eventual aim of an organisation may be to achieve transformation, possibly as part of a turnaround, but the organisation may lack the resources, skills, or finance to achieve transformation. Alternatively, the organisation may be in a crisis, and losing a lot of money, and therefore need to stop the rot before any longer-term change can be undertaken.

The most popular change path is that of reconstruction followed by evolution (see Figure 2.3). In fact, it has almost become a change formula in its own right. To give a well-known and popular example first, British Airways in the 1980s effected a much-cited cultural transformation. However, this followed a financial turnaround of the airline. Between 1981 to 1982 the workforce was downsized dramatically, particularly at the middle management level; unprofitable routes were closed; cargo-only services halted; offices, administration and staff clubs were cut; and a pay freeze imposed. Only then, in autumn 1982, was attention turned to changing the airline's image and culture from an organisation more about transportation to one focused on customer service.[6] The reconstruction resolved the financial crisis at the airline, and provided both money and time for the culture change. It also shook staff out of their complacency and into a recognition of the need for change. Similarly, change was initiated at GE, the international corporation with businesses as diverse as financial services, aircraft engines and lighting, by Jack Welch in the early 1980s, following his appointment as CEO. However, up until 1988, the changes had arguably been mainly to do with a series of reconstructions, such as altering the GE infrastructure, working practices and political make-up.[7] Come 1988, Welch realised that if a genuine transformation was to be achieved, culture change was also needed, and this couldn't be delivered through restructuring. Therefore, the initial change effort was extended into the 1990s by a 10-year programme called 'Work-Out'. However, it would not have been possible to put Work-Out in place had GE not already been through a change which left it in a financially sound position and created a desire and commitment for change. Another example is the transformation undertaken at Asda, the UK supermarket group, by Archie Norman in the 1990s, although here the evolution was set off almost in parallel with the reconstruction.[8] In 1991, when Norman took over as chief executive, ASDA was close to bankruptcy. Financial stability was restored within Norman's first year by restructuring, which involved selling off non-related parts of the business, property and some stores, and staff reductions. However, Norman wanted to create an involvement, customer-focused culture rather than a control culture and a wide range of additional initiatives were put in place to help this over the next few years.

Figure 2.3   Paths of change

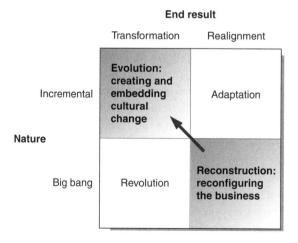

Illustration 2.2

change in action

Change at Scottish and Newcastle

Scottish & Newcastle (S&N) is one of Europe's largest brewers. Its Pubs and Restaurants arm, S&N Retail, has undergone significant change between 2000 and 2002. Starting in 2000, S&N Retail integrated the Greenalls pub estate and sold 900 smaller pubs, to focus on the top end of the market. Three clear businesses were created – restaurants and accommodation, branded pubs and unbranded pubs. Authority was pushed downwards in these new businesses. S&N Retail now employs 30,000 people instead of 40,000. In addition, to bring the different businesses together, S&N Retail moved to a new head office in Northampton in September, 2001. The old head office was a 1960s building known as the 'Kremlin'. A silo mentality existed, with adversarial attitudes between the functions spread over three sites. Staff characterised the management style as command-and-control, with little recognition of effort and poor communication. The move was used to provide impetus for a culture change programme, and was given a holiday theme, 'The Big Move'. The design of the new office incorporated feedback from a staff attitude survey.

A cross-functional working group, the 'Culture Club', was responsible for the planning of the move. Initially people were taken on pre-move 'tours' of the new head office on double-decker buses. They were invited on the 'tour' by postcards, and actors acted as tour guides. On each department's first morning in the new building, they went through a Great Start change management workshop. These workshops were for all levels of staff, including the chairman. In the new head office a 'passport' scheme was introduced to encourage people to talk to each other. Everyone was given a passport and encouraged to get it stamped by each department which meant going to see that department, and spend time there. External consultants were used to help create a different language for the new office. Two types of people were created drawing on the Winnie the Pooh stories – 'Tiggers' (bouncy, excited, positive) and 'Eeyores' (nothing is right). These labels were used to describe individuals' attitudes when they seemed either negative or positive. There was also a 'commitment wall' on which everybody had to write a brick saying what they would do differently. Staff have 'Kit-Kat breaks' so they can go back and reflect on their commitments and put Tigger and Eeyore stickers on people's bricks. They have to take them off afterwards to prevent the upset this might cause to others. There are also other initiatives aimed at ensuring head office staff become more knowledgeable of customer needs and business pressures outside of head office. Everybody has to work out in the pubs for 4 days of the year – from clerks to the board.

The aim of all of this has been to create a head office culture where people talk to each other, solve problems, help each other out and have a service attitude, but also to inject some fun into a hard-working business.

Source: Adapted from Maitland, A., 'Winnie the Pooh and beer too', *Financial Times*, 6 March 2002, p. 15; and Tyler, E. (21 March 2002) 'Going places', *People Management*, pp. 44–5.

The path of reconstruction followed by evolution is not the only change path. Illustration 2.2 describes the change process at S&N Retail, the pub and restaurant business of Scottish & Newcastle, one of Europe's largest brewers. For the head office staff, this is a route of reconstruction followed by revolution, with a short reconstruction phase involving the sell-off of pubs and business restructuring, followed by an attempt at a big-bang culture change process centred on a new office. In reality, the culture change may take longer to embed itself at head office. Furthermore, by mid-2003, S&N was seeking to sell S&N Retail.

Therefore, existing examples of change suggest that, dependent on the context of the organisation, it may be necessary to undertake an enabling realignment phase, either in the form of an adaptation or a reconstruction, before embarking on a longer-term transformation. Indeed, when organisations are underperforming badly, a rapid reconstruction focused on restoring profitability will be essential to the longer-term survival of the organisation and a necessary first step on the path to transformation. It may also be necessary, following a transformational change, to move to adaptation, to ensure that the changes are embedded throughout the organisation,[9] to sustain competitiveness. Subsequent reconstructions may also be needed. BA, for example, has been through a series of reconstructions in the 1990s and into 2002 as it fights to remain a key player in the fiercely competitive airline industry. The book will discuss how to decide on an appropriate change path in Chapters 3 and 4.

2.3 CHANGE START-POINT

Change start-point refers to where the change is initiated and developed, or rather the locus of control and influence. There are two main approaches – top-down or bottom-up. A more recent approach is through 'pockets of good practice'. In addition, whatever the start-point selected, change can also be implemented organisation-wide simultaneously, or more gradually via pilot sites.

2.3.1 Top-down change

Much of the prescriptive change literature has emphasised a top-down approach, in which the direction, control, and initiation of the changes come from the strategic apex of the organisation. It usually involves a programme of change determined and implemented by the top management or their representatives.

However, although top-down change is clearly driven by the top executives, this does not mean that a top-down change approach is never collaborative or participative – although this is the way some people interpret it and it is often portrayed. In top-down change initiatives the plans developed can be via collaboration with senior managers, and a wider group of individuals within the organisation (see Illustration 2.5 on change at UNHCR below). Similarly, part of the selling of the plans can be to use employee participation in workshops to work out some of the details of implementation. The change initiative might also include a comprehensive programme of staff involvement through road shows or workshops.

Top-down change may have to be imposed in a directive or coercive manner, particularly in a crisis or turnaround situation where there may be no alternative. For example, when Tim Parker took over at Clarks, the British shoe manufacturer, as chief executive in 1995, he sacked 10 per cent of the workforce and closed five factories shortly after his arrival, as part of a longer-term change strategy to revitalise the organisation.[10] In 2002 Opel, the German car manufacturer, introduced a restructuring plan which cut 2,500 jobs, and instituted a pay freeze and a 30-hour week without employee compensation. The dealer network was also to be halved in terms of size.[11] This directive form of top-down change design has the advantage of being speedy to implement. Staff can also feel that there is a clarity in the nature of the change, which can be an advantage at a time of uncertainty.

2.3.2 Bottom-up change

Emergent or bottom-up change has a very different starting point and logic from top-down change. Responsibility is passed downwards into the organisation to encourage ownership of the change process by employees, and to make change self-generating. This is partly because the assumption here is that responsibility for change should not just lie with the senior managers, but also because in certain change contexts, a top-down approach may not encourage the needed ownership and commitment to the required changes. Since bottom-up change is an emergent process, it can be much slower to mature than top-down change initiatives. Bottom-up change is also more unpredictable in its consequences as it is subject to interpretation and negotiation by the very staff who put the changes in place. Senior management have far less control over the process.

It is possible to combine a top-down approach with a bottom-up approach.[12] Advocates of this sort of approach argue that certain activities, such as mobilising support for change, may need to be done in a top-down way, whereas others, such as creating a vision for change, can be more participative. The leader of a change effort may be directive about the fact that the departments within a business unit must change to meet the aspirations of the vision. However, the leader then allows each department or section to choose the way in which they want to implement that vision, to ensure ownership and commitment. The changes that emerge within each department, and the new behaviours these changes engender, then need to be institutionalised and supported in the organisation through top-down actions, such as changes to organisation-wide systems and structures.

2.3.3 Pockets of good practice

The third approach, *pockets of good practice,* is less well known. Change is initiated in one part of an organisation by an individual or individuals within that department or division to, for example, take advantage of a new business opportunity, or to implement new best practice in terms of processes and systems. The department then becomes a pocket of good practice and provides a role model to the rest of the organisation.[13,14] Illustration 2.3 provides examples of pockets of good practice in two organisations, Ericsson and Jewson, a British builder's merchant. They both illustrate how individuals can create best practice in their part of the organisation that will encourage other parts of the organisation to do something similar, due to improved performance and the corporate reputation this then earns them.

Illustration 2.3   *change in action*

Pockets of good practice

Ericsson

The software design unit of Ericsson, Athlone, Ireland, created a pocket of good practice to aid the development of a group of highly competent engineers. The aim was to move away from a design organisation to a competence-based approach which aimed to retain and develop staff. Key technical and managerial competences were identified to support the unit's strategy, and then people were recruited and developed to attain them. Unit-specific development norms were created. Professional career paths were put in place along with tougher interview procedures for promotions and greater transparency of the process. Competence managers were appointed with responsibility to develop others. These managers were also made responsible for putting together project teams instead of the project leaders. These initiatives and the resulting performance improvements have earned the unit a corporate recognition, with other European units now wanting to emulate their approach.

Jewson

Jewson, a timber and builder's merchant in the UK, have instituted pockets of good practice in their branch network, led by their managing director of operations. The BM2000 initiative was designed to achieve sharing of best practice across branches. The top 30 managers were brought together monthly for 2 days to enable sharing of experiences and ideas. Both in-house and external speakers would attend these events to discuss developments in other areas of the business and particular topics. The group were also given financial incentives if they met new additional branch and group profitability targets. Individuals can drop out of the group and be replaced with others if their performance dips below forecast targets. Many changes have been implemented through the group, such as improved transport efficiency and flexible working. The success of this initiative, in terms of improved profitability and productivity, has led to other operational areas within Jewson doing similar things.

Source: Adapted from Butcher, D. and Atkinson, S. (2000) 'The bottom-up principle', *Management Review*, 89 (1), pp. 48–53; and Butcher, D. and Atkinson, S. (14 January 1999) 'Upwardly mobilised: against the grain – catalysing change at Jewson', *People Management*, pp. 28–33.

There are certain situations where this type of change approach can work well. This would not be a style to use to initiate rapid organisation-wide change. However, when an organisation is in a phase of incremental change, allowing managers to use their judgement to develop on-going change initiatives may be a useful way of delivering self-sustaining continuous improvement in organisational practices. It may also be a useful approach in organisations where change management expertise is patchy, or it is hard to gain buy-in to organisation-wide change. A danger is that this type of change will only lead to further organisational change if the practices established by the individuals concerned are then copied by others.

2.3.4 Pilot sites

Whichever approach is selected, this can be combined with an organisation-wide approach to change, or change based on *pilot sites* as the start-point. This may initially involve implementing change in just one department or division, or it may be by using a new start-up site. The advantages of pilot sites are many:

- It is possible to test the impact of new systems and procedures, and iron out any unforeseen faults or problems before the changes are made throughout the organisation. It is also possible to identify and rectify potential and actual problems and weaknesses with the accompanying change management interventions, such as training and communication.

- A successful pilot can be used to mobilise awareness of the need for change and support for the changes in an environment where change awareness is low.

- Pilot sites followed by a gradual roll-out programme reduce the amount of change management expertise and resources needed at any one time.

For these reasons, there are certain contexts that lend themselves to pilot sites. Organisations that are geographically dispersed, with many similar operations in different locations, such as retailers, are an obvious candidate for change implemented on a site-by-site basis. Large, global organisations may have many different manufacturing sites, for example, which are best dealt with individually as part of an on-going change programme. These sites may also have different levels of readiness and capability for change, which may make certain sites more suitable than others for early involvement. A pilot at one or a few site(s) can be improved and replicated for subsequent sites.[15]

Marriott, the hotel group, used pilot sites to implement an initiative designed to move away from its culture of 'face time' – the more hours you put in, the better. The long hours culture was making it hard to retain and attract talented staff. Marriott implemented a 6-month programme, Management Flexibility, at three hotels in the Northeast of the United States. The aim was to enable managers to work more effectively by eliminating unnecessary meetings and inefficient practices, but the pilots also involved an overhaul of the way managers thought about their work. The pilot was then rolled out in other sites in 2001 with a wider roll-out in 2002.[16]

Pilot schemes can also be used to implement a rolling series of change initiatives in one site or to introduce new ways of working on a department-by-department basis.[17] See Illustration 2.4 which describes a change process underway at the *Hull Daily Mail*, a regional newspaper. This also illustrates one of the problems of change through pilots, namely that the process can take longer and can be stalled when commitments and priorities change.

There are also other disadvantages to pilot sites:

● Each site and department involved in an implementation may be different. Changes made to the implementation approach to mitigate against the problems identified in one site may not be suitable for another site.

● The time it takes to run a pilot may give opponents of change more time to build their resistance, particularly if there is not a strong and powerful backer of the changes.

Illustration 2.4

change in action

Change through pilots at *Hull Daily Mail*

The *Hull Daily Mail* is a regional newspaper in the UK. The newspaper's parent company set challenging new profit targets. A project team was set up to investigate internal restructuring as a result. It became clear that the paper need radical and comprehensive change. The change process became known as Genesis. Every part of the business – editorial, production, advertising, distribution and sales – had to be taken back to basics and redesigned. There was also a need to ultimately shift the paper's culture from command and control, to delegation, trust and individual accountability. The first pilot scheme was in advertising. The advertising director led a project to streamline the advertising process, which involved merging the two previously separate jobs of sale and design. Staff worked as account managers, visiting the customers with a laptop and designing the ad on the spot. Costs of errors in advertisements were cut by 80 per cent, revenues went up 24 per cent because

customers liked the new service, and costs came down by 12 per cent because the new process was more efficient.

The next pilot scheme was the editorial department. The aim was to simplify procedures, cut out bottlenecks and raise quality for the reader. Individual journalists were to take responsibility for a whole page of the newspaper, to be developed through the day through a team of roving reporters. Subeditors were to become full-time writers enabling the paper to cover a wider geographical territory, leading ultimately, it was hoped, to a wider circulation. Training was to be provided as needed. Another aim was that the training and the wide range of experience that could be offered to staff would also cut turnover – another expense to the business. However, the managing director has been promoted to a group role, and it is not known if his successor will push ahead with the series of pilot schemes.

Source: Adapted from Simon Caulkin © (10 March 2002) 'A new angle to an old story', *The Observer*, p. 8.

- The use of pilot sites creates a prolonged period of change, and therefore uncertainty for staff, and the need for the use of parallel systems and processes for the organisation.

- Organisations have found it difficult to transfer changes made at new sites to existing sites and departments.

2.4 CHANGE STYLE

The style of change is to do with issues about how the process of change is managed. There are many classifications of management styles during change, but broadly change styles can be seen as sitting on a continuum from coercion, in which change is forced on people, to education and delegation in which change is delegated. (See Figure 2.4 for an explanation of the styles.)

2.4.1 Education and delegation

Education and delegation involves convincing employees of the need for change through means such as training, gaining their commitment and support for change, and then delegating change to them. This may involve more than just talking to employees. It could involve, for example, sending managers on bench-marking visits to other organisations to learn how things could be done better and then expecting the managers to implement the ideas and opportunities they identify. The change process at Lufthansa (see Illustration 2.9 below) describes this style of delivering change through the 'Explorer 21' network and the 'Climb 99' initiative. The 'Samurai of Change' group was also developed from an education and delegation intervention in the form of a four-week change management training course.

   This change style is easily confused with collaboration and participation. However, education and delegation is more to do with equipping employees with an understanding, and then encouraging them to use their learning to propose and implement change projects supportive of the organisational change goals. There are problems with this style of leading change:

- It can be difficult to generate commitment to action from it. Workshops and seminars can be seen as an interesting exercise, and fun to do, but change will only occur if a series of explicit actions are identified and carried out.

- It can be necessary to inject some energy, emotion and direction into the process. Otherwise, an awareness of the need for change may be developed, but this awareness will not translate into a commitment to doing something about it, especially if there is no onus on senior managers to take note of ideas that arise and act on them.

- It can be very time consuming and costly if there are large numbers of

Figure 2.4   Styles of managing change

STYLE	DESCRIPTION	ADVANTAGES	DISADVANTAGES
Education and delegation	Use small group briefings to discuss things with people and explain things to them. The aim is to gain support for change by generating understanding and commitment.	Spreads support for change. Also ensures a wide base of understanding.	Takes a long time. If radical change is needed, fact-based argument and logic may not be enough to convince others of need for change. Easy to voice support, then walk away and do nothing.
Collaboration	Widespread involvement of the employees on decisions about what and how to change.	Spreads not only support but ownership of change by increasing levels of involvement.	Time consuming. Little control over decisions made. May lead to change within paradigm.
Participation	Involvement of employees in how to deliver the desired changes. May also include limited collaboration over aspects of the 'how' to change as opposed to the 'what' of change.	Again, spreads ownership and support for change, but within a more controlled framework. Easier to shape decisions.	Can be perceived as manipulation.
Direction	Change leaders make the majority of decisions about what to change and how. Use of authority to direct change.	Less time consuming. Provides a clear change direction and focus.	Potentially less support and commitment, and therefore proposed changes may be resisted.
Coercion	Use of power to impose change.	Allows for prompt action.	Unlikely to achieve buy-in without a crisis.

employees to be convinced. A multinational company operating in many different countries with maybe thousands of employees could find such an approach
difficult to undertake.

2.4.2 Collaboration

In collaboration, there is widespread involvement of employees in both what to
change, and how to deliver the needed changes. Employees are asked to contribute to both the goals set for change and the means of achieving those goals.
This may be through participative face-to-face meetings, such as workshops or
focus groups, in which, for example, consultants introduce participants to analytical tools and frameworks that can provide new insights on the participants' business and lead to identification of the critical change issues and an explicit
consideration of actions to be taken, and by whom. The principle behind
collaboration is that the more employees are involved, the more likely they are to

---

Illustration 2.5   *change in action*

Achieving change at UNHCR

UNHCR, the Office of the United Nations High
Commissioner for Refugees, has undergone
rapid growth in recent years, fuelled by events
such as the Gulf War and the exodus of the
Kurds in 1991. UNHCR's expenditure has also
risen sharply (to $1.3 billion in 1995), against a
backdrop of greater competition for donor
community funds. The organisation needs to be
seen to be efficient, well managed and effective
if it is to maintain levels of funding. Head office
needed to become less bureaucratic, and more
responsive to the needs of the field.

The change agent, Lynn Wallis, led many
change initiatives following her appointment in
1992. The major change initiative was Project
Delphi, a highly collaborative initiative to review
the UNHCR operations, spearheaded by the
Change Management Group (CMG) created by
Wallis. The Delphi process involved staff in
thinking through the organisation's problems
themselves. Via *Delphi News*, a newsletter
launched in 1996, staff were introduced to the
Delphi Process. The Delphi concepts were to
do with improving efficiency and effectiveness.
Staff everywhere were asked to hold a Delphi
Day to brainstorm in small groups about how
their work could be changed to improve the
way UNHCR worked. Ideas were to be sent to
the CMG (anonymously if wished) before 1
March 1996.

A total of 2,200 ideas were collected from
100 Delphi groups in over 118 country offices
and fed back to staff. The CMG then devised a
list of actions and needs arising from these
ideas, through consultation with staff
worldwide. The next phase of Delphi was to be
the implementation of these ideas by a project
team supervised by the High Commissioner of
UNHCR herself.

Source: Adapted from Sayers, I. and Johnson, G. (1999) 'The UNHCR case – achieving the impossible', in *Exploring Corporate
Strategy*, 5th edn, Hemel Hempstead: Prentice Hall.

support and be committed to the changes that they have helped design, and the more likely they also are to sell those changes to others in the organisation. Furthermore, collaboration can be used not only to determine what to change and how, but also to create an awareness of the need for change by challenging complacency within the organisation.

Collaboration can also be used to bypass resistance. At Schlumberger, the chairman and chief executive experienced resistance to his restructuring ideas. He subsequently brought together a team of younger employees at a meeting called Forum 2005, and asked them to develop pictures of what Schlumberger should look like in 2005. He then adopted their proposed ideas.[18]

However, collaboration does not have to involve face-to-face situations. In organisations where employees are widespread, for example, this is difficult to achieve. Illustration 2.5 describes how the UNHCR, the international aid organisation, used a collaborative technique called Project Delphi to get involvement in change from a broad group of staff.

Collaboration can be a good management style to use when dealing with professionals, such as hospital clinicians, or even academics, who value the freedom and autonomy they normally have in their work. Such groups of people are likely to rebel against more directive interventions, which they perceive to be limiting their autonomy and their right to have a say in their future. However:

- Collaboration can be time consuming, and is therefore not a technique to use in a crisis situation.

- Employees may not come up with the suggestions or ideas wanted by senior managers, so there is a loss of control.

- If employees are consulted and then ignored, this will do more harm than good, as it can raise expectations about what it is possible to achieve. The employees will feel devalued, and perceive the senior managers to be practising tokenism in respect of collaboration.

- The ideas offered by existing employees could be within the existing way of thinking, or the existing organisational paradigm, and the existing way of working within the organisation. This could stifle creativity and transformational change. Some organisations use external facilitators and consultants to challenge ideas and thinking in order to overcome this problem.

2.4.3 Participation

Participation is limited collaboration. The principle that involvement will equal greater commitment still justifies this approach to change. However, employees are allowed only limited involvement in certain areas of change, such as *how* the desired changes can be achieved. For example, employees may be told of the overall vision and change goals for a firm, such as to achieve greater efficiency, greater productivity, and to eliminate waste. They can then be asked to think about what they need to do differently if they are going to help to deliver that vision. At Marriott, when they were implementing the programme 'Management Flexibility' to change their 'face time' culture (see section 2.3.4, Pilot sites), external consultants ran focus groups involving all the 165 managers from the three hotels involved in the pilot. The focus groups were used to generate ideas from the managers on what could be done differently to reduce inefficient practices. General Motors are using a scheme called 'Go Fast' in which groups of staff attend one-day workshops to resolve problems with a particular business issue. Each workshop is aimed at cutting costs and bureaucracy in a particular area of the business. Teams within each workshop compete to come up with the best solution.[19]

Alternatively, employees may be asked to contribute to the design and delivery of specific tasks which will assist the overall change process. A series of working parties may be set up to address issues, from new working practices to communications. In some change initiatives the participation is literally limited to consultation. Members of the change design team may hold workshops to tell staff of the change ideas being proposed and ask their opinion as a form of input to the process, but this is more a process of keeping staff informed and asking for their approval, than actively seeking input.

Obviously, the participation management style enables the change leaders to retain greater control over the outcome of the change process, as they are setting the overall goals if not the means of achieving the goals. Unfortunately, it may be seen by employees as a type of manipulation, an attempt to pay lip-service to employee involvement, particularly if participation is limited, or employees are told what outcome is expected from a workshop, or whatever type of forum is used to achieve their participation. Participation can also be a time-consuming way of delivering change, although less so than collaboration.

2.4.4 Direction

When those leading change make the majority of decisions about what to change and how, and use their authority to *direct* the achievement of change, this is a management style of direction. This approach effectively separates the thinkers from the doers. The thinkers come up with the change ideas and 'sell' them to the doers, who are then supposed to implement these plans and the ideas. There may still be an attempt to sell the changes to the employees, to encourage them to buy into the changes and support them. There can still be an extensive communication effort in which employees are involved in workshops to debate the implications of change for themselves. However, employees are not invited to contribute to the goals or means of change, except in a limited way. Many turnarounds, such as the examples of Clarks and Opel presented in section 2.3.1, Topdown change, involve this style of change.

The advantages of this approach are that it is easier to retain control over the direction and content of change, and decision making is faster than it would be under a style which involves consultation. Thus many organisations requiring a rapid change use this style. Other features of the organisational context may also lead organisations to use this style (see Chapters 3 and 4). The disadvantages are that:

- The lack of employee consultation and involvement might create more resistance to the proposed changes. As a change style it is more likely to be suitable in an organisation which is either in crisis, or in which there is a widespread awareness of the need for change. In such a situation, despite the lack of participation by employees, they are more likely to support the proposed changes.

- An imposed change process may result in impressive rhetoric within an organisation, with little change in actual behaviour or job and ultimately organisational performance. Staff may find it easy to repeat the language of the change process without really embracing the change at an emotional or behavioural level.[20]

2.4.5 Coercion

Coercion is an extension of direction. Here change is imposed on staff, rather than staff having the idea of change sold to them. It is a way of achieving rapid change, but as with direction, it may lead to greater resistance. Given the lack of effort devoted to explaining the need for change to staff, or to encouraging buy-in for the changes, this approach is unlikely to work unless there is a very *real* crisis that is felt by most staff within the organisation. However, unless the coercion is such that all aspects of behavioural change can be enforced in some way, the result may still be lip-service to the changes rather than actual change.

2.4.6 Examples of change styles

KPMG, the large international firm of accountants, initiated a change in 1992, to differentiate themselves from the other accountancy firms. Illustration 2.6 describes how Sharman, initially the partner in charge of the south-east region, created a recognition of the need for change in an organisation in which there was no crisis. As one of the partners at KPMG, Sharman had no power to *impose* change. He could only put in place interventions to trigger questioning and challenging of the status quo. A number of interventions were used, such as workshops, conferences and feedback. However, the style of change was different for different groups of staff. For the partners, Sharman put in place extensive *collaboration*. For the senior managers, their opinions were sought, but at a later stage, so for them, the style was more like *participation*. Those below senior manager level were never really consulted at all. They were informed of the decisions, and as such, the change style for them was *direction*. This illustrates that the context

Illustration 2.6

change in action

Initiating strategic change at KPMG

KPMG is a large international firm of accountants and consultants. Like many other such organisations, traditionally the primary interface to the market had been discipline-based practice units (audit, tax, consultancy). At the beginning of the 1990s Colin Sharman, partner in charge of the south-east region, perceived the need to change the firm into a client-focused organisation. Although the firm was increasingly run along corporate lines, each partner of the firm is, in effect, an owner–manager and has to agree, or at least not disagree, with any change. Given this partnership structure, and the fact that the firm was very successful in its existing form, Sharman had no mandate or authority to impose change. He initiated change in a way designed to obtain the support needed from a critical mass of partners.

As a first step a series of partner workshops were run, at which the partners considered the firm's strategy, the blockages to change and the actions needed. Sharman attended debriefing sessions at the end of each workshop, but did not direct the outcomes from the workshops. Subsequently, Sharman held evening feedback sessions attended by most of the partners, which were focused on building consensus on the need for change and what should be done. The Senior Managers Conference was also used as a way of getting those below the level of partner involved. The senior managers were asked to work through a similar process to that undertaken at the workshops by the partners. This was followed by more briefing meetings for partners and senior managers.

In 1992, a special partners conference was called where the '20:20 Vision', the blueprint for change, was presented to give impetus to the change process. Similar events were held for both senior and junior managers. Change was also communicated in a variety of other ways, including videos, glossy brochures, the personal repetition by Colin Sharman, and later on publicly through the financial media.

The decision-making context within the firm meant that strategic change was a lengthy process. Formulating the new strategy and getting partners to buy-in to it culminated in the launch of '20:20 Vision' in mid-1992. The actual processes of change continued beyond that.

Source: Adapted from the cases on KPMG (1999) in *Exploring Corporate Strategy*, 5th edn, Johnson, G. and Scholes, K., Hemel Hempstead: Prentice Hall.

determines the type of style that is likely to be effective, and that the approach may be different for different groups of staff. However, some observers would question whether it was right not to involve staff below the senior manager level in the workshops. Would they have had more commitment to the changes and the firm if they had been involved in a more participative change experience?

The description of the different change styles reveals a need to match style to the change context.[21] We discuss this in more detail in Chapters 3 and 4 as many contextual factors may impact on the choice of style.

2.5 CHANGE TARGET

An important design choice requiring consideration is the different organisational levels at which to intervene. Some change processes concentrate on attempting to change the values of employees, others emphasise behavioural change, whilst others may only seek to change the performance objectives or outputs of employees.

2.5.1 Outputs

Change can focus on changing the nature of outputs or performance objectives to in turn trigger a change in behaviours. The target is the *outcome* of what people do in terms of managerially determined outputs or objectives, for example profit margins, hourly sales levels, levels of customer response. This usually involves the redesign of performance measures, such as rewards and control systems.

A focus on outputs is useful when high levels of autonomy are required. Individual, national or functional business divisions may need a degree of independence from the parent corporation in order to manage the change in a way that is appropriate to their specific country's context or the nature of their staff. Alternatively, autonomy may be required by individual staff themselves as in the case of doctors or consultants or city traders. For example, an investment bank will employ many traders to make their financial deals for them. These traders are usually highly self-motivated and skilled, valuing the independence and autonomy in their jobs. Their primary motivation, and performance measure, is the achievement of their commercial targets and the high financial bonuses this earns them. Therefore, in any change situation, changing these measures and rewards is likely to be a more suitable target and effective intervention, than any attempt to prescribe their behaviours. The traders would not feel their autonomy was under threat. Similarly, when rapid performance improvements are needed, performance measures may be an appropriate target. At AlliedSignal Aerospace Repair and Overhaul in Singapore in the late 1990s, there was a need to greatly reduce the turnaround time for parts under repair as a first step in a more major change process. The master production schedule was used to set clear individual and departmental targets for tasks. These targets were monitored and followed up on in daily production meetings.[22]

However, care needs to be taken when targeting outputs. The manager of a regional theatre decided to improve levels of customer service by requiring his staff to answer the phone within a certain number of rings. The statistics from the telephone system suggested that levels of service were improving and the targets were being met. However, customers were not happy. When ringing into the theatre, at times their call would be answered, but then the line would go dead. The theatre staff had worked out that if they answered the phone and then cut off the person on the other end, the system still registered the call as answered and they met their targets. Such stories are common. Staff change their behaviours to meet the new performance metrics, potentially in ways other than intended. New performance measures alone can be dangerous leading to unintended outcomes.

2.5.2 Behaviours

An alternative approach is to focus primarily on enforcing new behaviours. Those that support this view argue that the individual can only change if the organisational system in which the individual operates is changed. Figure 2.5 summarises this argument.

Programmatic change targets individual attitude change to effect behaviour change.[23] The underlying principle of this approach is that ways of behaving are underpinned by individual attitudes and beliefs. So change should be aimed at individuals and their attitudes. Yet individual behaviour is constrained by the organisational system in which individuals work. Roles and responsibilities, and existing ways of working, force particular behaviours onto individuals if they are to function effectively in an organisation. If individuals learn new attitudes, but are then returned to the old organisational system, they will not be able to practise the new ways of behaving that accompany their new attitudes. If instead the

Figure 2.5 Attitudes versus behaviours

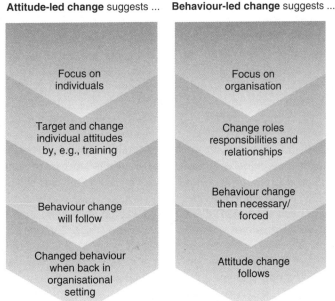

Attitude-led change suggests ...   **Behaviour-led change** suggests ...

Focus on individuals

Focus on organisation

Target and change individual attitudes by, e.g., training

Change roles responsibilities and relationships

Behaviour change will follow

Behaviour change then necessary/ forced

Changed behaviour when back in organisational setting

Attitude change follows

organisational system is changed (task alignment), and individuals are placed in job roles with different responsibilities and different relationships from their peers, subordinates and superiors, this will force them to behave differently, and ultimately to think differently leading to a change in attitudes.

A focus on work-based behaviours can therefore be used to effect behavioural and accompanying attitude change and maybe, ultimately, value change.[24] A target of behaviours may also be used for other reasons:

● Behaviours are an appropriate target in changes involving reconstruction or realignment, which require some degree of behavioural change without a fundamental change in the shared organisational values or beliefs.

Illustration 2.7   *change in action*

Behaviour change at the UK Hydrographic Office (UKHO)

UKHO's 900 employees produce and update marine charts used by all ships – from yachts to supertankers – to navigate. UKHO has produced charts and coastline drawings since 1795 and has 60 per cent of the global market. However, two factors triggered the need for change. Advances in digital technology will lead to the eventual replacement of craft-based methods of producing charts with electronic display that can be delivered on-line. In addition, UKHO has become a trading unit within the Ministry of Defence rather than an operation supported by the UK government. Thinking has had to shift from how to get money from the government to how to earn money from customers. This also required the organisation to be more cost-effective. To achieve this investments were made in new technology and training initiatives were put in place to create a climate of continuous improvement and change through behavioural change.

First the UKHO's IT systems were changed. Manual processes have been eliminated where possible and new software tracks the production process. Initially, individuals did not always use the systems in a timely manner leading to breakdowns. The new systems showed that managers had to understand the impact of their activities on those of other departments, and that there was a need for new skills such as marketing, IT and project management.

Two specialist companies were hired to run training and development programmes for nearly all staff. There were two programmes, First Steps and Inspire. Both programmes were to give employees the opportunity to discuss their problems, devise solutions and contribute to the future. First Steps was a corporate management training programme for the 300 most senior staff and 350 people from lower grades attended Inspire. First Steps divided managers into groups of 15 to 20 people from different grades, functions and departments. As part of the workshops managers had to suggest initiatives to create a climate of innovation and continuing excellence. They then split into action learning groups to pursue a project. The Inspire programme was similar. Now the board has set up cross-functional action groups to address future change, such as improving customer service. Future managers need to be trained to run what is becoming a commercial operation. Traditional 'techies' need to take a wider management role.

Source: Adapted from Golzen, G. (11 January 2001) 'Voyage of discovery', *People Management*, pp. 32–6.

- The prescription of behaviours may be useful in service outlets such as McDonald's where routinised procedures ensure quality of delivery or product.

- In a crisis situation where there is little time, the enforcement of behavioural change may be an appropriate initial intervention, since value change can take a long while to develop.

- Behaviours are an appropriate intervention level in situations where the employees concerned are all involved in the same core business or the same management function, because the intervention is aimed at an homogeneous group of employees with similar values and motivations. This is particularly true if the changes do not require a change in the shared organisational values. Illustration 2.7 describes how behaviours were changed at UKHO through a combination of new systems, processes and training. The intent was to build on existing organisational values, whilst making it clear that the status quo was untenable, and developing a greater cost efficiency and a climate of continuous innovation in working practices.

2.5.3 Employee values

Interest in values as a lever for change was particularly strong in the 1980s, associated as it was with developments in human resource management and the increasing popularity of culture change programmes.[25] In the 1980s, the belief was that if employees could be made to adhere to a predetermined set of corporate values, they could then be given licence to innovate freely. In other words, by prescribing shared values, appropriate employee behaviour would emerge in such a way that there would be less need for bureaucratic rules and regulations. Appropriate values would drive appropriate behaviour, reducing the need for other types of managerial controls on employees.

However, the evidence shows that this approach can be fraught with difficulty in certain organisational contexts:

- Many espoused value statements are devalued in employee eyes if these are not reflected in changed behaviours, particularly from senior managers. So values such as 'individuality' or 'people are our greatest asset' quickly became relegated to meaningless slogans in many companies.[26]

- An emphasis on managing values may lead to staff feeling manipulated or brainwashed, which can result in cynicism about the values themselves.

- The acknowledgement of all kinds of diversity within organisations may undermine the attainment of a common set of values. In hospitals, for example, there are consultants, nurses and managers, each with their own professional allegiances, and different professional values, identities and motivations. Can common values be achieved across such diverse professional and occupational groups, or for that matter, different national cultures or business divisions?[27]

In addition, some organisations feel that the dividing line between organis-ational values and individual values is hard to define. They therefore feel uncom-fortable with this level of intervention, and question the legitimacy of trying to alter something as personal to an individual as their set of values. Yet if an organ-isation needs to achieve fundamental, transformational change, this by its very nature requires a change in the assumptions and beliefs shared by the organis-ation's employees. Therefore, there are circumstances where targeting values, or if not values, the shared assumptions and beliefs, is appropriate, although value change can take a long while to achieve. (See Chapter 5, Illustration 5.6.)

2.6 CHANGE LEVERS

One of the issues facing any change agent is the range of levers and interventions to use. Organisations are composed of a number of interconnected and interde-pendent parts or subsystems, and are most effective when the major components are in alignment with each other,[28] just like a car engine. Given the interdepend-ency of these subsystems, it is difficult to change one part in isolation. Either other parts of the organisation with which the changed part interconnects will counteract the effect of the change, or the change made will force domino change effects, maybe unforeseen, in the other parts of the organisation.

Figure 2.6	The cultural web of an organisation

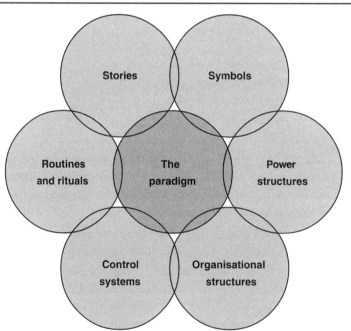

Source: Adapted from G. Johnson, 'Mapping and Re-mapping organisational culture', in V. Ambrosini, G. Johnson and K. Scholes (1998) *Exploring Techniques of Analysis and Evaluation in Strategic Management*, Hemel Hempstead: Prentice Hall.

Readers who have read *Exploring Corporate Strategy* will be familiar with one tool based on these principles – the cultural web shown in Figure 2.6, although there are others.[29] The cultural web suggests that organisations consist of a number of interlinked and interdependent subsystems all interconnected with the paradigm – a *technical* subsystem to do with organisation structures and control systems; a *political* subsystem to do with both formal and informal power structures; and a *cultural* subsystem to do with symbols, stories, and routines and rituals.

For those not familiar with the web, how to use it is explained briefly in Appendix 1. As with other such frameworks, it is suggested that to achieve effective change it is necessary to use interventions in all parts of the web. Transformational change initiatives, requiring a change in the shared assumptions and beliefs, in particular, are more likely to fail if change practitioners apply a change recipe which concentrates on the use of a range of levers and mechanisms from just one or two of the subsystems that make up the whole. This will be particularly true if these changes are introduced in isolation without considering how they link together to form a coherent change strategy.[30] Consideration should be given to both hard aspects, such as structures and systems, and the softer aspects, such as symbolism and communication.[31]

Illustration 2.8 shows the extent of change that occurred at Baxi Heating, the UK's leading gas domestic heating appliance manufacturer and the core business within the Baxi Partnership group of companies, during a change process designed to make the organisation more competitive and profitable during the late 1980s and early 1990s. The new paradigm shows that the changes involved a transformation from a solid, slow, manufacturing organisation, to a more dynamic, market-focused organisation. In order to support this transformation, the organisation structure and control systems have been changed, but also new ways of working and managing have been introduced (rituals and routines), and new symbols and stories more to do with success and change rather than the organisation's history have replaced the old ones.

Not all changes require a fundamental realignment of all subsystems. A change that only involves adaptation, or maybe even reconstruction, will not necessitate a fundamental shift in the paradigm. It is also likely that earlier decisions about design choices will determine what range of levers should be used. There is a link between the range of levers and mechanisms to use and the change target, as illustrated in Figure 2.7:

● If the target is *change outcomes* then it is likely that this can be achieved by changing rewards and performance measures and targets, particularly since this is only likely to be an appropriate intervention target if existing values remain appropriate.

● If the target is *change behaviours* then this is about putting in place interventions to do with organisation structure (particularly roles and responsibilities), performance management, control systems to support and measure the

Illustration 2.8

Change at Baxi

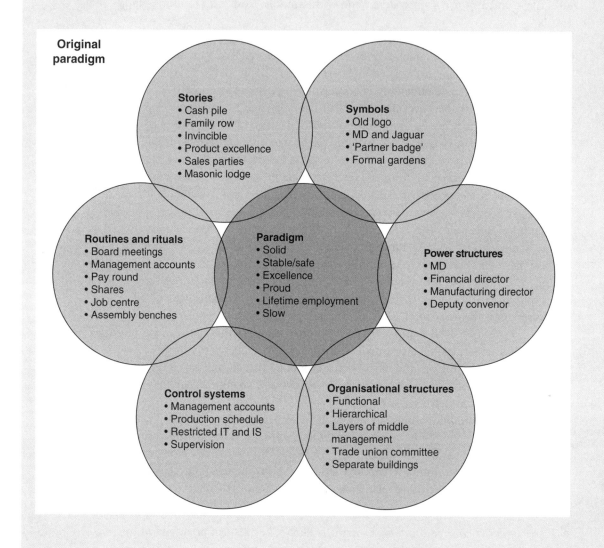

Original paradigm

Stories
- Cash pile
- Family row
- Invincible
- Product excellence
- Sales parties
- Masonic lodge

Symbols
- Old logo
- MD and Jaguar
- 'Partner badge'
- Formal gardens

Routines and rituals
- Board meetings
- Management accounts
- Pay round
- Shares
- Job centre
- Assembly benches

Paradigm
- Solid
- Stable/safe
- Excellence
- Proud
- Lifetime employment
- Slow

Power structures
- MD
- Financial director
- Manufacturing director
- Deputy convenor

Control systems
- Management accounts
- Production schedule
- Restricted IT and IS
- Supervision

Organisational structures
- Functional
- Hierarchical
- Layers of middle management
- Trade union committee
- Separate buildings

behavioural changes occurring, and supportive training. For example, see Illustration 2.7, Behaviour change at UKHO. However, mutually supportive and consistent changes may be needed in all organisational subsystems, including

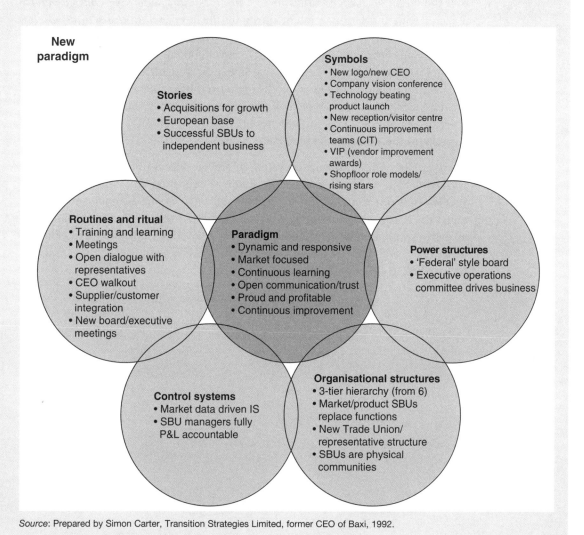

New paradigm

Stories
- Acquisitions for growth
- European base
- Successful SBUs to independent business

Symbols
- New logo/new CEO
- Company vision conference
- Technology beating product launch
- New reception/visitor centre
- Continuous improvement teams (CIT)
- VIP (vendor improvement awards)
- Shopfloor role models/ rising stars

Routines and ritual
- Training and learning
- Meetings
- Open dialogue with representatives
- CEO walkout
- Supplier/customer integration
- New board/executive meetings

Paradigm
- Dynamic and responsive
- Market focused
- Continuous learning
- Open communication/trust
- Proud and profitable
- Continuous improvement

Power structures
- 'Federal' style board
- Executive operations committee drives business

Control systems
- Market data driven IS
- SBU managers fully P&L accountable

Organisational structures
- 3-tier hierarchy (from 6)
- Market/product SBUs replace functions
- New Trade Union/ representative structure
- SBUs are physical communities

Source: Prepared by Simon Carter, Transition Strategies Limited, former CEO of Baxi, 1992.

symbols and routines, to ensure there are no contradictory messages sent to staff about the end goals of change. Many organisations have undergone change through a mixture of restructuring, downsizing and business process re-engineering initiatives throughout the 1990s in a response to increasing competition. A common complaint is that employees receive mixed messages about the intent of change, because supportive symbolic changes have not been made. Managers talk of innovation, quality, teamwork and empowerment, but continue to use old routine ways of behaving to punish mistakes, cut costs and reward individual performance.

● If the target is *change values or assumptions and beliefs* (or *change behaviours* with the ultimate intent of driving in new *assumptions and beliefs*), then the range of interventions to use has to include intensive communication, education, training, and personal development interventions, to help employees understand exactly what is expected of them in the new culture. These interventions will need to be supported by changes to all aspects of the web, as the Baxi illustration shows, to create a mutually supportive and consistent organisational system, which will enable and reinforce behaviours appropriate to the new values (see Figure 2.7).

There is, therefore, a fourth subsystem of change levers to consider – the *interpersonal* to do with communication, training, education and personal and management development. Whilst this subsystem only received significant mention under the heading of value change, as the examples used in this chapter illustrate, all forms of change usually require some level of communication and training. However, which change levers to use and when is a complicated topic and will be revisited in Chapters 4, 5 and 6.

Figure 2.7   Linking change target and change levers

(a) Targeting outputs

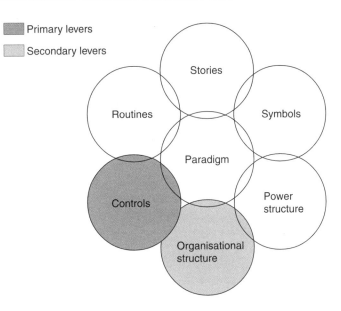

(b) Targeting behaviours

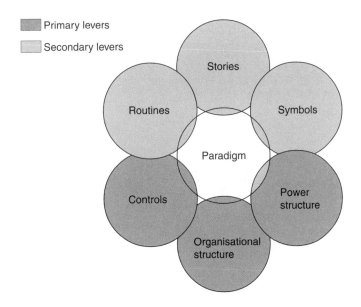

Figure 2.7   *Continued*

(c) Targeting behaviours to get value change

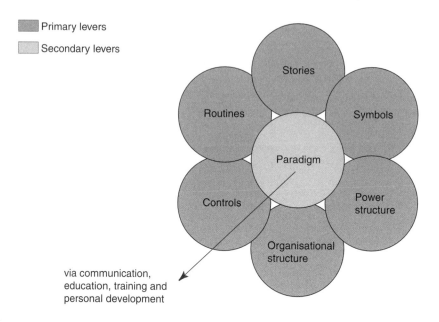

(d) Targeting values

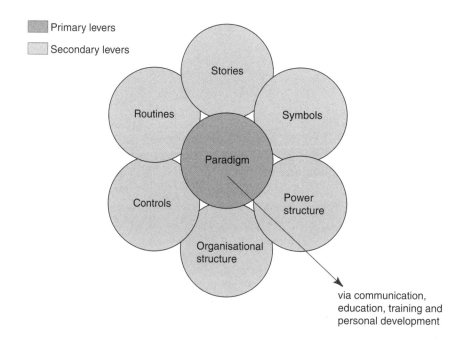

2.7 CHANGE ROLES

Change is only likely to succeed if someone is responsible for leading that change, although it is also accepted that this responsibility may not reside with just one person. A change agent needs to be supported by additional change agents. There is less faith placed in the one charismatic and heroic figure,[32] particularly since it is now recognised that change is complex and requires consideration and management of many different tasks. One individual could not hope to manage a major change effort entirely on his or her own. This is not to say that the role of leadership has been trivialised in any way. Major change efforts in particular are likely to require a champion who shows tremendous commitment to, and enthusiasm for, the vision he or she wants to see implemented in the organisation.

However, there are a number of different ways change can be managed, although none of them are mutually exclusive, and there are pros and cons for each role (see Figure 2.8). The primary change agent roles are:

- *Leadership*. The success of the change programme is based on a key, pivotal figure. The 'leader' may be the CEO, the MD, another senior manager acting as the internal change agent, or another director such as the HR Director. The new CEO of Philips, Gerard Kleisterlee, mentioned above, would be a good example of leadership during change. If the individual championing change is not the CEO or the MD, then they may need to gain the support of more powerful individuals within the organisation if they are to push change through. Alternatively, in bigger or more geographically dispersed organisations, a number of individuals may fulfil the leadership role with different individuals leading the change in different parts of the business. In such cases, there may be one overall leader, such as the chief executive, with local leaders or change champions in each organisational division or department.

- *External facilitation*. External consultants may be appointed and play a pivotal role in the change process.[33] This may be in the form of advice, providing change management training, or more active participation. Illustrations 2.1, 2.2 and 2.7 on Yuasa, S&N and UKHO all provide examples of this.

- *Change action team*. A team of people within the organisation may be appointed to lead the changes and this may be in the form of a steering committee. If this team does not consist of senior and influential people, the team is likely to need the support of a more powerful individual or group of individuals in major change efforts. Illustration 2.9 discusses the change process at Lufthansa in the 1990s. It illustrates many uses of change action teams, but the change effort also involved *leadership* from the CEO, Jurgen Weber, and extensive *functional support* from HR in the design of communication, performance management systems, and management development.

- *Functional delegation*. Change responsibility may be assigned to a particular function such as HR, or operations management. Some organisations even appoint a new senior manager to lead a particular change initiative, such as a

Illustration 2.9

change in action

Using change teams at Lufthansa

The transformation process at Lufthansa started in 1991, when the company was almost bankrupt. The transformation process involved three phases – an operational turnaround (1992–1994), structural change and privatisation (1994-1996) and finally strategic development (cost leadership, the STAR ALLIANCE, and moving to an aviation group). By 1998, the CEO was able to announce the company's best results ever. The change reversed a record loss of DM 730 million in 1992 to a record pre-tax profit of DM 2.5 billion in 1998.

The record losses in 1991 created some awareness of a crisis, but Lufthansa was a state-owned company – longevity was assumed. The first step of the change process was a change management programme in 1992 that led to the birth of a group called 'Samurai of Change'. This group convinced the CEO of the need for fundamental change. To take change forward and create a group of managers prepared to lead change, the CEO invited 20 selected senior managers to attend a workshop in June 1992 at the training centre in Seeheim. This meeting led to 'Program 93': 131 projects including staff reductions of 8000, downsizing the fleet (stationing aircraft in the desert), and increasing revenues. The Seeheim workshop was repeated three times with groups of 50 people, to encourage a wider ownership of change and to build commitment to the ambitious goals. Teams were appointed to head the projects, mostly led by members of the 'Sumarai of Change'. An Operations Team was put in overall charge. Communication was achieved through the use of town meetings. The CEO officer held these meetings himself when visiting the various Lufthansa units. About 70 per cent of the projects were delivered during the turnaround. The remaining longer-term strategic projects were launched later. Networks of change agents were developed through the establishment of the teams during the turnaround, that led to formal and informal groups implementing new ideas.

Corporate restructuring followed. Lufthansa was changed from a functional organisation into autonomous subsidiaries including cargo, technical maintenance, and systems, that could support the core business of the passenger airline. Problems with the pension fund had also been resolved so that privatisation, first discussed with the German government at the start of the turnaround, could now proceed and by 1997 the privatisation was complete. Attention was then focused on some of the outstanding strategic goals. First, Program 15 was launched to deliver cost leadership in the fiercely competitive airline business. It aimed to reduce costs by 20 per cent within 5 years and was led by a task force. This program is integrated into line managers objectives and performance evaluations. The task force emphasised the importance of the programme symbolically. It positioned its office next to the CEOs, talked about progress regularly in the town meetings and the staff journal, and publicised success stories. Second, the STAR ALLIANCE was initiated. Third, further moves were made to develop Lufthansa into an aviation group rather than an airline, by building on the subsidiary structure already in place.

To help sustain change, Lufthansa now has an 'Explorers 21' network (young professionals) and the 'Climb 99' initiative (an action learning network of experienced managers). Both programmes start with a leadership self-assessment. Participants then visit excellent companies worldwide to develop recommendations for Lufthansa. There are also congresses at which members discuss their ideas with senior management to agree concrete action plans. Participants are encouraged and supported to follow through on the change initiatives they propose.

Source: Adapted from Bruch, H. and Sattelberger, T. (2001) 'Lufthansa's transformation marathon: the process of liberating and focusing change energy', *Human Resource Management, Fall 21*, 40 (3), pp. 249–59; (2001) The turnaround at Lufthansa: learning from the change process, *Journal of Change Management*, 1 (4), 344–63; (2001) Lufthansa 2000: Maintaining the Change Momentum, London Business School Case, reference LBS–CS01–001.

Figure 2.8 The pros and cons of different change roles

	PROS	CONS
Leadership	● Can create drive, determination, and strong focus on the change project.	● Leader may not be credible/believed. ● Leader may not have track record of delivering on promises. ● Leader may lack time given other operational duties. ● Leader may lack change management skills/expertise. ● Leader may be part of problem (e.g. not acknowledging need for change). ● Multiple leaders in different parts of the organisation may pull change programme in different directions/lack co-ordination.
External consultants	● Have experience. ● Can be objective – carry no organisational baggage. ● Can be used as a scapegoat for bad news. ● Can facilitate, to open up conversations about the need for change. ● Can overcome organisational barriers/politics. ● Dedicated resource.	● Cost a lot. ● Cannot lead change as not seen as having any stake in the organisation's future. ● No accountability. ● May not know the business well. ● No ownership and need to deliver.
Change action team	● Good ownership for change initiatives. ● Knowledge of organisation and issues. ● Potentially influential with their peer groups. ● Sustainability and follow-through. ● Can involve individuals with change expertise (e.g. organisation development specialists).	● Can make design long-winded due to multiple inputs/perspectives. ● Can be time consuming. ● Can lead to compromises in design. ● May lack power.
Functional delegation	● Use of expertise (human resources, organisation development). ● Knowledge of area. ● Individuals may identify more strongly with their immediate manager.	● Individual(s) may lack power required to intervene in other parts of organisation. ● May be biased in favour of their part of the organisation. ● May focus only on their area at expense of others. ● May lack expertise.

total quality initiative like Six Sigma at Maple Leaf Foods. This may be appropriate when implementing change limited to a particular new function or if the skills and knowledge needed to manage the change reside within a particular department or individual. In major change efforts, unless the function head is endowed with a large amount of authority, the individual is also likely to need the backing of a more powerful figure such as the CEO.

Transition management is a time-consuming activity, and there may be a trade-off to be made between the amount of time managers need to devote to keeping the business going, and the amount of time they have to act as a change resource. For example, an organisation's MD may decide to lead the change, supported by a change team of other senior managers, but also appoint external consultants to provide advice and assistance, and additional resources when needed.

2.8 SUMMARY

A key issue when planning an appropriate change implementation approach is to decide which design choices to take. This chapter has explained that there are six main design choices a change agent needs to examine – the change path, the change style, the change start-point, the change target, the range of change levers, and the key change roles. All of these choices need consideration in relation to the context of change, to avoid the application of simplistic change recipes.

However, choosing which options to take is not straightforward. Within each of the choices there are a number of options, which creates a wide variety of possible permutations:

- The *change path* may involve more than one type of change, for example an enabling phase of adaptation or reconstruction, followed by evolution or revolution.

- The *change start-point* options include not just top-down or bottom-up change, but also some combination of the two or pockets of good practice. These choices can be exercised organisation-wide, or within pilot sites.

- The *change style* may vary from highly collaborative to coercive, and is not necessarily dictated by the change start-point. Top-down change, for example, can still be collaborative. The change style may also vary by staff level or occupational groupings.

- The *target of change interventions* may be attitudes and values, behaviours or outputs. However, outputs are normally used to indirectly achieve behaviour change, and behaviour change may be used to effect value change.

- The *range of change levers* is affected by the choice of change target, but may be other choices such as change style. The range of levers and interventions that can be used includes not just harder technical and political interventions such as structures and systems, but also softer cultural interventions such as symbols and routines, and interpersonal interventions to do with communication, education and training.

- The *change roles* are often some combination of leadership, functional delegation, the use of external consultants, and change action teams.

The first and most important choice is the change path. The other choices, such as change start-point, style, target and so on, then need to be made for each phase of the change path. None of these choices can be made without reference to the change context. Chapters 3 and 4 elaborate on this chapter to explain how to create linkages between the context and the design choices.

REFERENCES

1. This definition is taken from *Exploring Corporate Strategy*. The concept of the paradigm is also discussed extensively in *Exploring Corporate Strategy*, Chapters 2 and 5. An organisation's paradigm is the shared, although often taken-for-granted, assumptions and beliefs of the organisation that shapes the way things are done in an organisation. Also see Appendix 1, on the cultural web.
2. Stockport, G. and Norvall, G. (2002) 'Broken Hill Proprietary (BHP) Company Limited – turnaround strategy', in *Exploring Corporate Strategy*, 6th edn, Johnson, G. and Scholes, K. (eds) Harlow: Financial Times Prentice Hall.
3. Time, B. and Ibison, D. (13 December 2001) 'Trimming the costs in the nicest possible way', *Financial Times*, p. 13.
4. Schenker, J.L. (18 March 2002) 'Fine tuning a fuzzy image', *Time Magazine, Time Digital,* 159 (11), pp. 2–5.
5. Firn, D. and Wassener, B. (12 April 2002) 'A search for the ingredients of critical mass', *Financial Times*, p. 14.
6. There are many sources of information for the change process undertaken at British Airways in the 1980s. Two good sources are Goodstein, L.D. and Burke, W.W. (1991) 'Creating successful organization change', *Organizational Dynamics*, 19 (4), pp. 5–17, and Leahey, J. and Kotter, J.P. (1990) 'Changing the culture at British Airways', Harvard Business School, case number 9–491–009.
7. The story of the transformation at General Electric led by Jack Welch is told in Tichy, N.M. and Sherman, S. (1993) *Control Your Destiny, or Someone Else Will*, New York: Doubleday. Also by the same authors a summary of the Work-out programme, (1993) 'Walking the talk at GE', *Training and Development*, (June), pp. 26–35.
8. Van de Vliet (1995) 'ASDA's open plan', *Management Today*, (Dec), pp. 50–5.
9. For a discussion of change paths and other examples of matching change style to context, see, for example, Stace, D.A. (1996) 'Dominant ideologies, strategic change, and sustained performance', *Human Relations*, 49 (5), pp. 553–70.
10. Lynn, M. (12 April 1998) 'Parker kicks Clarks into shape', *The Sunday Times*, p. 7.
11. Harnischfeger, U. (19 November 2002) 'Bayer drug add potency to merger mix', *Financial Times*, p. 26.
12. For a fuller description of how to combine a top-down approach to change with a more bottom-up approach, see Beer, M., Eisenstat, R.A. and Spector, B. (1990) *The Critical Path to Corporate Renewal*, Boston, MA: Harvard Business School Press.
13. Clarke, M. and Meldrum, M. (1998) 'Creating change from below: early lessons for agents of change', *Leadership and Organizational Development Journal*, 20 (2), pp. 70–80.
14. Butcher, D., Harvey, P. and Atkinson, S. (1997) *Developing Businesses through Developing*

Individuals, Cranfield School of Management.

15. For an example of this see Mark, K. and Golden, B. (2002) 'Maple Leaf Foods: leading Six Sigma Change', Ivey Management Services, Case No. 9B01C032.

16. Munck, B. (2001) 'Changing a culture of Face Time', *Harvard Business Review*, 79 (10), pp. 125–31.

17. Pilot sites are often a good approach in organisations, such as hospitals, where there are many similarly functioning units and a need to retain standards of care during change. See, for example, Anson, B.R. (2000) 'Taking charge of change in a volatile healthcare market-place', *Human Resource Planning*, 23 (13), p. 21.

18. Edgecliffe-Johnson, A. (17 May 2002) 'Nurturing talent to oil the wheels of change', *Financial Times*, p. 14.

19. Burt, T. (24 June 2002) 'General Motors leaves its old self standing', *Financial Times*, p. 12.

20. For a discussion of imposed change see Willmott, H. (1993) 'Strength is ignorance: slavery is freedom: managing culture in modern organisations', *Journal of Management Studies*, 30 (4), pp. 515–52.

21. See reference 9 above.

22. Hwee, C., Demeester, L. and Pich, M. (2002) *AlliedSignal Aerospace Repair and Overhaul (Singapore) (A)*, INSEAD, Case number 602–034–1.

23. For a fuller discussion of the merits of attitude- versus behaviour-led change see Beer, M., Eisenstat, R.A. and Spector, B. (1990) 'Why change programs don't produce change', *Harvard Business Review*, 68 (6), pp. 158–66.

24. Whilst we know that behavioural change will lead to a shift in accompanying attitudes, as yet there is no evidence that a change in behaviours will lead to value change.

25. For a discussion of the role of values in change see Hope, V. and Hendry, J. (1995) 'Corporate cultural change – is it relevant for the organisations of the 1990s?' *Human Resource Management Journal*, 5 (4), pp. 61–73.

26. See reference 25 above.

27. For a discussion of the impact of diversity see Lawrence, P.R. and Lorsch, J.W. (1967) *Organisation and Environment,* Boston, MA: Harvard University Press. Also Purcell, J. (1989) 'The impact of corporate strategy on human resource management', in Storey, J. (ed.) *New Perspectives on Human Resource Management,* London: Routledge.

28. For an alternative way of analysing organisations and designing levers and mechanisms to achieve the desired future organisation in terms of three subsystems (technical, political and cultural), see Tichy, N.M. (1983) *Managing Strategic Change: Technical, Political and Cultural Dynamics*, New York: Wiley. Also Tichy, N.M. (1983) 'The essentials of strategic change management', *The Journal of Business Strategy*, 3 (4), pp. 55–67.

29. See reference 28 above.

30. See reference 28 above.

31. Tichy as in 28 above, and also see Orgland, M. and Von Krugh, G. (1998) 'Initiating, managing and sustaining corporate transformation', *European Management Journal*, 16 (1), pp. 31–8.

32. For a discussion of leadership during change see Pettigrew, A.M. and Whipp, R. (1991) *Managing Change for Competitive Success,* Oxford: Blackwell. Also Nadler, D.A. and Tushman, M.L. (1989) 'Organizational frame bending: principles for managing reorientation', *The Academy of Management Executive*, 3 (3), pp. 194–204.

33. For a comparison of internal and external change agency roles see Ginsberg, A. and Abrahamson, E. (1991) 'Champions of change and strategic shifts: The role of internal and external change advocates', *Journal of Management Studies*, 28 (2), pp. 173–99.

WORK ASSIGNMENTS

2.1 Identify different organisations undergoing change from newspaper articles or another source. What types of change (transformation versus realignment) do these organisations need to implement and why?

2.2 Consider why examples of bottom-up change are rare.

2.3 Consider an organisation with a wide number of different stakeholder groups, like a hospital or a university. Identify the different stakeholder groups and how this might affect your choice of change styles.

2.4 For the organisations you identified in question 2.1, what change targets would you select and why?

2.5 What are the advantages and disadvantages of the different change targets?

3

Analysing the change context: the change kaleidoscope

3.1 INTRODUCTION

Chapters 1 and 2 have already introduced the change kaleidoscope as a framework to aid the development of context-sensitive approaches to change. Chapter 2 has explained the different design choices from the kaleidoscope and the options within each choice. This chapter builds on this. It:

- Reminds the reader of the perils of formulaic change and the importance of taking the change context into account when designing change.
- Introduces and explains the contextual features in the change kaleidoscope – scope, time, preservation, diversity, capability, capacity, readiness for change and power – which influence the design choices.
- Discusses the implications of each of the contextual features for the design of change.

The aim of this chapter is to examine each contextual feature of the kaleidoscope in depth, but also to give examples of the implications of each of these features for the design of change.

3.2 THE PERILS OF FORMULAIC CHANGE

Successful change, by its very nature, depends heavily on context and circumstance. We have explained in Chapter 1 that it is dangerous to apply change formulae that worked in one context directly into another. Longitudinal research examining best practice change management in successful companies[1] has established that these companies do not follow trends or change recipes, but instead customise their change approach to meet the needs of their organisation at any one time. It has to be appreciated that even organisations that seem very similar are in reality very different. Unfortunately the complexity of the change task can make existing models look attractive, and it is tempting for managers to use one of these 'off-the-shelf' solutions.

The use of past experience, even within the same company, can also be dangerous. What worked well at one time may be a poor indicator of what will work well in the current context. This is not to say that previous experience is irrelevant. However, it is important for a change agent to remember what was unique about a specific change situation and what was generalisable or replicable in other organisations or at other times. Similarly, it is important that they appreciate and acknowledge what is *unique* and *specific* about the current context in which they are working. *Contextual judgement* becomes the competence required of a change agent.

Chapters 3 and 4 use the kaleidoscope to show how the framework can help change agents exercise such judgement. First it is necessary to carry out a detailed analysis of the organisational change context through the contextual features, which this chapter deals with. Then it is necessary to determine which aspects of the current context are most critical, and how this affects the design choices made. This is the focus of Chapter 4.

3.3 CHANGE CONTEXT: THE CONTEXTUAL FEATURES

As Chapter 1 has already explained, the change kaleidoscope (see Figure 3.1) is a diagnostic framework which enables change agents to pinpoint the key contextual features of their change context. Here we focus on explaining the contextual features and how they can be derived for an organisation. The eight contextual features are:

Time: How quickly is change needed? Is the organisation in crisis or is it concerned with longer-term strategic development?

Scope: What degree of change is needed? Realignment or transformation? Does the change affect the whole organisation or only part of it?

Preservation: What organisational assets, characteristics and practices need to be maintained and protected during change?

Diversity: Are the different staff/professional groups and divisions within the organisation relatively homogeneous or more diverse in terms of values, norms and attitudes?

Capability: What is the level of organisational, managerial and personal capability to implement change?

Capacity: How much resource can the organisation invest in the proposed change in terms of cash, people and time?

Readiness for change: How ready for change are the employees within the organisation? Are they both aware of the need for change and motivated to deliver the changes?

Power: Where is power vested within the organisation? How much latitude of discretion does the unit needing to change and the change leader possess?

Figure 3.1   **The change kaleidoscope**

The *Oxford English Dictionary* defines a kaleidoscope as '*a constantly changing group* of bright objects; a tube through which are seen symmetrical figures produced by reflections of pieces of coloured glass and *varied by rotation of the tube*'. The kaleidoscope does not give predictable configurations that lead to more formulaic change recipes. Instead the pieces of coloured glass, the eight contextual features, remain the same but are *constantly reconfigured* to produce different pictures for each organisational change situation they are used to assess. Therefore the change designs will also vary. Certain features infer certain design choices, but the potential permutations are endless. This chapter can only give a few examples for each feature.

The framework of the kaleidoscope is often used within companies to raise staff awareness of the implications of change, to stimulate debate about difficult areas and to encourage managers to consider what design choices are appropriate to the context of their own organisation.

3.4 TIME

Time is to do with how long an organisation has to achieve change (Figure 3.2). Is the organisation in crisis or is it concerned with longer-term strategic development? Time can also be affected by stakeholder attitudes. Is the stock market, for example, expecting short- or long-term results from change?

3.4.1 Assessing time

How much time an organisation has to deliver change should have been determined by the strategic analysis. It may be that an organisation is in a crisis situation, with rapidly declining market share and profitability, and therefore in need of a reactive, rapid turnaround and recovery change process. This may be due to a change in the competitive conditions the organisation is facing, such as the arrival of new competitors and/or the development by competitors of different products and services. Alternatively it could be that an organisation has become complacent and failed to keep up with the trends in its marketplace, continuing

Figure 3.2   **Contextual feature: time**

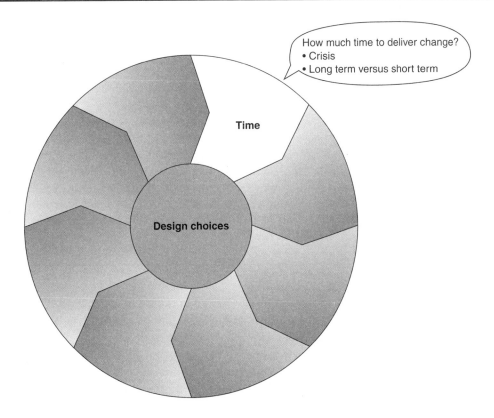

Illustration 3.1

change in action

Transformation at the UK engineering group Senior

Senior is a UK engineering group that grew rapidly during the 1990s through the aggressive acquisition of companies. Such expansion took the group far from its core flexible tubing business and on to the screens of analysts and investors. It was then that controversial accounting policies drew attention to Senior's practices. Following three consecutive profit warnings, the last of which was prompted by revelations of improper accounting at a US subsidiary, the chief executive resigned to launch a management buy-out of Senior. When both the MBO and a subsequent search for a buyer failed, Graham Menzies, who was recruited to shepherd the company through the MBO process, was left with the challenge of rebuilding a company demoralised by months of media scrutiny and driven by internal political battles. He was under considerable pressure from shareholders and the financial institutions to present an immediate turnaround of fortunes.

In his first week as chief executive in March 2000, Menzies flew to the USA to start a tour of the group's overseas operations. As a symbolic first decision, he insisted that from then on the group should operate in a spartan management style. Senior executives were to travel by taxi rather than limousine, and the Wedgwood china was replaced with Styrofoam cups. Subsequently he also eliminated biscuits at board meetings, sold an expensive office in Tokyo, and dismissed half the head office staff

and let the empty space. Such symbolic gestures were meant to send immediate signals to employees and shareholders alike that the group was going to take restructuring seriously. In addition he instituted an open door policy for himself and let employees know they could e-mail him in an attempt to break down closed groups and foster teamwork.

Two months after his flying US tour, Menzies gathered his managers at an airport in Massachusetts, where he mapped out his strategy for transforming the organisation. The reforms would focus on three areas – strengthening communications between subsidiaries and the head office; improving the quality of financial and accounting information about the business both inside and outside the group; and jettisoning unprofitable divisions and business practices. Changes were to commence immediately. Executives were pushed to provide more accurate profit and revenue statements. He also replaced Arthur Andersen as the company's auditor in the light of the Enron scandal.

Building on his early cost-cutting drive, Menzies initiated essential organisational restructuring. This included the elimination of 500 jobs, the sale of five units and the closing or merging of two others. Net debt fell from more than £160 million to about £123 million by mid-2002, while free cash flow improved from about £20 million to nearly £30 million in 2002.

Source: Adapted from Harney, A. 'Tough talk at a Boston tea party', *Financial Times*, 2 May 2002, p. 14.

instead to pursue strategies still rooted in the ways of behaving that used to lead to success, placing the organisation in an uncompetitive position (see the example of Marks & Spencer, Chapter 1: section 1.2).

An organisation may also need to implement proactive change rapidly, either to pre-empt fast competitor imitation, or to meet changing customer needs. Stock market and shareholder pressures may also lead to the need for rapid change.

Illustration 3.1 describes the fast action required by Graham Menzies in the face of shareholder and competitive pressure to secure the survival of the engineering group, Senior, in 2000.

From a change management perspective a crisis situation can appear attractive. It is easier to start or trigger change when there is an emergency. People seem to overcome their reluctance to change when it is a matter of survival. The needs of an emergency can serve to legitimise methods and measures that in normal times would not be accepted, such as longer working hours, pay cuts or freezes, or redundancy programmes. However, there are also real disadvantages to crisis-driven change management. It is tempting to respond to a financial crisis with short-term measures only, such as strict cost-cutting strategies that may include downsizing programmes. These may appear to deliver a solution to the share-holders, but if the fundamental problems leading to poor performance over time are ignored, then crisis may loom large again in the future, leading to a downward spiral with reconstruction after reconstruction. In addition, whilst crisis may give an organisation's managers the impetus to start change, there may be no cash to invest in the transformation.

Alternatively, like KPMG (Chapter 2, Illustration 2.6), an organisation may have the luxury of time on its side and be able to implement change in a pre-emptive manner, before the organisation is showing many visible signs of decline in com-petitiveness. In such circumstances there is more time and resource available to invest in a transformation. However, the problem in such non-crisis-driven change situations is how to generate readiness for change. There is no 'burning platform'[2] for change. Why engage in something as risky and painful as change when there is no obvious need? These issues have an impact on the design choices made, and explain why some texts on change advocate the exploitation of, or the creation of, a crisis to trigger change.

3.4.2 Time and design choices

If there is *limited time* available to the change agent, particularly if the organis-ation is in a crisis for whatever reason, then some design choices become auto-matic. Initial change initiatives are likely to involve some type of *realignment*, probably via *big-bang reconstruction* as at Senior, as opposed to a more *incre-mental* approach, since the immediate need is to stem the decline in the organis-ation's competitive position. This then places an organisation in a position where it can embark on longer-term and more fundamental transformation if this is needed. Chapter 2 describes how this path is taken by many organisations. If there is money available, maybe from a parent group or other stakeholders such as national governments who are prepared to invest in the turnaround process, it may be possible to go for a more revolutionary approach from the start.

Such *big-bang* approaches, whether reconstruction or revolution, are also likely to be more *top-down* and *directive* in approach, and supported by a *leadership change role.* This is partly because there is not the time for more participative approaches, but also because the crisis legitimises the action and there is likely to be a greater willingness among staff to follow top management edicts. However, if an organisation needs to change rapidly, but there is not a felt need for change, then the change agent may need to force change in order to trigger the realisation of the inevitability of action among employees. It should not be assumed that a crisis will create a felt need for change at all organisational levels. The attitude of more junior employees may be that it is the responsibility of the senior managers to resolve the problems. The *change target*, particularly with reconstruction where the aim is not an immediate shift in values, will be *behaviours*, or even *outputs* to effect rapid change. Change will therefore be delivered via harder interventions to do with structures and control systems, which may include new rewards to incentivise different behaviours. In addition, as Illustration 3.1 shows, a *big-bang* approach may also involve the use of symbolic *levers* such as the closure of certain parts of the business, or the closure of executive dining rooms and the removal of other staff perks, to indicate that times are hard and things must be done differently if the organisation is to survive.

If organisations have the luxury of *time* then this enlarges the design choices available to the change agent. For instance, they can choose to map a particular change *path* whereby the organisation starts with one form of change, which over time develops into another type of change. Organisations can start with adaptation aimed at increasing the organisational and individual capability for change, and then move into more fundamental and transformational evolution. Similarly when time is not an issue it is possible to consider change processes which are educative, participative or collaborative in *style*. Highly participative or collaborative change processes take time to cascade through an organisation. Furthermore, if there is no obvious need for change, such participative approaches may be needed to gain a recognition of the need for, and a buy-in to, change.

Decisions about the change *start-point* can work either way. If awareness of the need for change is low, then getting the change process started may still require a *top-down* approach. Other contextual features also affect the choice. If there is a low capability for change among staff, then the approach may have to be *directive* in style as well. On the other hand, there may be parts of the organisation that are more ready for change, or have senior managers more willing to embrace change than some other managers, enabling change to be initiated via *pilot sites*. Alternatively, the time for change and the capability for change among staff may allow for the creation of awareness of the need for change, and the development of what should be changed, via a more *bottom-up* approach. Staff diversity also has an impact here. Even in circumstances where there is a low readiness for change, staff groups that value their autonomy may need to be involved through a more participative approach if they are to buy-in to change.

In terms of change *targets*, when there is more time available and some sort of transformation is required, then it may be possible to target *values*, although of course a change agent could still choose to target *behaviours* to drive in *value change* as would need to be done in circumstances where there was less time. This in turn impacts on the change *levers*. Longer-term change interventions, particularly those where the intention is to aid value change, include communication, management development programmes and personal development initiatives such as coaching or mentoring.

Time also affects the choice of change *roles*. Change agents need to ask whether there is sufficient time to establish and develop a change action team. Also the potential champions of the change – be it the chief executive, the HR Director, or another change agent – need to be screened for competence and capability. If they require a great deal of coaching in change leadership, yet there is no time to develop this, then support may be needed from external consultants or champions. If time is available then teams can be established to spread the vision and required changes throughout the organisation.

3.5 SCOPE

Scope is the required outcome of the change, varying from realignment through to more radical change aimed at transformation of an organisation (Figure 3.3).

| **Figure 3.3** | **Contextual feature: scope** |

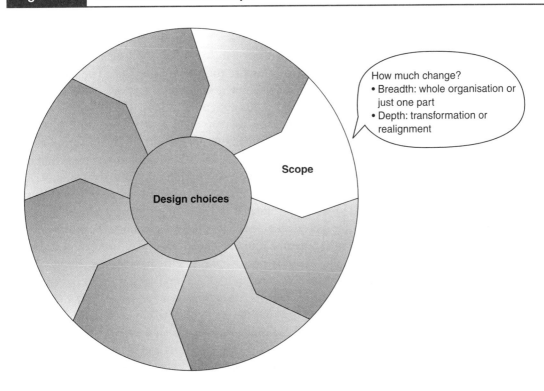

Whether the whole organisation needs to change, or just one division or department, also affects scope.

3.5.1 Assessing scope

The scope of the change determines just how much change is necessary. There are two aspects to scope – the depth of the change required in an organisation and the physical spread of change across the organisation.

The *depth of change* required is equivalent to the extent of change discussed in Chapter 2 when considering the types of change to be undertaken and the change path to be followed. As such, it is one of the key determinants of the type of change, although by no means the only one. It also impacts on design choices other than the type and path of change. When considering the depth of change, it is therefore necessary to consider whether the desired changes involve *transformation*, a change which cannot be handled within the existing paradigm and organisational routines and entails a change in the taken-for-granted assumptions and 'the way of doing things around here'; or a *realignment*, a change to the way of doing things that does not involve a fundamental reappraisal of the central assumptions and beliefs within the organisation. We can illustrate the difference between the two with reference to the retail banking industry in the UK. The banking industry until the late 1990s had undergone several forms of change but in retrospect these changes had all fundamentally been forms of realignment. This is because the changes never altered the fundamental purpose of the banks – banking. The new entrants into the marketplace in the 1990s, in the form of direct telephone banking and the supermarkets, coupled with growing customer sophistication and demand, required the banks to respond in a more fundamental fashion. The banks had to switch from being bankers to being retailers of financial services. This necessitated a shift in the fundamental beliefs and assumptions of these organisations.

A useful framework that can be used to help assess the scope of change required is the cultural web. This framework has already been introduced in Chapter 2 as a way of considering the range of levers and interventions that need to be used to effect change, and is explained in more detail in Appendix 1.

By drawing up a current cultural web for an organisation, and then an outline web of the sort of organisation needed if the desired changes are to become a reality, the extent of required change can be determined, since the two webs provide a picture of how different the future organisation will need to be from the current one. If the changes also impact what sits in the paradigm, then the change is likely to be transformational in nature (see Illustration 2.9 on Baxi). To return to the banking example, the changes carried out by retail banks in the 1980s and into the 1990s did little to shift the internally focused, conservative, risk-averse nature of the banks. Whereas if a move to a retailer of financial products is to be successful, this requires a change in the assumptions and beliefs to ones that support the notion of a responsive, customer-focused organisation.

The questions about the *physical spread* of the change process concern formal structures rather than informal cultures. Is change limited to a small department, or a particular national division, or a particular layer of management? Or, alternatively, is it a change process that should affect the whole organisation? In the course of the privatisation of Posten, the Swedish post office, new departments were created such as sales and marketing. The people recruited into these units and the structures created reflected the newly privatised vision for the organisation. On the other hand there were other divisions, some of which were hundreds of years old. These were the mail-delivery divisions and the post office branch network. Although Posten wished to implement a common corporate vision, in reality the majority of investment in terms of time, people and money needed to be directed at the mature divisions who needed paradigmatic change – the newly created divisions did not.

3.5.2 Scope and design choices

The depth or extent of change obviously impacts on the *type* of change required in terms of *adaptation, reconstruction, evolution* or *revolution*, and therefore the choice of *change path*. However, other contextual features, such as time, capacity and capability, also affect the change path. If the *scope* of change suggests a need for *realignment* rather than transformation, the other main factor is likely to be time. A short timescale points to reconstruction with the associated design choices described above under time. A longer timescale suggests adaptation, which brings with it a wider range of design choices – again see 'Time' above.

If the *scope* of change points to *transformation*, then the choice of change path is more complex. The discussion above on the impact of time on design choices explains how when in a crisis, an organisation has little time to effect change, and probably a low capacity in terms of cash to invest in the change process, and therefore may need to initially undertake reconstruction, even if the ultimate aim of the change process is transformation rather than realignment. The implications of this for the other design choices are also explained above and will not be repeated here. However, once the reconstruction has been delivered, the organisation then needs to consider how it delivers the transformation that is still required. Furthermore, the deeper and broader the change, the more difficult it is to manage, particularly in international organisations, as it takes a long time, and carries more risk if it goes wrong. Illustration 3.2 shows the extent of the change that was necessary within Motorola in order to regain its market share during 2002. As well as management and cultural change, design and product development were targeted as a critical area for transformation, alongside cost-cutting measures.

If the organisation has more *time* to effect a *transformation*, or has carried out a reconstruction that has in turn gained the organisation more time, then there is

Illustration 3.2

change in action

Motorola answers a wake-up call

Motorola pioneered the concept of cellular phones, introducing its first car phones as early as 1946. However, by 1998, Motorola had seen its global dominance in the phone market wrested away by Nokia, the Finnish group. Its loss of market share had been swift and embarrassing – from 31 per cent in 1995 to 15 per cent in 2001. Motorola needed to undertake radical change in order to cope with increasing competition and innovative developments in the cellular phone market. The scope of the change required would need to be sufficient to reverse a steady decline in Motorola's position in the global market, and would therefore need to embrace a number of aspects of the company.

● *Management and culture changes:* New people were introduced into the top management team. At the end of 2002, of the 16 executives reporting directly to Tom Lynch, the new president, 12 were new to their roles since 2001. This was driven by the recognition of the need to change Motorola's notoriously engineer-oriented mindset to one focused on consumers, and to foster a more creative environment. Recent funky adverts of youthful models showing off flip-top Motorola mobiles under slogans such as 'bangbangmoto' are an indication of this attempt to restore the company's brand image.

● *Design and innovation:* The drive for innovation was also reflected in a shift in the designs of Motorola's handsets. Design was considered a service, now it is seen as a force in its own right. There is an array of new phones, including a rotating design and models customised to different operators' needs. Motorola also used to work around dozens of handset platforms. Now, having declared 'war on complexity', it has greatly reduced the number of platforms.

● *Cost cutting:* In conjunction with the changes in Motorola's approach to product design, there was a drive to cut costs. Some 18,000 jobs were cut out of a total of nearly 33,000, as Motorola moved towards increased outsourcing of its non-core business activities. Subsequently, Motorola introduced a global supply chain, and began implementing a plan to cut inventory by sharing information with carriers and high street retailers.

Motorola announced that following its programme of change its market share in the USA has risen to 18 per cent. Operating earnings increased four-fold, and margins also improved. Motorola still faces a challenge in resuming growth in a market in which mobile phones are becoming more of a commodity, and competition is increasing, but the extensive scope of the changes undertaken seem to have allowed Motorola to get back into the game.

Source: Adapted from Daniel, C., 'Motorola answers a wake-up call', *Financial Times*, 24 October 2002, Inside Track, p. 14.

---

a wider range of design choices from which to choose. These have also been discussed above. However, when needing to carry out a transformation, with or without time on its side, an organisation can still be constrained from revolution or evolution by aspects such as a lack of readiness for change or a lack of capability for change. This may point to the need for some sort of realignment first, either with personal development interventions to build a capability for change, and/or the use of maybe more participative change approaches to build a readiness for change. See section 3.8 on capability and 3.10 on readiness. Alternatively, the power of the change agent to deliver transformation may be limited, in which case early interventions may be to do with the use of political levers aimed at building support and a stronger power base for the change agent.

The scope of change also has implications for the change *target*. Ultimately, if an organisation is to deliver transformation it needs to drive in change to the central assumptions and beliefs in the paradigm, which means that at some stage it may need to *target values*, or at least *behaviours* with the intention of driving in *value* change. This also has implications for the range of *levers and interventions* as explained in Chapter 2, as at some point it will be necessary to invest in education, training and personal development interventions. If the organisation is not cash-rich, this may limit their ability to invest in such change levers. In such circumstances it may be necessary to first target behaviours via a full range of levers and interventions, such as structures, systems, routines and symbols, and then support these changes through time with appropriate education and training.

The issue of physical spread throughout an organisation also brings other dimensions into consideration. If, for instance, the change is limited to one functional division which is located within one nation state and employing similar types of staff, then the change process is less complex than trying to lead a change over a multi divisional global corporation. See section 3.7, Diversity.

3.6 PRESERVATION

Preservation is the extent to which it is essential to maintain continuity in certain practices or preserve specific assets, either because they constitute invaluable resources, or they contribute towards a valued stability of culture or identity within an organisation (Figure 3.4). Assets include tangibles such as money, buildings and technology but also include intangibles such as know-how, and staff loyalty or pride in the employer or product.

3.6.1 Assessing preservation

A key criterion for the change agent to consider is the extent to which there is a need to preserve the status quo within an organisation. There are two aspects to preservation. The first is to be clear about what the organisation's assets are, both tangible and intangible. The second is to decide upon what should or should not be preserved in a change process.

Tangible assets are to do with physical, human and financial resources. These can be identified from a simple resource audit,[3] which lists the assets in each category. Intangible assets are more to do with know-how, or the 'tacit knowledge' of particular staff. Tacit knowledge is about knowing more than you can tell – it

Figure 3.4   Contextual feature: preservation

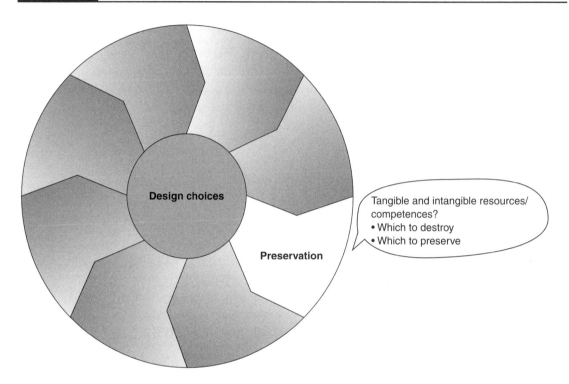

is informal, not codified and therefore difficult to talk about. This knowledge could be about understanding, for example, customers or causes of organisational success, and is often acquired through experience. The important aspect of tacit knowledge is that it is not formally held within an organisation in the form of standard operating procedures or practices. Since it is not written down or systematised in any way, it is hard to imitate and pass on to others. When this informal knowledge gives competitive advantage, it is often referred to as an organisation's core competence.[4] It is important that all resources that contribute to an organisation's competitive advantage are retained during the change process, but it is particularly important that the change process does not lead to the loss of the more intangible resources that are unique and difficult to imitate, and often embedded in an organisation's culture.

Some of the downsizing that went on in the early 1990s resulted in the precipitous removal of more experienced managers from corporations. They were often perceived as an easy target for redundancy because of their age and pension holdings. However, their hasty removal from the organisation often resulted in a loss of tacit knowledge. Many companies continue to risk losing expertise through downsizing and cost-cutting exercises, and the associated costs can be significantly greater when such cuts cause companies to lose experienced people who know how things work. If a change agent does not understand what aspects of the existing organisation need to be preserved, or how such assets can be replaced if lost, the change process may have unanticipated and damaging outcomes.

In extreme cases, the loss of specialists, and the emergence of a remaining middle management structure that does not understand its staff's daily operational routines and rituals, can have catastrophic results. This issue was at the heart of the conclusions drawn in the Cullen inquiry, following a fatal UK rail crash in 1999. It found that many new recruits to jobs at UK Rail where safety was at stake were inexperienced or inadequately trained, and the loss of 'corporate memory' led to inconsistency and confusion over procedures for train drivers.[5] In the case of UK Rail the loss of specialist staff and the introduction of poorly trained new recruits led to a situation where this loss of corporate memory was critical to the safety of passengers.

There may also be cultural aspects of the organisation that need to be retained in addition to particular groups of staff, such as staff loyalty, a team sprit, or extensive staff collaboration which in turn leads to sources of advantage such as creativity or better customer service. If an organisation's competitive position is based on its staff's creativity or customer service, then any change process that unwittingly destroys these features of the culture will damage the organisation.

Aspects such as staff loyalty or team spirit can also be used to help facilitate the painful process of change. Warburtons, a UK fast-moving consumer goods firm, is still a family-owned business. The business has been in existence since 1876. It is extremely successful and pursuing impressive expansionist strategies. However, the culture of the company is still dominated by the family values of caring for staff, and the staff in return are loyal to the family. At the beginning of the twenty-first century these practices may appear out of date. Yet the family believe that this culture is a source of competitive advantage. Being a family baker is part of their brand. They also record very high levels of staff commitment and have created an employment climate that is attractive to new recruits.

The extent of preservation is in part dependent on the scope of change. Arguably the more that has to be retained, the less the scope of change. Yet it is necessary to address preservation as a separate question. If an organisation needs to undergo transformation, it is possible to overlook the existing sources of competitive advantage that reside within the organisation. The baby gets thrown out with the bath water.

A cultural web analysis can help identify some of the softer organisational aspects that need to be retained. Therefore such an analysis needs to be used in two ways – to consider first, what aspects of the organisation need to be changed, and second, what aspects of the organisation need to be specifically *retained*, either because they contribute to competitiveness, or because they can be used to facilitate the change process.

3.6.2 Preservation and design choices

If preservation of hard-to-replace assets is important, particularly intangible assets embedded in the existing culture, then a number of design choices become clear. For instance, *revolution* in which many aspects of the organisation are changed simultaneously would be a risky change path. Similarly, a *target of outputs* could be dangerous as this could lead to many unintended behavioural side effects.

If preservation is more to do with the retention of particular staff groups, particularly if these people are seen as highly desirable assets in the external labour market, this has implications for the *style of change*. To avoid alienating them a *collaborative or educative* style of change may be a safer route than a directive approach. If the staff group concerned is a group that values their autonomy and independence, such as university lecturers, then *direction* and prescription of *behaviours* or *values* is likely to be inappropriate, and it might be that a *change target* of *outputs* would then be appropriate.

On the other hand, organisations seeking true transformational change will have to give up, or even destroy, features of organisational life that in the past might have been assets but now represent barriers to change. The emotional attachment to such features may make this hard to do. Managerial and staff mindsets about what leads to success, and about what is the right way of doing things, may need to be abandoned. This is about 'unlearning'. Unlearning implies that people have to throw out unhelpful behaviours or ways of thinking to make room for new ways of thinking. If these old ways of thinking have become taken-for-granted assumptions for individuals, then challenging them and giving them up can be a painful process for staff. This may mean that change needs to follow in a more *top-down, directive* approach.

The need for unlearning also has implication for the *range of levers* to be used. If there is sufficient time and money, unlearning can be achieved by investment in *levers* to do with *training and development*. However, if inapplicable practices are deeply embedded within an organisation, particularly if there is little time for change, the imposition of changes to working practices via structures and systems may be necessary, accompanied by visible destruction of aspects of the organisation that symbolised the past. A forceful and directive approach may mean that staff who cannot adjust to the changes asked of them given the rapid-change timescale, leave. On the other hand, if staff are unable to adapt to the new ways of working required of them, they can become a liability to the organisation rather than an asset.

3.7 DIVERSITY

Diversity is to do with the degree of diversity that exists among the staff group(s) affected by change (Figure 3.5). Essentially it is asking the question: 'Is the organisation heterogeneous or homogeneous?' Change may affect groups or divisions

Figure 3.5 Contextual feature: diversity

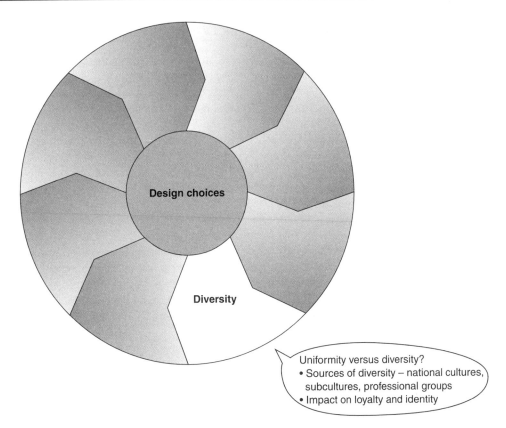

with different subcultures, or different national cultures. Staff may also differ in the way they identify with the organisation – through their team, job, department, division or the whole organisation. Professional groups may identify more with their profession than their employing organisation.

3.7.1 Assessing diversity

Many change texts assume that organisations are homogeneous. This is usually far from the truth. There are three aspects to diversity that can impact on the appropriateness of any change approach:

- The extent to which there is uniformity or diversity within an organisation. Diversity can occur within an organisation because of the existence of different *national cultures,* different *subcultures,* or different *professional* or *occupational groups* between divisions and departments.
- The impact of these differences on staff loyalty and commitment to the overall organisation.

Illustration 3.3

Bayer: creating a pan-European organisation

In 1998 Chris Tobin was appointed Senior Vice-President of Bayer Diagnostics Europe (Bayer DS EU), a subsidiary of the German company Bayer AG. In response to the continuing trend of convergence in the European diagnostic market, and an internal drive within the company to improve performance, he was given the remit of transforming the Bayer Diagnostics operations, creating a pan-European organisation with a shared strategy across the individual European operations.

With over 1,800 employees, covering 20 different countries, the diversity of the organisation in Bayer DS EU was considerable, and proved a major obstacle in implementing a change strategy aimed at uniting the region. Historically, each major country operation in Europe reported individually to Headquarters in the USA, resulting in minimal strategic visibility and poor communication between country operations. This lack of communication reflected a strong element of independence in each country operation. This was further accentuated by the fact that legislation on diagnostics varied considerably between different countries. Whilst there was a trend of consolidation and integration in Europe, it was far from a single market. Therefore, operations had developed largely according to domestic requirements and needs, with little concern for European homogeneity.

One of Chris Tobin's first steps in attempting to foster a culture of sharing and unity was to form a European Leadership Team (ELT) to act as the forum for developing and implementing the strategy for pan-Europeanisation. The ELT comprised the 90 most senior managers across the European operations. In this way, the different operations across Europe were made to feel closely involved in, and committed to, the change programme. The ELT also presented a new opportunity for colleagues to meet and network across national borders. At the same time, a Leadership Development Programme was rolled out, providing other opportunities for Bayer DS EU's senior managers to network with colleagues in a way that had never been done before.

The drive for pan-Europeanisation highlighted the differences among the different country operations. Bayer realised that whilst it was important to maintain local responsiveness, the diversity in the group provided an opportunity to undertake internal benchmarking. Through cross-national, cross-functional teams, a period of internal analysis was undertaken, with the aim of identifying best practices. These were then implemented across the region. The larger country operations provided the greatest source of best practice, and allowed the smaller regions to be pulled up to a higher, European, standard.

At the outset, a centralised strategic marketing unit was set up in the European Centre, designed to roll out consistent and standard marketing strategies across Europe. These were then tailored at the national level by country operations to reflect more closely domestic needs.

Throughout the programme for pan-Europeanisation, Chris Tobin and his team had to handle the dual needs of implementing an overlying strategic structure that pulled European operations together, whilst recognising some strong independent needs at a national level. This resulted in a structure in which strategic decision making was centralised, whilst operational decision making was left at a national level, to enable continued local responsiveness. In this way, the positive aspects of diversity within Bayer DS EU were not lost by the implementation of a pan-European strategy. The results have been impressive. Bayer DS EU has increased its profit margin and sales faster than static market growth, with much of this success attributed to the change programme's ability to harness the group's diversity in a positive manner.

● The extent to which the change agent wishes to reduce or increase levels of diversity as part of the intended outcomes of the change process.

If a corporation is spread over several different countries then issues of diverse *national cultures* must be taken into account. A change initiative designed in California may be quite unacceptable to a South-east Asian national culture. The issue of cross-cultural management becomes less of an issue in truly global corporations where the culture of their staff is so international that common approaches are possible despite different geographic locations. However, truly global or transnational corporations remain rare. The more diverse the operations and national units, the more difficult it is to introduce common change processes at anything more than a visionary level. The implementation of the new vision may have to be left to the discretion of the geographic unit concerned. Illustration 3.3 describes how Bayer had to balance diversity with integration as it introduced a pan-European approach across its different national and divisional cultures within the region.

Another source of diversity is that of *professional groups*, such as doctors and nurses in a hospital, or academics and administrators in a university. There can also be *departmental* or *divisional* subcultures. Within a pharmaceutical company such as Glaxo SmithKline there are differences between the culture of the sales units and the culture of the Research and Development scientists. This means that any change process would have to be able to appeal to all groups. Alternatively different change strategies might be adopted for different parts of the organisation: 'different strokes for different folks' may be a more effective way of persuading people to change than corporate-wide change implementation that assumes that employees are all the same. The more subcultures that exist, the more complex the design process.

These different sources of diversity in turn affect employee loyalties and commitment. If the source of diversity is national culture, to what extent would a local employee in a developing country agree to a corporate change if he or she felt that it threatened the national security or safety of his or her country? Similarly staff who are members of professional or vocational bodies, such as lawyers and doctors, may put their allegiance to their professional norms, values and professional bodies, before their allegiance to any one particular organisation. Alternatively, employees may show more loyalty to their trade or staff union. The very existence of a tradition such as collective bargaining within an organisation should alert change agents or managers to the possible existence of diversity within the workforce.

At a more basic level staff may identify more with their immediate work or peer group rather than the notion of their whole employing organisation.[6] Sometimes Head Office staff identify more with an organisation than geographically dispersed field staff. Research shows that within some large corporations there has been a significant decline in the loyalty felt towards both the corporation and the senior management team over the last decade.[7] However, loyalty to the immediate boss had not declined. Senior managers can erroneously assume that the rest of the staff shares their strong allegiance to the employing organisation. Change agents should not assume that the staff feel that the 'organisation' is worth the pain of individual change.

Having identified the levels of diversity or uniformity within an organisation, the change agent may consider addressing these as part of the change process. An organisation may be too diverse with insufficient unifying elements for commercial effectiveness or the maintenance of management control. This can often happen as a result of rapid growth or increasing internationalisation where units start to grasp too much autonomy from the centre. Alternatively it may result from many mergers and acquisitions and inadequate periods of consolidation, which in turn enables employees to retain the identity and cultures of their old organisations. In all these cases the change decision is how to promote more unity of purpose. The case study on Bayer (Illustration 3.3) illustrates this well.

The increasing trend for mergers and acquisitions that transcend national boundaries can also create considerable cultural change challenges. As an example, in 2000, Tata Tea of India took over Tetley in the UK. Although the two companies are continuing to operate independently until debt levels are such that the balance sheets and operations of the two companies can be merged, integration is required to enable the use of the Tetley brand name to penetrate new global markets. To this end, a new common culture and vision are required.[8]

Conversely, the organisation may have become too uniform, with conflict or dissent eradicated from everyday working behaviours. Alternative ideas are not considered and different personality types are either not allowed to enter the organisation or are ejected once inside. The result can be a company of clones who all think and behave alike and have fixed views on how business should be conducted. Whilst their views fit the marketplace the business may succeed. However, if the market changes they may struggle to change in order to meet new forms of customer or competitor demand. Here the change issue becomes one of promoting diversity within the organisation.

3.7.2 Diversity and design choices

If there are *high levels of diversity* based around different national cultures, then a *target* of *value*-led change, if time allows, can cross these boundaries. Likewise common output targets can be prescribed across the globe. Hewlett-Packard, until its recent merger with Compaq, was a multinational corporation which existed with the same values statement for over 60 years – the HP Way. Furthermore that values statement was used throughout its operations across the globe. The values statement had a universal message about respect for other people that was meaningful for people wherever they lived and whatever their religion. They also had a business planning system and performance management system which were common to all national and business divisions within the corporation. Thus staff objectives were derived from a common set of measurements. What Hewlett-Packard did not do is to prescribe common behaviours across its multinational corporations. A programme that emphasises tightly prescribed behaviours is hard to introduce across diverse national groups within the same organisation because it would clash with behavioural norms within national societies.

A high level of diversity also has implications for change *roles*. In a large corporation, either national or international, local staff may identify more with the head of their business division rather than the overall chief executive of the whole corporation. Therefore in identifying change leaders it may be wise to devolve responsibility down to business unit heads. On the other hand, a strong organisational identity may mean that the Chief Executive is seen as a leader for all staff, and therefore is the natural choice for the role of leading change.

Diversity can also affect the *change path*. When undertaking a merger or acquisition, the initial change phase may concentrate on unifying the cultures of the two organisations involved. Similarly, if an organisation already has subcultures within it as a result of, for example, previous acquisitions or mergers, and this diversity needs to be reduced for the planned changes to work, then again the initial change phase may involve interventions aimed at unifying the different cultures. However, in other acquisitions, such as the Tata/Tetley acquisition, other issues may need to be tackled first. Debt reduction has been necessary at Tetley before a full merger can occur, and only now is attention turning to cultural issues.

The presence of diverse professional or vocational identities means that any change process has to take that into account, particularly if the groups are powerful. A *role* could be created for a professional representative within the change design team, in the same way that union involvement would be sought, to increase the acceptability of proposed changes. Many hospitals involve representatives from the different professional groups, such as consultants and nurses, in change teams. If this is not possible, then a change *style* that incorporates education and collaboration may be necessary to engender a better sense of ownership for change among the different groups. Behavioural prescription is also less likely to be received well by professionals because they often have a great need for high levels of autonomy. Teachers, for example, are likely to react negatively to the imposition of directives that limit their discretion in the classroom. However, this may point to the need for a mix of change styles. Whilst a directive style may be inappropriate for professional groups within an organisation, it may be appropriate for administrative staff groups.

3.8 CAPABILITY

Capability assesses how capable the organisation is at managing change (Figure 3.6). Capability should not be confused with experience. Many organisations experience change but neither handle it well nor learn from their mistakes. It is also important to distinguish between capability for different types and ways of delivering change. An organisation, and the individuals within it, may be very good at delivering operational change, such as rolling out new operating procedures, or sharing best practice from one part of the organisation to another. However, this does not give the organisation a capability in more transformational change. Furthermore, delivering change as a planned and deliberate intervention requires one set of capabilities, and delivering change on a more continuous basis to keep pace with a changing environment a different set.

To assess change capability it is useful to differentiate between two forms of capability. One form of capability resides at the level of the individual. How flexible and adaptable are managers and non-managerial staff in terms of their skills, behaviours and attitudes? The more adaptable the staff, the more able they will be at handling personal and organisational transition. Some employers specifically target their recruitment at attracting people who display these personal attributes. The frenetic pace of many investment banks is possible because the banks only select people who display adaptability. All levels of employees will be

Figure 3.6   Contextual feature: capability

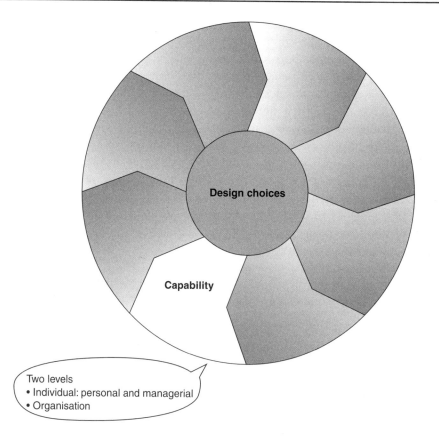

Design choices

Capability

Two levels
• Individual: personal and managerial
• Organisation

expected to travel, work long hours when necessary and move about departments within the bank with little difficulty. Such employers often are more
interested in finding highly flexible and intelligent people than in recruiting to
specific job descriptions.

The second form of capability is located within the organisation itself.
Organisations could, for example, be expert at particular types of change, such as
mergers and acquisitions, and post-acquisition integration. This capability may
rest in established practices and procedures for handling acquisitions, and in
specialist teams of people who are responsible for the integration process. GKN,
for example, a focused automotive and aerospace engineering group active in
more than 30 countries in Europe, the Americas and Asia-Pacific, undertakes
many acquisitions and has established teams and procedures for dealing with
them. Other organisations may have sophisticated and well-developed HR systems which they can then use as levers to deliver change. Chapter 6 (Illustration
6.4) describes how effective use of performance management and management
development systems enabled Kraft Foods to move from a strategy of growth by
acquisition to one of innovation. However, it might also be that an organisation's
systems allow it to co-ordinate change on a more continual basis in response to a
changing environment. These systems might be information systems, business
planning systems or production systems. Such systems can contribute to an
organisation's 'dynamic capability',[9] the capability of an organisation to reconfigure existing processes and create new ones, to deliver on-going competitive
advantage.

3.8.1 Assessing capability

It is important to question whether an organisation possesses the necessary skills
and abilities to manage change on either an individual or organisational level
before embarking on change design and implementation.

The first aspect of capability at the individual level is *personal capability,* the
ability of individuals within an organisation to manage change within themselves.
Anyone who has lived through a personal crisis such as a bereavement or divorce
will understand that personal change can be an overwhelming experience.
However, the more reflective the individual, the more they can expect to learn
from the experience, and hopefully then be able to manage the process more
effectively if it recurs. The more an individual has experienced change, and
reflected on it, the higher their personal capability for change should be. Various
models for understanding the process of personal transition are described in
Chapter 5.

Some organisations use personal development interventions, such as MBA
Programmes and Senior Executive Development programmes, to help their managers develop a change capability. The programmes usually incorporate some
form of experiential learning, through which individual staff members can

develop a competence for handling change at a personal level. The organisations that sponsor employees on these courses know they gain if their staff become more capable of managing the personal impact of organisational change. Staff with a personal capability for change may show less resistance to change, or may need less persuasion from their peers or managers to undertake change. Resistance at an individual level is often not directed at the change but towards the change process itself.

The second aspect of capability at the individual level is *managerial capability*. How able are line and general managers to counsel and help their staff through the process of change (see Chapter 5, The transition curve)? Does the organisation's management possess the appropriate communication skills to convey a clarity about the change and a commitment to their staff? Do they possess change-counselling skills? Are any managers experienced in dealing with a number of different change initiatives at one time? Does the organisation know which managers within their staff have a high degree of competence at managing change?

Research has concluded that line manager capability is a key differentiator in accounting for the differences between success and failure in the different change histories of companies.[10] In companies that successfully transformed or changed the researchers found:

- Line managers followed through consistently on change initiatives, whereas, in companies that struggled with change, line manager response was inconsistent.

- There was a focus on a few clustered and coherent interventions. Thus, their line managers were not faced with a bewildering array of change initiatives.

- Managers were assessed and held accountable for managing change and were also rewarded for their efforts in this area.

At the *organisational* level specialist change units can be established anywhere within an organisation. Some change experts may be located within strategic planning units, Chief Executive Offices, Human Resource functions or specialist change units called Organisational Development departments. As well as displaying expertise within the broad subject of change, they may be specialists in their own right in the areas such as management development, top team development, management of high-potential or fast-track staff, or internal communications. All these functions contribute to an organisation's overall capability in handling change.

When assessing organisational change capability, consideration should be given not just to the individual functions mentioned above, but also to the extent to which they can integrate their approaches. Knowledge management, for example, is an area where information systems and human resource systems must be delivered in an integrated way in order to maximise the investment made in both areas. There is no advantage in having each function following leading-edge practices in their own areas if the systems cannot co-ordinate with each other across the whole organisation. This is particularly true in change, where systems that do not reinforce each other can be a strong barrier to change.

By their very nature *big-bang* change programmes attract greater attention. Research has shown that companies who possess a competence at this level also display certain other skills.[11] They know which levers to pull in order to achieve rapid change. Senior managers know which change initiatives can instantly tap into sources of motivation. For instance, investment bankers are primarily motivated by rewards and bonus systems. Adjusting the criteria by which bonuses are achieved is a rapid way of delivering behavioural or output change. These are, therefore, potentially key levers in achieving change within investment banks. Different levers may well be more important in other organisations. Research suggests[12] that a capability in more continuous, incremental change is based upon a set of different skills: constantly scanning the external environment; using management systems as information and communication systems; promoting flexible organisational structures; and maintaining a relative stable set of cultural values for the purpose of consistency. This is, of course, fine as long as the changes required do not challenge the core values.

The people process model[13] can be used to assess levels of change capability within an organisation. Specifically it checks out transformational competence in three areas – organisational transformation, transformation of future leaders, and the ability to transform the workforce. This model assesses the strength of linkage between individual behaviour and corporate strategy through the sophisticated use of people management processes and systems. For more details of this framework and how to use it see Appendix 2.

Capability is a difficult feature to assess in the short term. At an individual level there exists a plethora of psychometric tests that can indicate change capabilities, particularly among managerial staff. At the level of the organisation it may simply require a database of skills and different contractual arrangements. Surprisingly enough, depending on the size of the organisation, a simple questionnaire or focus group sessions with staff may uncover valuable information in this area.

3.8.2 Capability and design choices

A change agent should not design an implementation process that the organisation is not capable of delivering. Levels of change capability affect the level of sophistication with which change can be tackled.

Capability influences the choice of *change path*. Transformational change, whether evolution or revolution, is harder to achieve. This may mean that whilst transformation is the preferred change path for an organisation, it is not an option because the organisation lacks the capabilities listed in the previous section. The organisation needs to start with adaptation or reconstruction first. For instance, earlier change may entail developing managerial capability. Managers may need

Illustration 3.4   change in action

Modernising the Ministry of Defence

This case looks at the efforts of the MoD, traditionally a risk-averse organisation, to address the institution's capabilities to effect change in the late 1990s. There was a need to transform the organisation's hierarchical culture to improve teamwork and break down the boundaries between military and civilian staff. Following an office relocation from London to a greenfield, modern building in Bristol, and a reorganisation into integrated, multidisciplinary teams from specialist units, it became apparent that in order to effect a major cultural change, and foster innovation, the existing bureaucratic management structure needed to change. Traditionally characterised by a rigid hierarchy whereby people were not encouraged to speak directly to individuals who were more than two grades above them, the channels of interaction in the MoD were very regimented. Teams worked in isolation without much thought for the needs of others. A distinct split between civil servants and military personnel existed, leading to conflicting leadership styles.

The proposed transformation to a more entrepreneurial culture made managers rethink the accepted norms of their office, many of which were inherited from the armed forces. However, the prevailing culture at the MoD was ill suited to handling change, even though a high percentage of people thought change was needed. A comprehensive training programme designed to foster a climate of openness and consensus was introduced. A 50-strong MoD central training department, along with dozens of external trainers, rolled out a programme to over 6,000 civil servants and military staff. The programme involved a combination of team-building, management development and culture-change workshops. It was designed to go some way towards changing the 'bunker mentality' of many who work at the MoD, by encouraging a different way of working, where people are more able to overcome barriers between different teams. The intent was to create a learning environment in which both leaders and team members could experiment with new behaviours. The task driven culture of the MoD typically gives individuals little time to reflect on how well they are doing.

Source: Adapted from Littlefield, D. (6 July 2000) 'The big push', *People Management*, pp. 38–40.

to be taken through training and planned personal development initiatives to enhance their understanding of change and change management techniques. If the ultimate aim is evolution, business planning systems, including performance management systems, may need to be established to aid an incremental approach. Illustration 3.4 describes the management development initiatives that were necessary in order to create a change capability within the UK Ministry of Defence (MoD).

When considering *change targets*, value-led change is probably the hardest form of change to achieve as it requires skill to purposefully and successfully penetrate the values and attitudes of staff and to change them. At the very least the organisation would need to be able to demonstrate an Organisational Development capability, with perhaps a team of development specialists who have a knowledge of personal change. Some organisations have change consultancy teams with such capabilities who act as internal contractors within the organisations. A *change style* of *collaboration*, for example, may also require particular skills such as facilitation. Capability, therefore, also affects the choice of *change roles*. Consultants may need to be involved in a change process to compensate for a lack of change capability within an organisation.

Capability can affect the choice of *change levers*. Symbolism can be used as a powerful change lever but in inexperienced hands symbolic change can be counterproductive (see Chapter 6). Similarly, using Human Resource Management systems as change levers, such as recruitment and selection or reward systems, requires the staff in the Human Resources function to possess both an operational excellence in these areas and a strategic understanding of these systems' power as change mechanisms (again, see Chapter 6). In addition, as stressed above, if an organisation lacks the necessary levels of individual capability, training and personal development interventions aimed at building this capability in individuals, maybe through training on models such as the transition curve discussed in Chapter 5, will be needed.

Unfortunately, the easiest options, such as top-down and directive change, often seem the most attractive. The problem is that these options may not be the most appropriate way to inculcate change within a specific organisation. The research on change is littered with examples of organisations who either implemented inappropriate change designs, or attempted change designs that were too sophisticated for their levels of change competence. This is also why many of the change initiatives that are heralded as transformational actually result in reconstructive change.

3.9 CAPACITY

Capacity considers how much resource the organisation can invest in the proposed change both in terms of cash and staff. How much time managers have to devote to change is also an issue (Figure 3.7).

3.9.1 Assessing capacity

Many of the change programmes written up as showcase pieces feature large corporations undertaking change. The danger is that small to medium-sized enterprises try to mimic these larger programmes but without the same capacity available for investment in initiatives. The result can be over-ambitious changes announced at senior management level which fizzle out at lower levels because there is no means to manage a big-bang change. It is therefore necessary to consider which key resources are limited in any specific change scenario.

Capacity can be divided into three main areas – cash, time and people:

Figure 3.7   **Contextual feature: capacity**

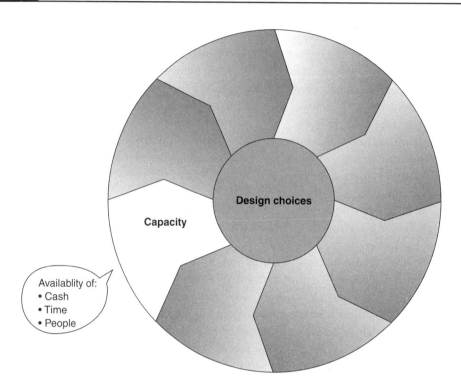

- *Cash*: Any change interventions that involve management development programmes, particularly off-site, are likely to be expensive and require considerable investment. Physical change assets, such as new technology, can also be expensive. Symbolic change, such as the relocation of offices or redesigning existing office layouts, can also require cash investment.

- *Time*: During change, time is a very valuable resource. Difficult questions need to be addressed about how much time is available for senior managers to devote to leading the change. Middle managers often feel squeezed by the pressures of change. All too often they are expected to implement several different change initiatives whilst at the same time continuing to deliver on all their normal performance targets. If a change agent wants line or general managers to give attention to change initiatives then he or she needs to consider creating time for them. Some organisations remove managers' responsibility for certain routine tasks for a limited period of time in order to create time for the implementation of change. These issues are discussed in Chapter 7.

- *People*: The issue of capability has already been considered, but quantity is also relevant. Are there sufficient people or managers who are competent in the management of change and committed to the change itself? Are these people sufficient to create the momentum needed for the change to be carried out?

Illustration 3.5

change in action

Canon, capacity and change

Canon, the Japanese electronics firm, has managed to sustain an unprecedented period of performance, reporting in October 2002 a 53 per cent jump in profits in the third quarter. This equated to expected earnings of ¥175 billion ($1.43 billion) for the full year, and would deliver the firm's third consecutive year of record profits, and maintain an 11–12 per cent return on equity that puts most Japanese companies to shame. All this during a period when a dismal home market and sliding exports crippled other Japanese electronics firms.

Much of Canon's ability to maintain its profitability in such an adverse market environment stems from its capacity to blend its traditional Japanese formula of winning technology battles, with the adoption of more prosaic Western business practices to cut costs. Fujio Mitarai, Canon's president and chief executive, has applied some of the lessons he learned during his 23 years at Canon

in America. He has narrowed the focus of Canon, by quitting businesses such as personal computers, typewriters and liquid crystal displays. In addition he has introduced new methods on the factory floor, and better cash flow management. His approach is that high market share is not enough on its own. It must generate profits and high returns. Cost-cutting is used to reinforce this approach.

However, Mr Mitarai is also willing to invest in leading-edge technology. By ploughing almost 8 per cent of revenues into R&D, Canon has protected and improved on the core technologies that give it an edge in the printer and copier markets. Such investment has allowed Canon to build up a capacity not just to churn out patents, but also to achieve and sustain market leadership. Canon now accounts for nearly 60 per cent of the profitable laser printing market, along with high-margin printer consumables such as toner cartridges.

Source: Adapted from 'Canon: Hard to copy', *The Economist*, 2 November 2002, 365 (8297), p. 79.

Illustration 3.5 describes the investment of time and resources that the CEO of Canon, the Japanese electronics firm, and his fellow managers have invested in continuous change to deliver both improved business processes and new technologies. These investments have enabled Canon to retain its competitive edge.

3.9.2 Capacity and design choices

Cash capacity affects the choice of *change path*. Big-bang programmes may be costly. Incremental change may require less investment, in terms of cash and resources, upfront, but only if the management system infrastructure and line manager capability is already in place. If not, then substantial investment will be needed to build up the systems and capability.

Likewise value-led change, if it is to be successful, involves a heavy investment in the participative/collaborative/educative change levers that will need to be used to achieve the *target* of value-driven change. Investment is needed in the form of both managerial time and money. Changing outputs or behaviours is much cheaper in terms of investing time and money but may not deliver the change that is needed.

Higher levels of capacity, in terms of time, cash and people, are needed for collaborative, educative or participative *styles* of change. Less time and money is needed in the short term for directive styles of change – although there is always the risk that managing the resistance to extreme forms of direction may be more costly in the longer term.

Choosing the right people for the key *roles* in change management also raises questions of capacity. The chief executive may be the company's most charismatic leader but if he or she simply has not time to devote to the leadership of the change process then alternative candidates need to be considered. If the company has little time but does have cash then there is the option of bringing in an external change consultancy to help manage the change, or assembling an internal change action team to lead it through the organisation.

3.10 READINESS

Readiness for change exists at two levels. The first is the extent to which staff are aware of the need for change. The second is the amount of personal commitment there is towards changing individual skills, attitudes, behaviours or work prac-

Figure 3.8   Contextual feature: readiness

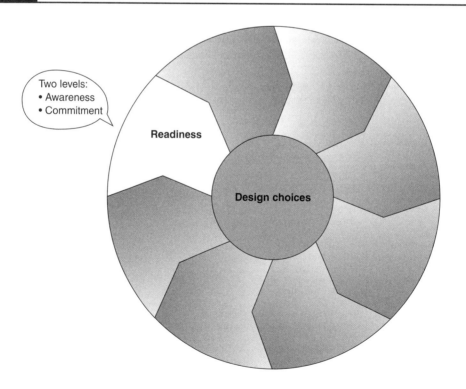

tices (Figure 3.8). This is a critical feature within the change context and accurate assessment of staff readiness at the earliest opportunity can make a fundamental difference to the design of the change, and therefore the likelihood of success.

3.10.1 Assessing readiness

This feature helps change agents to assess how prepared staff are for change. Change agents therefore need to understand the degree to which staff are aware that change is necessary, and the degree of motivation staff feel towards change. Staff can be aware at a rational level of the need for change but be unprepared at an emotional level to embrace change personally.

Low awareness of the need for change is primarily a reflection of the inadequacy of communication in an organisation about the need for change and relates to issues such as channels of communication, and the content of the information sent through the channels (see Chapter 6). Achieving awareness of change through communication is relatively easy. Commitment to change exists at a very personal level and is harder to create. It is linked to the idea of personal transition which is explored further in Chapter 5. Low commitment for change can exist for a variety of reasons but many of them stem from self-interest. At a simple level the change may be disadvantageous to the individual. For instance, it may lead to a loss of power or status, or potentially a loss of job. At a deeper level the individual may fear the prospect of change. Research has shown that employees can be ambivalent about change – they can think that the proposed change is a good idea but at the same time be frightened by the thought of what is involved.[14]

Retail bank cashiers in the high street branches of banks were originally employed on the basis of their reliability with figures and willingness to conform to tightly regulated procedures and systems. They have had their jobs transformed through the introduction of a sales environment into the branch networks as more of the basic transactional banking is removed onto the lower-cost telephone and Internet channels. Most of them understand full well the reason for the change and what it involves. However, their personal commitment to change may be low for a number of reasons. One is that the prospect of change after years of stable employment is daunting in itself. However, there is also the threat of unemployment if they cannot succeed in developing the new skills required within a sales organisation. With employment experience only within the retail banking system they may find themselves with few transferable skills and therefore low employability outside the banking sector. For such reasons there will be low commitment to change. Chapter 4 considers the case of change at a retail bank over a ten-year period and explores many of these issues.

Not only will there be different forms of readiness within an organisation, but usually the awareness and commitment levels will vary according to the level of employee within the organisation. This often presents problems in the implementation of change. For instance, a senior team of an organisation may be expert at anticipating future market trends over the next five to ten years. As a result, the team may recognise that the organisation needs to start to change now in order to be able to respond competitively to the changing environment. However, if the organisation is in good health, with excellent profits and high staff satisfaction, the problem the senior managers face is how to demonstrate the need for change to lower levels of staff.

The case of Glaxo at the end of the 1980s illustrates this gap of understanding. Senior managers were aware that their successful drug Zantac was due to come off-patent in the mid-1990s. As this superdrug accounted for nearly half of Glaxo's turnover at that time its patent expiry would bring massive changes to the fortunes of the company. However, at the end of the 1980s the company was

---

Illustration 3.6   *change in action*

Readiness for change in a state orchestra

In the early 1990s, Brazil's state-owned São Paulo State Symphony Orchestra (Osesp) fell on hard times. Lacking funding for new facilities, the orchestra was reduced to rehearsing in a canteen. Aware of how serious the situation had become, by 1995 the government decided Osesp was in need of a radical overhaul. The task of rebuilding the organisation was given to John Neschling, who became conductor and artistic director in 1997. Mr Neschling's experience convinced him that if he were going to run Osesp, he would need better facilities and more flexibility. He convinced the government that if the changes were to succeed, he would need a new concert hall, decent salaries and the freedom to hire and fire musicians. The new hall, the Sala São Paulo, was constructed in a flamboyant, British-built railway station in the inner city, at a cost of £23 million. This showed the government's willingness to support much-needed change, and an understanding of what would be required to make the change successful.

Mr Neschling also focused his attention on achieving significant changes within the orchestra itself. He asked for, and eventually achieved, a major reshuffle of the musicians, many of whom in the past had been guaranteed jobs for life as state employees. Musicians agreed to be taken off the state payroll and be hired under service contracts. In recompense, it was agreed that salaries would almost triple, so as to attract foreign players. Mr Neschling then set up rigorous auditions in São Paolo, New York and Bucharest. New musicians and Osesp's existing players alike had to pass. About half of the musicians, mostly the younger ones, stayed on. The changes were not accepted by all, and seven musicians who objected to the new contracts and Mr Neschling's management style were fired after they began organising protests.

Osesp's first few seasons were hugely successful. The repertoire is broad, and the young orchestra has been reinvigorated, with a clean, stylistic image. The orchestra now plays to a capacity crowd of 1,500 twice a week.

Unquestionably, the successful transformation was due to a large extent to the awareness by both the government and Osesp staff of the need for change, and their readiness to make difficult choices in bringing it about.

Source: Adapted from Wheatley, J., 'A new arrangement for a troubled orchestra', *Financial Times*, 31 October 2002, Inside Track, p. 15.

highly successful and the employees highly trusting of their senior management's ability to lead them through change. The task was to make them aware of the need to change in the first instance, and in the second to test out staff's commitment to change at a personal level.

The case of the Brazilian State Orchestra (Illustration 3.6) describes what can be achieved when there is a crisis and correspondingly a high readiness for change. The conductor was able to negotiate changes to working practices that would have been impossible to achieve had the musicians been unaware or uncommitted to change. Paradoxically sometimes a high readiness for change may raise expectations for speed and effectiveness of change within customers and staff that managers then fail to deliver against. For instance, the concept of privatisation of nationalised industries is often sold to the electorate on the promise of immediate improvements in cost-effectiveness and customer service. Yet often the paradigmatic change that is required within these sorts of organisations can take years to implement, and in the interim the customer base can get frustrated or feel cheated by the slow response. In other organisations, a lack of action from senior managers when staff are ready to embrace change can leave staff frustrated and result in a high turnover.

3.10.2 Readiness and design choices

A low readiness for change has implications for the *change path* selected. If an organisation has a complacent workforce, the change may need to take a change *path* that is big-bang in nature but only achieves (deliberately) realignment rather than transformation for the organisation. This high-impact change design may be necessary in order to shake staff out of their complacency in readiness for a subsequent more fundamental change initiative. This is what was done at Glaxo (see above) at the beginning of the 1990s to achieve some level of readiness among staff.

If personal change is not perceived as necessary by staff, this also impacts *the change style*. If time allows, the change agent may need to lead a participative or collaborative campaign that engages the personalities of the staff involved. Merely directing staff to change may be insufficient. Likewise if there is low readiness for change it may be impossible to expect change to *start* at the bottom of the organisation and percolate upwards. Instead, top-down change may be necessary to kick-start the process. Alternatively, change agents could consider using pockets of good practice or pilot sites to start change initiatives. These pilot sites could symbolically act as role models for the rest of the organisation. Chapter 5 discusses these issues and tactics for developing readiness in more detail.

A low readiness for change is likely to necessitate a *change role* of leadership. Anyone who is to lead the change must demonstrate two things to the rest of the organisation: an absolute belief or passion in the need for change and a commitment to change themselves. The change leader must also demonstrate the visible manifestation of that change to all staff in the organisation. Therefore, senior managers who are potential change champions need to be assessed against these criteria. Otherwise, they may espouse the need to change to the rest of the organisation, whilst contradicting what they espouse by not changing their own working practices.

Change levers to be considered when there is low readiness for change include personal development courses for senior managers and other levels of staff which are designed to encourage them to recognise the need for change. Where staff understand the meaning of the change but perceive little gain from it, the change agent may need to accept that some staff will not change and therefore contemplate voluntary or compulsory exits from the organisation.

When the organisation displays a high readiness for change then change champions may find themselves pushing on an open door. The menu of design choices is increased.

3.11 POWER

A consideration of power examines where power is vested within an organisation (Figure 3.9). It is to do with the identification of the major stakeholders (within

Figure 3.9   Contextual feature: power

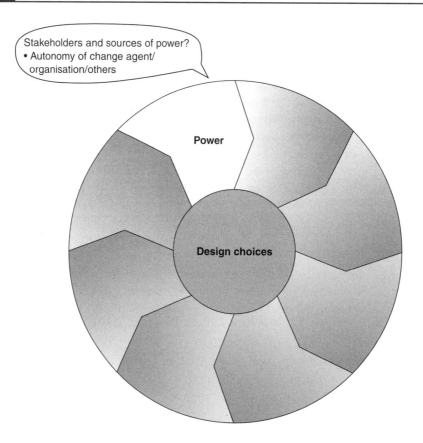

and outside the organisation) and individuals or departments that hold power in the organisation. Other issues include whose support must be canvassed and how much discretion the change unit holds.

3.11.1 Assessing power

Power can be understood on many levels. Here it is considered from two perspectives – the personal power exercised within organisations by individuals or groups of people, and the power of the organisation to determine its own future.

Understanding the personal power and politics within an organisation, and identifying the major power brokers, is critical. The best choice in design terms may not be achievable because of powerful coalitions who may block the change because of their own agendas. To give a practical illustration, in the health service the medical consultants are powerful figures. Any change agent within a hospital needs to be able to convince a critical mass of consultants that the change is necessary in order to get processes implemented. Similarly, at KPMG, Sharman had to convince a critical mass of other partners of the need for change (see Chapter 2, Illustration 2.6), since he did not have the power to push change on to his fellow partners.

In organisational terms, many change texts assume that an organisation's management team have full latitude of discretion in terms of the choices they can make about change. In reality, many organisations are constrained in what they can undertake by their relationship with other institutions. This is particularly true of public sector organisations contemplating change. They may not be allowed to choose the obvious or best course of action because of constraints placed on them by their political masters. However, this lack of room for manoeuvre is not restricted to sectors with government involvement. In private sector organisations change agents face other constraints on their decision making because of forces beyond the organisation. For instance, membership of a group of companies can be a constraint. The WH Smith example in the next chapter illustrates a change situation where the division concerned is unable to release itself from its role as cash cow within the broader group, which impacts upon its choice of change approach.

Shareholders or institutions like the stock market can also have an impact on change. Illustration 3.7 briefly describes the high-profile case of the difficulties experienced by Carly Fiorino when negotiating the proposed merger between HP and Compaq with the shareholders of HP. It details a painful lesson in the risks of failing to ensure the commitment of key stakeholders to a deal, and the extent to which powerful groups can be mobilised when they believe the soul or culture of a company is under attack.

A useful way of assessing who has power and their position on the proposed change is to use stakeholder analysis (see Appendix 3). A stakeholder analysis enables a change agent to consider what they can do to gain support for their

Illustration 3.7

change in action

Carly Fiorina and the HP/Compaq merger

The planned merger between Hewlett-Packard (HP) and Compaq dominated business headlines for many reasons, not least because of the extraordinary power struggle between stakeholders in determining the outcome of the most controversial acquisition in the history of the computer industry.

Carly Fiorina was appointed CEO of HP in 1999, with a mandate for radical change. By early 2001, HP was grappling with a severe economic downturn which served to highlight its weaknesses. Squeezed at the bottom end of the market by Dell Computer, HP was also facing stiff competition from Sun Microsystems in the server market, and remained a weak challenger to IBM in high-end computing and consulting. The aim of the HP/Compaq merger was that together, the two companies would have the scale and breadth to challenge Sun Microsystems and IBM by providing considerable synergies and complementary market competences, boosting lucrative services revenues. HP would be transformed into a computing powerhouse that could provide end-to-end products and services.

Despite the rhetoric, it quickly became apparent that investors were not impressed. HP's shares fell 22 per cent the week the acquisition was announced. Market concerns revolved around the recognition that the deal would increase HP's exposure to the money-losing PC business, and there were doubts about the quality of the services business. Another concern was with the difficulty of integrating two such large businesses. However, Ms Fiorina's attempts to convince the majority of institutional shareholders to support the acquisition initially had an impact, with

investors indicating that they had begun to believe the deal could go through. Then Walter Hewlett, a board member and son of the company's co-founder, publicly confirmed in November 2001 that he was opposing the deal. Ms Fiorina had failed to sell her vision to a man who was not only a board member, but also the second most important shareholder. Furthermore, in December the Packard board also came out against the deal. All of HP's heirs, controlling 18 per cent of the company, were now against the acquisition.

It is a tribute to Ms Fiorina's determination that the deal did not fall apart then. Compaq's nerves were starting to fray, and HP's management had to allay their fears. The uncertainty over the deal could be damaging to both companies if it was not cleared up quickly. Importantly, HP's board did not waver, and non-executive board members spoke out in Ms Fiorina's favour. This allowed HP to embark on an offensive aimed at dismissing Mr Hewlett's objections to the acquisition. A bitter and public battle to win the support of the shareholders ensued. A poll sponsored by David Packard, son of the other company's co-founder, claimed that two-thirds of staff was against the deal. HP countered with its own survey, showing that 66 per cent of staff supported the acquisition.

Eventually, Ms Fiorina's proposal won, but only by the narrowest of margins. However, this was a painful lesson in the risks of failing to ensure the commitment of key stakeholders to the deal, and the danger of over-optimism demonstrated by the HP management, leading to a bitter proxy battle for the soul of the company.

Source: Adapted from Abrahams, P., Kehoe, L., Morrison, S. and Wine, E., 'The battle is over – the struggle begins', *Financial Times*, 1 May 2002, Companies & Finance, p. 28.

proposed changes from those who hold power and are against the changes or are ambivalent to them. It also enables a change agent to consider how weaker stakeholders can be used to help endorse change.

3.11.2 Power and design choices

Power, or lack of it, can influence the choice of change *path* taken. A business division may badly need transformational change, but its managers can be prevented from embarking upon such a route because other more powerful divisions, or the group's centre, block their actions. Equally a powerful parent can be a strong facilitator of change.

Powerful individuals may block the change path in the same way. A powerful chief executive who feels a potential threat from the proposed change can squash a plan for transformation in favour of more modest realignment routes. Equally, an overpowerful change agent or executive can insist on a change process which is disproportionately large in comparison to the problem the organisation is trying to address. However, the agent or executive concerned may see this as a way of raising their profile and visibility within the organisation and the wider business community.

Powerful individuals, such as managing directors or chief executives, can push through directive change. However, where the agent has identified powerful groups within the organisation whose support and commitment needs to be retained, then a more collaborative style is appropriate. Paradoxically, highly powerful individuals such as chief executive officers who take a leadership role can be counterproductive when the *target* for change is values and the culture they are trying to remove is one based on blame and fear. If the CEO is seen as a bully but leads the change, staff will merely start to mimic the desired values because they feel threatened. This will not lead to significant change and the issue will never be addressed due to the atmosphere of fear.

Power is critical when assigning *roles* within a change process. If a change champion or leader is to be appointed then the change agent needs to pick a powerful individual or provide the individual with powerful backing. Then they also need to consider other stakeholder groups and whether or not to incorporate them in some way into the change process, particularly if these groups could be obstructive.

Specific *levers* to deal with power include techniques such as breaking and reforming both formal and informal power structures within organisations; using the existence of cliques, networks and those with influence to gain buy-in for change; and drawing on resistance management techniques (see Chapter 7).

3.12 SUMMARY

In this chapter we have discussed the need to analyse the change context in order to avoid using inappropriate change formulae. This contextual analysis is the key to successful change for it is the context that should drive the design choices that are made rather than personal bias on the part of the change agent. In particular the chapter has:

- Explained the use of the change kaleidoscope as a diagnostic framework for mapping the change context.
- Described each of the eight contextual features of time, scope, preservation, diversity, capability, capacity, readiness for change and power from the kaleidoscope.
- Discussed the design implications of each of the contextual features.

This chapter has also outlined the various diagnostic frameworks that can be used to understand these contextual features. The next chapter explores the interaction between these features of change context and the design choices through several case studies.

REFERENCES

1. For more information on this research see Gratton, L., Hope Hailey, V., Stiles, P. and Truss, C. (2004) *Lessons from the Leading Edge*, Oxford: Oxford University Press.
2. The term 'burning platform' is a popular term used for a compelling reason and vision for change.
3. For more details on how to carry out a resource audit see Chapter 4, *Exploring Corporate Strategy*, 6th edition.
4. For more information on tacit capabilities, see Barney, J.B. (1995) 'Looking inside for competitive advantage', *Academy of Management Executive*, IX (4), 49–61; and Prahalad, C.K. and Hamel, G. (1990) 'The core competence of the corporation', *Harvard Business Review*, 68 (3), 79–91. Chapter 4, *Exploring Corporate Strategy*, 6th edition, also discusses how to identify more intangible resources.
5. For more information on the UK Rail example see Maitland, A. (16 October 2001) 'If downsizing, protect the corporate memory', *Financial Times*, p. 18. Also see Ambrosini, V. (2002) 'Organisational success and its vulnerability', *Management Focus*, 19, Winter, Cranfield School of Management, for more information on the impact of downsizing on organisational success.
6. See Wright, P.M. and Snell, S. (1998) 'Towards a unifying framework for exploring fit and flexibility in Strategic Human Resource Management', *Academy of Management Review*, 23 (4), 756–72.
7. See reference 1 above.
8. See Fernandes, E. (5 December 2002) 'Tea producer seeks a stronger brew', *Financial Times*, p. 13.
9. Teece, D., Pisano, G. and Shuen, A. (1997) 'Dynamic capabilities and strategic management', *Strategic Management Journal*, 18 (7), 509–33.
10. See Gratton, L., Hope Hailey, V., Stiles, P. and Truss, C. (1999) *Strategic Human Resource Management*, Oxford: Oxford University Press.
11. See reference 10 above.

12. See Hope Hailey, V. (2004) 'Crafting agility – the case for flexibility', in Gratton, L., Hope Hailey, V., Stiles, P. and Truss, C. (eds) *Lessons from the Leading Edge*, Oxford: Oxford University Press.
13. See reference 10 above.
14. Piderit, S.K. (2000) 'Rethinking resistance and recognizing ambivalence', *Academy of Management Review*, 25 (4), 783–94.

WORK ASSIGNMENTS

3.1 There are many textbooks and articles on 'how to do change'. Read two or three of these to identify the different change recipes advocated.

3.2 Consider an organisation with which you are familiar. Identify the aspects of the organisation that would need to be preserved in any change initiative and explain why.

3.3 Identify an organisation with low diversity and another organisation with high diversity. What are the implications for change for both these organisations?

3.4 How would you evaluate change capability within an organisation? What sources of information, for example, would you draw on?

3.5 How does a lack of capacity (cash/people/time) limit your design choices?

3.6 How might a change agent heighten readiness using technical, political, cultural, and interpersonal interventions?

Analysing the change context: making change judgements

4.1 INTRODUCTION

The previous chapter explained how to analyse the change context using the change kaleidoscope. Eight change contextual features were outlined: time, scope, preservation, diversity, capability, readiness, capacity and power. This chapter uses three extended case studies to develop the readers' understanding of how to use the change kaleidoscope. Its aim is to help the reader to identify the critical contextual features in each case and understand their implications for the design choices.

This chapter is deliberately different in style from the other chapters due to the nature of the material used. The descriptions are as rich in contextual features as space permits, although in a real situation the change agent would seek much more detail. Each change feature within the kaleidoscope is analysed in every case. Through this case study analysis the chapter examines:

- How to understand change context using the change kaleidoscope.
- How to identify which contextual features are critical.
- How the analysis of context is linked to the decisions made about change.

4.2 BAYER DIAGNOSTICS EUROPE

This case study examines one company's strategy to address a shift in market trends across Europe and also to seize an opportunity to create a pan-European organisation (Illustration 4.1). The objectives for the change process were to (1) create greater organisational and cultural cohesion, (2) achieve cost savings and (3) improve customer service.

Illustration 4.1

change in action

Bayer Diagnostics Europe: a case study on pan-Europeanisation

In late 1998, Chris Tobin, then a senior manager in Bayer Pharmaceuticals, was promoted to Senior Vice-President, heading Bayer Diagnostics Europe (Bayer DS EU), another division within the Bayer AG organisation. Bayer DS EU comprised 20 national operations, had 1,800 employees and an annual turnover of €600 million. His appointment was made against a background of patchy performance across the various countries. Chris Tobin's remit was clear; to radically improve Bayer DS EU's performance and put in place a strategic model that would serve as the foundation for sustainable growth.

The European market was changing. There was a trend towards European convergence. Customer needs in different European countries were becoming more similar, illustrating significant convergence of market needs. This heralded a likely move away from fragmented, nationally independent markets. The reasons for such an erosion of cultural and national distinctions were converging European legislation, greater cross-border transparency and increasingly similar national standards and behaviour.

Further, as a consequence of technological advancement, diagnostic healthcare providers throughout Europe were engaged in a process of consolidation of their laboratory sites. Rather than investing in small dedicated laboratories and technologies, healthcare providers were investing in fewer, automated, full-scope laboratories. Such a shift was also manifested in product development, where the industry was showing a trend of increasing commoditisation, resulting in greater uniformity in products across Europe.

As a result, Bayer Diagnostics was facing a changing market, moving away from fragmented nationally based domains towards greater convergence and consolidation. Therefore, the drivers for Bayer Diagnostics' pan-Europeanisation were market convergence, greater price transparency, increasing commoditisation of products and much more intense competition. These factors identified a two-pronged need for change; greater consistency in operations and functions across all European entities, and a new approach for adding value beyond the traditional product offering.

The initial approach for Europe was to be focused on adding a greater dimension of integration and control of the different constituent countries, whilst not losing the level of local responsiveness and operation currently in place. A small central team was envisaged with the aim of adding value through stretching performance, sharing ideas across Europe and leveraging the scale that a combined European organisation could provide. These measures were aimed at creating '*a Centre that was staffed by a small team focused on long term, allowing countries to run their business*'. The approach was to be communicated as '*regional leadership*'.

How Chris Tobin and his management team were to go about implementing the strategy was clearly critical. A great deal of attention was paid to rolling out the strategy and the '**Vision**' **phase** successfully. Right from the beginning, in early 1999, a **European Leadership Team** (ELT) was formed, with the top 90 managers from all the European operations. This was to constitute the driving body for formulating and implementing the strategic plan for Europeanisation. The ELT would meet regularly, providing the forum for communicating the Vision and establishing the new European culture. The ELT was based on trust and participation, and reduced the need for an implementation team.

One of the key drivers for change was the need to create consistency among all European operations. This was to be achieved through various initiatives designed around '**best practice**' – taking procedures and practices from the countries with the best performance and applying them across Europe. This was to be achieved through part-time cross-national teams, drawn from the ELT, looking at functions from a Europe-wide perspective.

A key development resulting from the establishment of the Centre was the opportunity to measure, control and set consistent targets for all the European countries – something that had not been possible previously. The Centre therefore gave itself the task of setting **stretch targets** for its ELT members, and encouraging clearer, more frequent communication among countries. This afforded the Centre a greater degree of authority over planning and control.

Other new initiatives resulting from the strategy changes were focused on people development. A **Leadership Development Programme** was introduced, aimed at providing better training and support for members of the ELT. This was supported by a **rewards system** that was introduced in parallel with the change initiatives. Finally, from early on in the change the ELT designed a '**balanced scorecard**', providing the first opportunity to apply a uniform system throughout Europe that allowed greater visibility within operations.

Despite progress achieved by initiatives emerging from the early phase of change, in June 1999 Chris Tobin received a '**provocation**' from the Bayer President Rolf Classon, challenging why Europe needed significantly more people to run its business than the USA, despite very similar levels of sales. In response to this the DS EU centre developed proposals for a more integrated European approach.

The philosophy for Europeanisation therefore encouraged national operations to focus their efforts on customer facing activities, whilst the expanded Centre pooled non-core back-office activities and took greater ownership of systems and processes. The rationale behind this structure lay in the recognition that to delight a customer in a distinctive market (Europe was converging, but was still not one homogenous market), customer service needed to be tailored to meet national characteristics, and the best people to do that were at a local level. Also, sales and operational marketing activities were the functions best represented at national levels. On the other hand, business management activities, such as warehousing, accounting, strategic planning and HR, could all be pooled, as they didn't reflect the country offices' core competences. There was duplication of resources and processes in the country operations that could be cut.

The result of this strategic development was that the Centre would have two roles. One to provide strategic guidance without interfering in operational activities, the other to provide 'shared services' for the 'back-office' functions where economies of scale could be achieved. In this way the centre hoped to avoid the ivory tower phenomenon of some headquarters, by offering a shared services structure, rather than centralisation.

Despite the networks that had been created and the opening up of communications across European countries, the Europeanisation philosophy was resisted by a number of the country organisations who genuinely believed that moving any functions out of the countries would be detrimental to their ability to service customers.

However, in June 2000, Bayer Diagnostics globally ran into trouble with significant additional costs due to exchange rate changes. In response to this Bayer Diagnostics launched **Project CURE**, a far-reaching turnaround exercise. In Europe, Project CURE focused on customer profitability and implementing the integrated European structure for marketing, supply chain, customer support and back-office operations.

In light of the imperative to turn around the performance of Bayer Diagnostics, Europeanisation and the tough new targets set by the Centre for each country operation met little resistance.

One of the early visible successes emerging from Project CURE was the project on 'Customer Profitability'. An index of Bayer DS EU's customers' profitability was drawn up across Europe. Customer profitability proved to be subject to a Pareto effect, whereby 80 per cent of the profits were derived from 20 per cent of customers whilst some 15 per cent of customers were loss making to the organisation. Bayer DS EU adjusted their management of those customers and developed a process for monitoring all customer accounts. This project provided a valuable source of revenue improvement and, for the first time, a clear and consistent customer management strategy across Europe. The Customer Profitability Project would not have been possible if the networks initiated in 1999 had not been established.

During Project CURE, the strategic **centralisation of European marketing** was completed, resulting in marketing directors overseeing from the Centre the emergence of consistent and structured strategies across Europe. Where previously each country was responsible for designing and running its own marketing approach (resulting even in different product packaging), the centralised marketing team ensured that a consistent strategy was devised, allowing local marketing teams to tailor the strategy to their domestic needs.

By 2001 a new phase of the change transformation was initiated. **Project Enterprise**, an investment in enabling technology, was designed to implement a common IT system across Europe. The change would introduce consistent and transparent standards, along with consistent management information, across all European operations and, importantly, enable a reduction in the number of warehouses in Europe from 16 to just 2, serving northern and southern Europe.

All the above initiatives were designed to pull the Bayer DS EU organisation irrevocably towards a pan-European structure and culture through three distinct levers identified by senior management at the start. These levers were stretching people and performance (e.g. stretch targets, ELT and Leadership Development Training), sharing best practices (e.g. centralised marketing and Customer Profitability) and leveraging economies of scale (Projects CURE and Enterprise).

Since the change project for pan-Europeanisation was initiated in early 1999, Bayer DS EU have managed to increase their profit margin and market share. Chris Tobin and his management team attribute much of this success to the ongoing change programme, and in particular the initiatives associated with Project Cure.

At the time of writing, Project Enterprise, the common IT system, has been implemented in the Iberia, Benelux and France branches.

In the last year Bayer AG, Bayer DS EU's parent company, announced plans to merge its five distinct healthcare divisions (Diagnostics, Pharmaceuticals, Animal Health, Consumer Care, Biological Products) into one entity, Bayer HealthCare. This new change will provide yet more opportunities and further challenges to DS EU to improve its contribution to the Bayer business, yet again testing its ability to effectively manage transition.

Therefore, in late 2002, after almost four years, Bayer DS EU was still in the midst of change. There have been some clear successes. However, question marks still remain over the future role of the Centre in pooling resources and functions, and synthesising Europe's strategy with that of global strategy.

Source: © Paul Arnold, 2002. We acknowledge with thanks the help of Peter Morgan of Bayer DS EU in the preparation of this case.

4.2.1 The kaleidoscope of Bayer Diagnostics

Illustration 4.1 shows that *time* was not a major problem for Bayer DS EU in the late 1990s as the change process had about three to five years to deliver the change. Nevertheless, presumably the falling performance of Bayer Diagnostics overall resulted in an awareness that some immediate cost savings were necessary. Therefore there was initial pressure to do 'something', with a longer-term *scope* of more transformational change.

In fact, the changes put in place by Chris Tobin targeted the senior managers and back-office operations, but not the front-office sales personnel. He wanted to impact as little as possible the people at the coalface. Customer-facing staff were allowed to continue to operate, more or less, as they always had, to maintain local customer responsiveness. The intent was to shift the senior managers and the individual back-office operations in each country away from existing assumptions of independence, autonomy and locally developed procedures, to integration, centralised decision making/control, and shared common services. The *scope* was also broad as well as deep. It affected all European operations. In the longer term the change also affected the operation of Bayer Diagnostics worldwide, as global operations would need to be adjusted to meet the demands of a pan-European organisation. The extent to which this was apparent at the outset of the restructure is unclear. By mid-2002 the impact on worldwide operations was being felt. Similarly, by 2002, it was necessary to think about the front-office European operations.

Bayer wanted to *preserve* the brand and product quality and also staff commitment. The biggest threat to the change lay in the *diversity* of the European organisation. There was large heterogeneity in terms of national culture but also in terms of size and maturity of the different country units. The branches also operated independently of each other. The change meant that each country lost power, headcount and ability to set its own strategy. This was the most significant barrier to change. The *capability* for change was mixed across the company, and the internal economic pressures experienced by Bayer Diagnostics worldwide meant there was little *capacity* with which to run the change.

Although there was rational acceptance of the strategy there was questionable emotional *readiness* for change. That is understandable given that countries, and the individuals within them, had much to lose in terms of power, status, budget and control. Some of the managers were long serving members of staff. Since there was no burning platform for change these personal feelings acted as restraints on the whole change process.

The *power* was one of the most positive influences upon the change context. Chris Tobin had clear authority at the outset of the change, and was fortunate to have support from Bayer HQ.

4.2.2 Key contextual features of Bayer Diagnostics

See Figure 4.1.

4.2.3 Design implications for Bayer Diagnostics

To appreciate the full design implications for Bayer DS EU it is necessary to take into account the findings from a change progress evaluation in mid-2002 by an independent consultant. The majority of managers accepted the strategy and vision. People felt the new direction was a breath of fresh air and Chris Tobin's leadership style was perceived to be participative. The early ELT meetings were seen as useful in encouraging a common culture and networking among managers. Likewise the LDC training was well received, and most unusually for a change process, communication was unanimously praised. The smaller European divisions viewed the concept of best practice very positively.

Inevitably concerns were expressed. Some felt that the strategy and structure had been developed too fast. The new Centre came in for criticism with remarks such as 'it takes but does not give' from its location in the UK. Not all the units had seen immediate benefits from the centralised marketing. Some interviewees

Figure 4.1 **Key contextual features for Bayer Diagnostics (1999)**

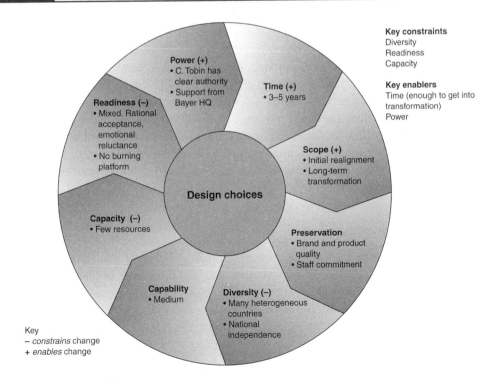

still felt confused over the new roles – 'Who is my boss?' Similarly the problems of the diversity of Europe were still there, although to a lesser extent.

There was a danger that the change could lose momentum as communication had started to tail off. The consultant concluded that whilst the change had been a success, there was now a need to focus on some softer levers for change. He also recommended that new initiatives, such as the ELT, were subject to constant development and evaluation as needs changed over time.

Change path

There was time for the changes to be evolutionary in nature and, as part of the change process, to build required levels of readiness and capability. However, at the time of the evaluation of the change there remained a need to sustain the change path by introducing new softer elements to achieve the full back-office transformation.

Start-point

The change start-point was top-down. Given the diversity and mixed readiness within the business it would have been difficult to adopt any other approach. However, the top-down approach was criticised in terms of 'best practice' as managers felt that it had been developed too quickly with insufficient internal benchmarking. Likewise, Project Enterprise was criticised for the way it was implemented as it was seen as too uniform and not tailored to meet local needs.

Change style

Within the top-down approach, the CEO, Chris Tobin, practised a very participative style of leadership, which drew in key stakeholders from the diverse European units. This helped him to gain general acceptance for the new strategy. The ELT meetings and the cross-functional teams were used to ensure that the ELT members felt involved. However, given the diversity within Europe, perhaps he could have adapted the style to a more collaborative approach over time, particularly over difficult issues such as 'best practice' or 'Project Enterprise'. Time was not a sufficient issue to rule out collaboration.

Change roles

The CEO took the change leadership role for himself. Given his past reputation for a participative style of management, and the extent of diversity he needed to harness, this was clearly the right decision for a change that would inevitably not please all of the people all of the time. An external consultant who provided challenge and objectivity throughout the process assisted him. However, there was evidence that the cross-functional working teams needed to be supported in their work in the field.

Change target

The target for the change combined both outputs and behaviours, which matched the project deliverables on costs and the capacity constraints on the change process, but potentially limited the extent of transformation. As cost reductions needed to be delivered, new outputs were defined early on through stretch targets in performance. The restructuring and job redesign resulting from the establishment of the Centre and the shared services meant that over time behaviours would change. These changes were supported by initiatives such as the Leadership Training and the ELT meetings. However this behavioural change was mainly required at a senior managerial level – many of the lower levels of staff remained unaffected.

Change levers

The levers used appear to have been primarily technical – structures and systems. These interventions were important in bringing together and reducing some of the diversity in operations – a key aim of the changes. There is some evidence of interpersonal levers in the Leadership development and the ELT. Clearly the technical changes were communicated well and this helped their implementation, as did Chris Tobin's style of leadership.

However, some change challenges remained post-2002. Softer symbolic aspects were missed from the change levers. For instance, the Centre was criticised for being too 'anglicised' in its approach. The location of central offices sends a very powerful message to employees. The repercussions of it being offshore from mainland Europe are reflected in these criticisms.

Perhaps more could have been done symbolically to erode the idea of a 'British' regional office. Furthermore, more cultural changes need to be introduced to sustain the change so that it becomes fully embedded. This may require an accompanying shift in the target of the interventions.

4.3 WH SMITH NEWS DIVISION

This case looks at the change experienced by one division within the WH Smith Group. At the time that this case was written the WH Smith Group in the UK was predominately a retail group with a large chain of newsagents/booksellers, specialist bookshops, music/media shops and a distribution business. The distribution business is the subject of the case study (see Illustration 4.2). The case study describes the change process put in place by the division at the end of the 1980s and the beginning of the 1990s. The case brings out the problems faced by mature corporations that are seeking corporate renewal.

This case demonstrates the constraints on change design that can flow from having a low capacity and capability for change. It also shows how powerful

Illustration 4.2

WH Smith News Distribution

WH Smith News was the largest distributor of newspapers and magazines in the UK by market share and turnover and was part of the WH Smith Group. News had 4,300 employees in 72 wholesale houses and over 22,000 retail customers. The group set broad financial and growth targets for the News division, which had a large degree of autonomy on how to achieve them. Since the News Division was the cash-rich division within the Group, effectiveness in achieving financial targets was vital. In 1989 the WH Smith Group instigated a process of corporate renewal. The need for change in the News Division was particularly strong as in 1988 the division had lost £40 million of business overnight to the non-unionised rival TNT.

The prevailing style of management was characterised by the Group CEO as 'autocratic, tempered by paternalism. The values of the business were loyalty, security and obedience to orders.' The nature of work within the News Division also brought strong traditions. The business is '24 hours a day, 7 days a week, 364 days a year' (only Christmas Day is not worked). The hours are long, deadlines are tight and much of the work, particularly in the warehouse, is physically demanding, all of which has engendered a 'macho' culture. However, the pace and deadline-driven nature of the business together with clear success criteria generated a high level of excitement and motivation among staff, despite low wages. As one manager said: 'once you are in it becomes a way of life and there is a very strong sense of identity among employees'. The company has always prided itself on being a caring company, an expression of the paternalism which runs throughout the division. There are two clear messages for staff: do not challenge the house manager's status or authority and do not challenge decisions.

It was decided to instigate a process of cultural change in order to implement a new managerial style of 'directness, openness to ideas, commitment to the success of others, a willingness to accept personal accountability and the strong development of teamwork and trust'. This was seen to be crucial in order to deliver the strategic intent of *enhanced customer focus and increased productivity*. In part the responsibility for this lay with the HR function.

The house managers were key to the change process but they could not be overtly attacked at first as they were also key in terms of maintaining the cash cow relationship that the division provided for the rest of the group. They also held tacit knowledge in the form of 'the way things are

---

stakeholders can limit the choices available to the change agent. Finally, it illustrates how the concept of the change path allows for change as a multi-staged process. Capacity and capability may need to be developed within an organisation before the desired scope of change can be implemented.

4.3.1 Analysis of WH Smith News

A cultural web and a stakeholder analysis (see Figures 4.2 and 4.3) are included to illustrate the scope of change required and the power blocks that existed. As pointed out in Chapter 3, such frameworks should always be used where possible to help assess the features of scope and power.

done around here'. The absence of any kind of systematic recruitment, selection, appraisal or communication system meant that a textbook transformational change would be difficult without any systems to support it. Equally, for the HR function to demand a strategic role and dictate the changes may have alienated the managers. The division also needed to maintain the cohesion and strong staff commitment that had been elicited through the paternalistic culture. Due to their position within the Group as a cash cow, the low profit margins and the resultant inability to invest in staff, there were severe constraints on their capacity to implement change.

A female personnel manager was appointed from within the group. She was one of very few women managers within the division and certainly the most senior. She did not demand a place on the executive council initially but instead set about formalising personnel systems and offering to take some of the administrative burden from house managers. Thus she started to handle recruitment and selection, delivering many of their training needs for them and handling the collective bargaining. She gradually established a personnel function which dealt with

all their human resource issues.

She also introduced a management style survey with the aim of countering what was seen as the strongly deferential culture within the division. The document was sent to all News Division staff by post and allowed them to comment on the performance of their manager on a series of 30 different characteristics. The data on an aggregate basis was published and shared among all employees. The fact that this information was generated bottom-up gave the personnel function permission and legitimacy to action the insight that they already possessed before the survey was completed.

In adopting a more bureaucratic service to the line managers and by seeking to assist rather than confront or overwhelm through more value-led cultural change, the personnel function won many friends and few enemies. Shortly after her arrival the personnel manager was invited to join the executive board for the division. By slowly formalising and systemising the personnel systems and restructuring the division, the business may now be capable of the more radical transformational change that is desirable but was not originally achievable.

Source: Adapted from Gratton, L., Hope Hailey, V., Stiles, P. and Truss, C. (1999) *Strategic Human Resource Management*, Oxford: Oxford University Press.

4.3.2 The kaleidoscope of WH Smith News

If we move around the kaleidoscope we can see clearly how the organisation shapes up against the various contextual features, and that WH Smith News faced a difficult change situation. Due to the increased competitive pressures within their industry the organisation needed to instigate some form of change fairly quickly as *time* was not on their side. They had lost a large amount of business to TNT. However, their position within the WH Smith Group meant that they provided an important cash cow function to their partner divisions. As the stakeholder analysis shows, this meant that the organisation's *power* was constrained because of its membership of the larger group, even though the larger group was supportive towards the changes. The house managers were also tremendously

Figure 4.2   **WH Smith News cultural web**

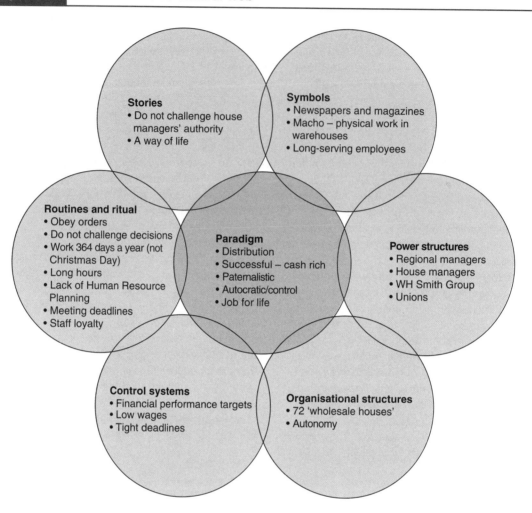

Stories
- Do not challenge house managers' authority
- A way of life

Symbols
- Newspapers and magazines
- Macho – physical work in warehouses
- Long-serving employees

Routines and ritual
- Obey orders
- Do not challenge decisions
- Work 364 days a year (not Christmas Day)
- Long hours
- Lack of Human Resource Planning
- Meeting deadlines
- Staff loyalty

Paradigm
- Distribution
- Successful – cash rich
- Paternalistic
- Autocratic/control
- Job for life

Power structures
- Regional managers
- House managers
- WH Smith Group
- Unions

Control systems
- Financial performance targets
- Low wages
- Tight deadlines

Organisational structures
- 72 'wholesale houses'
- Autonomy

powerful and the change agent needed to work with them rather than against them. Part of the reason for this was that the house managers had valuable tacit knowledge about how the business worked which needed to be *preserved*. Until that knowledge was formalised and therefore shared, it was crucial for keeping business going as usual through the change process. Thus the house managers were both the means through which to achieve change and yet also the blocks that were preventing change from taking place.

There were some positive aspects to the change context. All employees, managerial and non-managerial, felt a strong *identity* with the organisation. This translated itself into loyalty and staff commitment which the senior management wished to *preserve*. If they lost the staff's loyalty they were not in a position to buy it back using financial inducements. The strong identification with the pater-

Figure 4.3   WH Smith News stakeholder analysis

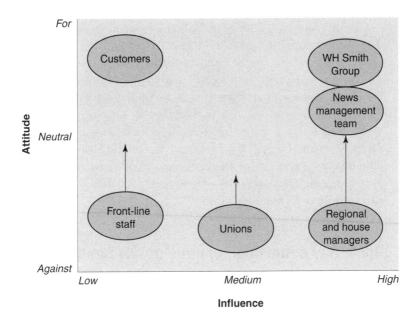

nalistic company also allowed it to extract long working hours from the staff. The organisation was relatively homogeneous with few subcultures existing within the division. There was therefore a low degree of *diversity*.

As the cultural web shows, the pre-change paradigm of the organisation was one of success with a paternalistic control culture and employees who were unquestioningly loyal yet expecting jobs for life. As such a cultural change to 'directness, openness to ideas, commitment to the success of others, a willingness to accept personal accountability and the strong development of teamwork and trust' challenged some of the most deeply ingrained historical ways of behaving. Therefore, in terms of *scope* the organisation needed to undertake fundamental transformational change.

The major gaps were in the two aspects of *capacity* and *capability*. In terms of capacity, the division's relationship within the Group meant that the division had to meet its financial obligations first. Furthermore, the industry sector itself was a low-profit margin business, which meant that compared with businesses such as pharmaceuticals or financial services, the business had little surplus cash for investment in a change process. In addition, the change capability was very low: staff had never had the chance to develop an expertise in this area. There was a strong internal labour market hence their exposure to change in other contexts was extremely limited. Their managers had extremely limited experience of managing staff through change processes, and little understanding of the nature of personal transition. At an organisational level within the division there was no specific change unit or department with a change expertise. Indeed the training and development department was very underdeveloped. Having said that they did have the expertise of the WH Smith Group HR department at their disposal.

Last, but not least, the organisation's **readiness for change** was very low. The house managers were reluctant to break from tradition, and given the poor history of communication throughout the division, had little understanding of their role and contribution within the group as a whole. They needed strong persuasion that change was in their best interests. Rather than confronting them head-on with the barrage of changes necessary, an alternative route was adopted whereby their support was sought in return for services given to them by the HR manager. By offering to provide basic personnel administrative services to them, the manager started to centralise, standardise and formalise those services. All of this was achieved without appearing to threaten their power base.

4.3.3 Key contextual features of WH Smith News

See Figure 4.4.

Figure 4.4 **Key contextual features for WH Smith News (end of 1980s)**

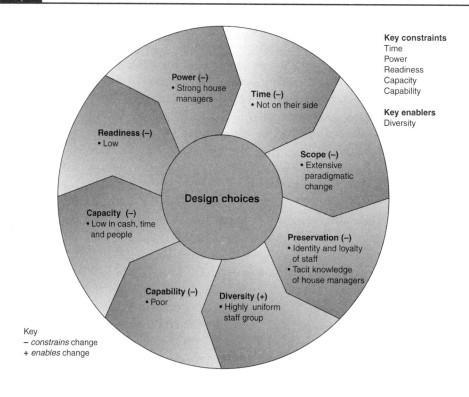

Key constraints
Time
Power
Readiness
Capacity
Capability

Key enablers
Diversity

Power (–)
• Strong house managers

Time (–)
• Not on their side

Readiness (–)
• Low

Scope (–)
• Extensive paradigmatic change

Design choices

Capacity (–)
• Low in cash, time and people

Preservation (–)
• Identity and loyalty of staff
• Tacit knowledge of house managers

Capability (–)
• Poor

Diversity (+)
• Highly uniform staff group

Key
– *constrains* change
+ *enables* change

4.3.4 Design implications for WH Smith News

Change path

The organisation's change in business strategy meant that the workforce needed to become more customer-focused. The desired results of the changes (increasing personal accountability, directness, openness and teamwork and trust) required a paradigmatic change in the basic assumptions and beliefs of the workforce, both managerial and non-managerial. The appropriate change path might have appeared to be transformational change through evolution. Yet, this was not possible because the division lacked the formal infrastructure of performance management systems and the informal management know-how that is needed. In short, they lacked the capacity and capability to implement transformational incremental change. Readiness was also very low.

When considering the nature of change, because time was of the essence, a big-bang radical approach appeared to be necessary, but there were also constraints. The division could not attempt big-bang change initially as it might have alienated the house managers. They possessed a great deal of the tacit knowledge that kept the business going. Until that could be formalised and centralised within the division any sudden change might have jeopardised the smooth running of the business. Furthermore the division's cash cow position within the group was another constraint on rapid change as it might have threatened the cash flow through to the other businesses. There were also union relations to consider. Therefore the division lacked the capacity and capability to effect big-bang change in a radical fashion.

The only option left open to them was to follow a two-phase change path, with a first phase of adaptation, which allowed the personnel manager to build up the infrastructure necessary for a subsequent incremental and transformational change (evolution) as the second phase.

Change target

Although the desired change in the longer term involved changing staff's values, neither behaviours or values were tackled in the short term. The priority was to design a process that built up the organisation's capability at a systems and infrastructure level, and tackled the politics of the situation. In the medium term targeting behaviours would be possible. This was because of the high uniformity and compliance of the non-managerial staff who were not likely to resist the tight prescription of behavioural change. Further change initiatives geared towards values could then be implemented in the longer term.

Change roles

At this stage in the organisation's development the change could not have been led by a complete outsider to the business or group. Outsiders would have lacked the legitimacy needed to work with the house managers. In contrast, it could not be designed from within since there did not appear to be any change competence within the division. Therefore the choice was made to appoint the current senior management team to lead the change process, with an insider/outsider, the HR manager from within the larger group, to help.

Change style

The process needed to be delivered using different styles for different levels. Given the power position of the house managers the process needed to either involve them collaboratively in its design, or be implemented in a participative fashion. With the non-managerial staff, directive styles of change would be acceptable and needed given the low levels of readiness and capability. However, the risk with that choice was that the directive nature of the process itself would serve to reinforce the old command and control type culture that the change was meant to erode. As readiness and capability developed, the change process could experiment with more participative forms of change for the warehouse staff.

Change start-point

Change was unlikely to take off through bottom-up initiatives. Staff at the lower levels of the organisation may have had potential for initiative, but they only had experience of top-down-driven management ideas. And again, the low readiness and capability of staff for change had to be taken into account. In the medium term relying totally on top-down change may also be risky as senior managers themselves may be ambivalent about the need for fundamental change. Having established the infrastructure needed in the initial change phase there would be strong arguments for starting pockets of good practice in the medium term throughout the division. If the personnel manager targeted change initiatives at particular managers whose current managerial style came close to the new espoused values, then those managers could start to act as role models for the rest of the organisation. This would allow the personnel manager to test out the effectiveness of the transformation change strategy using pilot sites before implementing it throughout the organisation.

Change levers

In the first phase of adaptation two forms of change levers were employed to address the balance of power, and build readiness and capability. First, the personnel manager established new control systems in the form of human resource management policies and procedures in the division. This allowed her to centralise some procedures and take control away from the house managers. It also allowed her to gain information on staff performance. The management style survey and the customer satisfaction survey added information to the central database, but they were also political in nature. Had the personnel manager started to impose changes in management style on to the house managers based on her own judgements, she could have been accused of not understanding the business. By using the views of both the workforce and customers she was armed with powerful reasons for persuading the senior and house managers that change was necessary. She also started to generate some readiness for change in the workforce through the communication of the survey findings.

Phase 2: evolution

The changes made by the personnel manager in the first phase of the change path may only have led to adaptation at WH Smith News, but they also changed the change context. The changes built some level of change capability within the organisation in the form of new human resource management systems, shifted the balance of power in favour of the personnel manager, and generated some awareness of the need for change. The context was now one more enabling of evolutionary change. The first phase of change was used to reconfigure the change context in a way that enabled the transformational change required.

4.4 LENDCO: A RETAIL BANK

This case study (Illustration 4.3) looks at a high street retail bank that needed to undergo incremental transformational change. The case brings out the problems of achieving such change when there is low capability and an equally low awareness of the need for change. It also shows the complexities of employee loyalty and the problems associated with over reliance on formal change levers such as structures and systems.

4.4.1 The kaleidoscope of Lendco

Time was not a major issue at first for Lendco as there was no immediate crisis. However, as the decade wore on the situation changed. One factor affecting this was that there were less and less costs that could be taken out of the business once the immediate gains had been made. Hence acquisition activity became essential in order to continue cost stripping and growing shareholder value. Once merger and acquisition activity was halted, the bank needed to turn to something new. The second factor running in parallel to this on-going upheaval was the growing competition from new entrants. Rather than disappearing from the marketplace, as predicted by some, these 'start-ups' began to take more of the market share.

In terms of *scope*, the bank needed to achieve a transformation over the long term within the branch network. It needed to transform from being a banking

Illustration 4.3

Lendco Bank

(At the end of the twentieth century the retail banking industry was a radically changing business. Three clear forces were driving change: deregulation, increasing competition and new technology. Prompted by an active policy of deregulation by government, the traditional demarcation lines between different types of financial institution have been largely eliminated). Competition has intensified as former building societies began to compete with banks by offering current accounts, and banks hit back by offering mortgages. The impact of new technology has been considerable in driving down costs within the branches, improving important aspects of product delivery, and taking away the human element in calculating the risk in lending decisions. This has helped to break down barriers between markets and has also opened markets to new entrants such as supermarkets. The biggest driver for change since the mid-1990s has been the difference in costs between the three main channels of distribution for the banks: the branches, the telephone and the net. The branch network is the highest-cost channel. This has meant that in order to stay open, the bricks and mortar part of retail banking has had to reinvent itself as a seller of financial services products. However, this reinvention had to take place in the context of its existing culture and staff.

Historically most staff joined a retail bank at an early age because it offered them job security, a fair salary plus a certain status associated with banking. In return for these benefits the staff were to be diligent protectors of risk through meticulous attention to detailed procedures that safeguarded the financial transactions of the customer. The branch had an important role in the local community and the local branch manager would be seen as a reliable and responsible figurehead within that community.

Yet by the end of the 1990s, the majority of banks were shifting performance measures so that employees in the branches were assessed on the number of financial services products they managed to sell to customers. The branches have become retail outlets in the same way that any local high street store such as Woolworth's is merely an outlet for the larger brand. The bank cashiers are encouraged to see themselves as sales representatives. The old role of local bank manager is obsolete, replaced in the majority of cases by product sales managers with only one branch manager for perhaps 6 or 8 branches. This challenges both the cultural paradigm of what it means to be a bank and the identity of its employees.

The internal environment

The response of Lendco to these structural challenges was to adopt a strategy that focused on selective market leadership rather than global growth, and to place shareholder value as the governing objective of the business. Measures of market value and share price were adopted. This embracing of shareholder value as a governing objective had strong repercussions for the structure of the business. Previously the processes of the bank (marketing, retailing, manufacturing) were tightly bundled together with the branch as the main economic unit and profit centre. In the 1990s the bank centralised many processes and branches ceased to be individual profit centres.

Lendco Bank had a strong bureaucratic culture, with a direct command and control style of management built upon a rigid hierarchical structure. Paternalistic and authoritarian managers moulded a largely compliant and dependent workforce, and because of the nature of the banking business before deregulation, they also created a climate of insularity from the realities of the marketplace. The financial success of the bank, together with its size and longevity, had brought strong expectations from employees concerning their careers. Promotions were largely automatic and the bank was expected to manage entirely the career progression of employees.

However, the new competitive environment brought with it the need for substantial internal change. The existing culture at the start of the 1990s was seen as insufficiently focused on the rapidly changing nature of customer demand, and as failing to make the best use of the bank's resources. The stated aim of the new culture was to move away from the authoritarian culture, towards one that emphasised personal responsibility and the effective management of people, through performance measurement. Lendco chose to implement this change without cultural change programmes. Instead Lendco focussed on the use of continual formal restructurings, job redesigns, overhauls of reward and incentive systems, job cutting through natural wastage, and a headcount freeze throughout the branch network.

Despite the formal changes going on around them, the strength of the old banking culture made it extremely difficult for employees to adapt:

> People's expectations were that they had a job for life and that they would be promoted on a regular basis. We have betrayed them and they have no trust in us, because we are fundamentally telling them a story which was not what they expected when they joined Lendco Bank at all.   (Senior Manager)

A large part of the problem stemmed from the employees' perception that the old culture was being dismantled without any clear replacement to put in its place. The result was that:

> every change which is implemented seems like another blow to the old accepted way of doing things, rather than something new and better being introduced.   (Senior Manager)

Long lines of communication and a lack of clarity on what the end result of the changes actually looked like exacerbated the situation. The head office was resented:

> There is a great distrust of the bank, a them and us feeling . . . There are demands and communications from the top but not much going up.   (Line Manager)

However, 'esprit de corps' and teamwork was quite high at branch level. The morale and lack of trust was directed at the bank as a whole or more specifically at senior management. Consequently the branch managers aligned themselves with the lower levels of staff:

> Branch managers are well loved, although it may be that they have jumped in to the trenches with the staff.

In the middle of the 1990s Lendco bought a building society, and then merged with another banking group. This flurry of merger and acquisition activity resulted in an appointment of a new CEO. New members of the senior management team were appointed, some from outside the industry. A plethora of change initiatives were put in place but, with little

integration between them, staff felt a barrage of change raining down upon them, with little sense of priorities. The uncertainty created by the merger, the shock of job insecurity and the experience of continual change, contributed to lowering morale. Eighty per cent believed that there was less job security, 86 per cent believed there was more pressure at work and 46 per cent believed that working conditions had worsened over the last two years. Eighty-two per cent believed the organisation would achieve its aims, but only 16 per cent believed that senior management were well informed about what people think and do.

> There is a lot of fear. People are a little scared of going off on their own and using their own initiative. It is all very well higher up and for me to speak like this because I have nothing to lose. But lower down, people have a lot to lose.   (Branch Manager)

Some of the problems were due to the inability of those at a senior level to envision the future for the branch staff:

> What we are not very good at at the moment is actually trying to paint a picture of the future in terms of business strategy, in terms of how we are going to behave, in terms of what are the key issues, to actually get people to raise their sights slightly higher from next week or next year in to what sort of company we want to be in 3–5 years time . . . we are not providing the big picture.

The bank's senior management started to trade on the staff loyalty achieved through the old culture and business model. Managers claim that it is not the merger and acquisition activity alone that is complex but the changes within the banking activity itself. Two groups of employees have emerged – old-timers who are employed on one set of terms and conditions, still harbouring at an attitudinal level paternalistic expectations or grudges about the bank, and newcomers without that baggage, but who do not stay long because the old culture persists in parts. The skills gap also remains a problem. The challenges remain the increasing diversity and complexity within the workforce, and the continuing need to drive down costs, through whatever means.

Source: © Veronica Hope Hailey, 2002.

business to being a retailer of financial services. This would require the bank to fundamentally change the way they did business in terms of beliefs, assumptions and behaviours. When considering depth, it could be argued persuasively that whilst the senior management in Lendco understood the depth of change to their current business model, they failed to understand the depth of personal and cultural transformation required of their long-serving and loyal staff to deliver the changes.

The issue of **preservation** is also interesting. In order to preserve continuing market performance and a good public image they could not go for any change that was too radical and sudden. Several of their competitors had been lambasted in the press for closing branches within remote rural areas. A less overt approach to change was required. Likewise, they could not afford to go for a massive redundancy programme because they were recording excellent business results and they risked losing customer goodwill.

To make the change happen, the organisation assumed that the levels of loyalty it had enjoyed in the past would see it through. Yet it did not want to preserve a commitment to long-term contracts of employment and job security. As the bank's identity shifted through its mergers and acquisitions, so the loyalty to the organisation decreased. What took its place was a fear of job loss.

What the bank wanted to destroy was clearer – the massive cost base within the branch network, the archaic work practices, the longevity of service and job security, and the dominant position of the branches as the main distribution channel in terms of volume.

The bank enjoyed low **diversity**. At the start of the 1990s, despite differences between the branch network and the international or investment divisions, the branches of the banks were very homogeneous in culture, staff groups, roles and customers. By the end of the decade, however, diversity had increased significantly. This increase was due to the merger and acquisition activity of the bank. It was also a result of replacement of staff cut through natural wastage (voluntary severance, retirements etc.) by new types of employees. New recruits were brought into employment on different terms, both formally and contractually, and in terms of informal expectations.

At the start of the incremental transformation the bank did not have a **capability** in change management terms. At a resource level, far from being adaptable and flexible, the majority of branch staff were highly institutionalised in terms of their narrow skill base, entrenched attitudes and routinised behaviours. The most important individuals in the implementation of change were the branch managers. Yet few of them had experienced change outside of Lendco, and the proposed changes within the banking sector implied a loss of status and power for many of them. Little was invested in developing a capability for change management within these branch managers. Whilst they regularly incorporated technical banking changes into their work, the management of culture in order to deliver business strategy was less familiar to them. In the middle of the 1990s the bank also reduced the number of dedicated human resource specialists working in the network, by centralising much of the personnel administration processing into shared service centres. Although this was an astute move in terms of cost reduction, it removed the only human face of the central head office functions from the employees' view.

Almost all business systems were underdeveloped at the start of the change. Resources were pumped into developing information systems, and shared service centres were introduced in the mid-1990s, which enabled more flexibility in structure and staff numbers across the branches. The human resource systems were also undeveloped as control or communication systems at the start of the change, but they were substantially reviewed and redesigned after the merger and acquisition activity. A substantial investment was made in this area to try to mimic best practice in these systems.

In terms of *capacity* for change, the bank had some financial capacity to invest in change management but only if senior management deemed it necessary. Committed as they were to a strategy of enhancing shareholder value, it was difficult for the board to cut dividends to shareholders in the short term in order to invest in change programmes that would build the organisation's sustainability. Employee time was also an issue. As headcount was reduced in the branches and a recruitment freeze was imposed, work intensified. Simultaneously a laudable initiative of computer-based training was launched. Most branches received a workstation, which allowed employees to update their skills base whilst at work. However, the reality was that due to staff shortages with the headcount freeze, branch staff were not released from counterwork to work on the computers.

The immediate lack of financial crisis contributed to the low *readiness* for change within the branch network. Whilst senior managers and some head office staff understood the need for change at a rational level, employees in the field offices did not share this. Lendco did launch a communications campaign which increased the rational awareness of the need for change. However, commitment to change was more difficult to generate for good reasons. For many, the personal transition required of them to make the move from cashier to sales assistant would be painful. Little training was offered initially to help with this shift. Even with training, some would not be successful and may then face the prospect of leaving the bank. Their employability at the start of the 1990s was low as the transferability of their skills was low. The majority of staff in the branch network had only had one employer in their life – the bank. Furthermore, few alternative employers could offer them the good terms and conditions of employment that they enjoyed at the bank. The end result was that they were not committed to change, but nor were they going to leave!

In terms of *power* the structure of the retail banks in the UK was such that there was a significant divide between the branches scattered all over the country and the head office functions. The head office functions assumed themselves to be quite powerful because that was where the senior managers were located. However, the power to change the behaviour and attitudes of the employees in the branches lay with the branch managers. Furthermore, these branch managers were in a strong position. They were scattered all over the country, and could not be directly supervised. Admittedly developments in new technology have meant that their work flow and targets could be closely monitored, but their ability to influence remains uncontrolled. In the early years of the incremental transformation the branch managers were the main source of both communication and interpretation of head office edicts to branch staff; they could therefore put whatever spin they wished on information as it cascaded down through the organisation. Over the ten years the employee loyalty to their immediate bosses has not diminished.

Yet the standardisation of approach required by the bank's retailing strategy, also required more centralised forms of control. Much of the bank's activity over time could be interpreted as gradually trying to extract power from the branch networks and much of the noise in the system can be seen as the branches' reaction to that power struggle.

4.4.2 Key contextual features of Lendco

See Figure 4.5.

Figure 4.5   **Key contextual features for Lendco (early 1990s)**

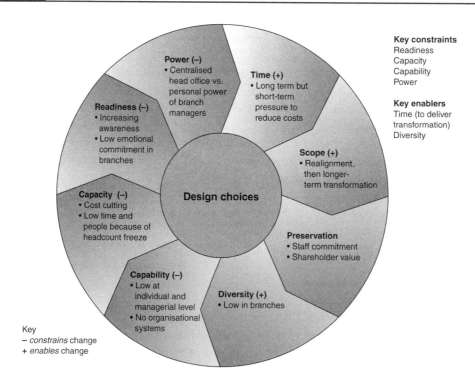

4.4.3 Design implications for Lendco

Change path

One of the difficulties of implementing incremental change is knowing when to deepen the impact of the change if transformation is to be achieved. The financial services industry as a sector is not characterised by revolutionary change for a number of reasons – heritage, products and the customer base. The senior managers at Lendco knew the long-term impact of technology, new entrants into the marketplace and the competing forms of distribution through the net and telephone banking. The change path started as gradual adaptation, but needed to change into evolution as the years went on. This was because the shift towards a retail culture required a paradigmatic change within the organisation, and a fundamental shift in values for the staff. However, the way the change was designed failed to transform the values and culture within the branch network.

Change start-point

The lack of crisis or momentum for change within the whole organisation meant that initially the change needed to be implemented top-down. However, after the initial shift much more could have been done to encourage bottom-up initiatives to emerge had some levels of readiness and capability been developed. This would have been helpful in creating a sense of ownership and breaking down the branch–head office divide that only grew over the ten-year period. Instead the senior management of the bank continued to issue directives in a way that assumed that the staff still felt the same degree of loyalty and commitment they had within the former culture.

Change style

The style was directive initially, although as the change proceeded more participatory approaches were used. Given the scope of the change, the lack of readiness and capability, it was unlikely that the approach could have been anything other than directive at the outset.

Change target

By focusing on change using structures and systems as the main levers the primary targets were behaviours. Removing managerial layers from the branch network and job redesign forced employees to adapt their behaviour. Performance targets and criteria for promotion were also changed and these reinforced the behavioural change. However, little attention was given to defining a future vision for the organisation or building the new values required for a transformation. This resulted in staff being aware of what they were changing from but not what they were changing to! Without knowledge of a new vision and values that could underpin the bank in the future, the employees derived one based on their own perceptions of their everyday working life. They perceived that the new values driving the business were shareholder value through cost reduction, with little consideration for the employees. This contributed to low staff morale.

Change levers

The change was primarily driven through the technical and structural interventions of mergers and acquisitions, job and organisational redesign, new performance management systems incorporating personal objectives, and new rewards and incentives. Most of these appeared to be driven out of head office by the need to deliver shareholder value through ruthless cost reduction.

Lendco provides a stark example of the need to use cultural and interpersonal levers in order to achieve transformational change. Technical changes were not supported by, for example, positive symbolic interventions that represented the future. Training and management development interventions that could aid understanding of the need for change, and also equip staff with the skills to deal with change, were not invested in. Thus Lendco did not help its employees to feel supportive of the change. In the short term the lack of commitment did not threaten the business strategy of cost reduction, but should the bank need to shift strategy in the future to one based on employee motivation it will be severely challenged.

Change roles

The change needed to be led initially by the senior management in the bank for a number of reasons. The branch staff were not fully aware of the need to change, and there was no immediate crisis that would galvanise action. However, leadership for the change should then have been delegated to branch manager level. It was the branch manager who motivated employees. This cohort of managers did not display great change management capability but the organisation could have chosen to invest in developing their skills in this area. In addition, the leadership style of the senior team, whilst attractive to the City, did not demonstrate a firm commitment to the welfare of the employees.

The change context in 2002

By 2002, the changes to date had reconfigured the change context. (See Figure 4.6.) However, whereas changes made in the first phase of change at WH Smith News had created a more favourable change context for the needed transformation, this was not the case for Lendco. If anything, readiness was lower than in the early 1990s with old staff now cynical and jaundiced given their change experiences over the last 10 years. New staff were relatively indifferent. There

| Figure 4.6 | Key contextual features for Lendco (2002) |

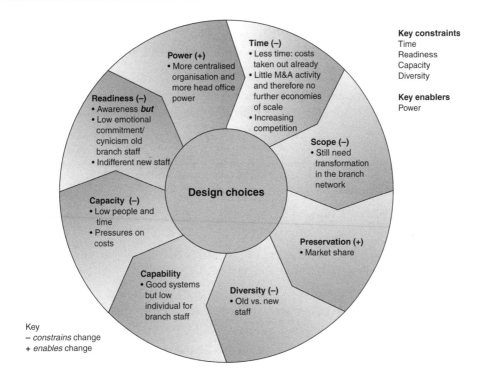

was less time now that competition was greater and most opportunities for cost savings had been exhausted. There was still no capacity for change, and although the organisational change capability was higher, individually, staff in the branch network still had a low personal capability. In addition, diversity was now higher.

4.5 SUMMARY

This chapter has explored the use of the change kaleidoscope through three extended case studies of companies undergoing change. These cases have illustrated both the complexity of change and the interrelated nature of all the kaleidoscope features. None of the individual features can be considered in isolation from the other seven aspects of context. Furthermore, the contextual features shift through time as illustrated by the WH Smith News and the Lendco case studies. The pattern of features at one time will be altered by the changes put in place. The features, therefore, have to be reassessed before choices are made about future changes.

In particular the chapter has considered three main areas:

● How to use the change kaleidoscope to understand the change context in depth.

- How to identify the key contextual features in any change situation that influence the design choices and therefore the change approach. As the case studies illustrate, certain contextual features may be critical in one organisation and of minor significance in another.

- How to link the assessment of the contextual features through to the design of change.

Having established the link between change context and change design choices, the next three chapters explore the design and management of the transition process.

WORK ASSIGNMENTS

4.1 Develop a stakeholder analysis for Lendco as at 2002. What are the key change issues this raises?

4.2 Drawing on the Bayer case study in this chapter, what lessons can be learned about managing change in a multinational enterprise?

4.3 Compare the three case studies in this chapter and reflect on why the design choices taken were appropriate or inappropriate. Were there other options that you would have considered?

4.4 For WH Smith News and Lendco, what should the design choices be for the next phase of change?

Transforming Glaxo Wellcome through the 1990s

Nardine Collier • Veronica Hope Hailey • Julia Balogun

This case describes the changes undertaken by Glaxo Pharma throughout the 1990s. It can be used to help students and other readers of the book deepen their understanding of how to apply the change kaleidoscope in practice, and how to develop change judgement. Assignment questions are at the end of the case.

Since the late 1980s Glaxo, and then Glaxo Wellcome, have rolled out a succession of change programmes in order to develop their internal capability to match market change. This case study will examine the investment in change management by Glaxo Pharma, the UK sales division, in order to identify to what extent they succeeded.

BACKGROUND

Prior to its merger with SmithKlineBeecham in December 2000, Glaxo was an international pharmaceuticals company, specialising in supplying drugs, with the British National Health Service (NHS) as the UK company's core customer base. From its origin as a general trading company in New Zealand in 1873, GSK has grown into a giant, with a combined turnover of £10.5 billion, operating in 70 countries and employing over 54,000 people. Built on strong market dominance and a portfolio of successful patented drugs, by the early 1990s Glaxo had developed an impressive reputation, coupled with considerable revenue streams. The Glaxo group had moved from being ranked at number 36 in the world in the 1980s to number 2 by the 1990s.

The original interview and survey data was sponsored by the Leading Edge Forum Research Consortium. We gratefully acknowledge the use of reports and information supplied by the research team: Lynda Gratton, Veronica Hope Hailey, Philip Stiles and Katie Truss.

PART 1: 1988–93

External problems

Glaxo's continued dominance in the market was threatened by a number of external factors that risked undermining its competitive position and profitability. Across the pharmaceuticals industry as a whole the nature of customer demand was continually changing. Doctors used to dominate customer demand despite the fact that their role as prescribers was separate from those who actually paid for the cost of drugs, the government or insurers. Under that business climate the main strategy for companies such as Glaxo was to persuade doctors that its products were superior to its competitors.

However, reforms of the NHS resulted in doctors becoming 'fund holders' and, as such, responsible for their own budgets. This resulted in greater cost consciousness in purchasing drugs. Other government initiatives also contributed to an overall squeezing of costs with a consequential shrinking of profit growth for pharmaceuticals companies.

Another major factor that threatened to impact Glaxo in particular was the patent expiry on its lucrative drug Zantac in 1996. Such a move represented a serious threat to Glaxo's revenue stream, because at its peak Zantac contributed £220 million in annual sales. There was grave concern that once the patent expired on Zantac the market would be flooded with cheaper generic versions of the drug. The generics would be an attractive option for GPs in such a cost-conscious environment.

Therefore, unlike many organisations, Glaxo Pharma embarked on a proactive change programme at a time of success, in anticipation of future industry and product changes.

Internal problems – survey

In response to the external problems, Glaxo Pharma commissioned an attitude survey to be completed throughout the company in 1988 and 1989. The results of the survey 'made disturbing reading'. It showed some worrying attitudes and organisational characteristics which, if not tackled, would severely affect the critical success factors that had been established for the business strategy.

The survey revealed three key issues. First, as a direct result of Glaxo's success and dominance over previous decades, there was an attitude of complacency and arrogance among the staff. Staff recognised that the nature of the marketplace within which Glaxo operated was changing, but believed the senior management team could address these issues, with little need for the staff themselves to do anything differently to ensure future success. Sixty-nine per cent of employees believed the organisation was flexible enough to cope with the change, and 56 per cent felt management could cope with a crisis. In effect there was insufficient awareness of the responsibility and contribution necessary on the part of each member of staff in order to sustain the success of the company.

Baronial, parochial, few cross-functional teams, unfluid, hierarchical, inflexible … which was probably appropriate for the 60s and 70s because we were in a stable healthcare market, but this is now inappropriate to the market and the type of people we employ.   (Senior Manager)

Second, slow decision making was identified as an organisational characteristic. This was potentially threatening Glaxo's ability to respond quickly to the needs of an evolving marketplace. Finally, the existence of strong functional divisions within the organisation further contributed to the slow pace of decision making. These divisions significantly limited both communication and understanding, and had hindered the development of any sense of shared responsibility for business success.

During one of their meetings the senior management team pondered the survey results and designed a set of behaviours for the organisation aimed at supporting and complementing business success in light of the future external problems. The HR Director was then given the task of turning these behaviours into a reality.

First change programme – RATIO

The behaviours formed the basis of a planned cultural change programme, introduced in late 1990 called RATIO. One of its primary objectives was to make it clear that a continuation with the status quo was untenable. Initially the change initiative focused on behaviours rather than values, with each letter of the acronym RATIO representing a desired behaviour: Role clarity; Acceptance of change; Teamwork; Innovation; and Output orientation. These were devised in conjunction with consultants from a management college. The behaviour defined and promoted through RATIO was a framework applicable to each individual's job or task. For example, the work practices that demonstrated innovation might be different for a sales manager as compared to an accountant. However they all supported the same aim – the promotion of more innovative practices. The staff were expected to expand or adapt the behaviours, and tailor them to their own jobs and roles.

At the suggestion of the consultants, the senior management team went on an outdoor development course which enabled them to understand and experiment with the new behaviours, and comprehend at a personal level the depth of change that was necessary from the staff. The course also prevented the cultural change from becoming a prayer to be memorised and recited, instead it was based around actions rather than purely thoughts. The course proved so successful, and so revelatory for the senior management team in terms of understanding the depth of personal change the new behaviours required, that the experience was repeated for a further 700 staff members within the organisation, and completed by mid-1991. The senior management team had not initially planned to put such significant management development resources into the RATIO initiative. They only did so because of their personal experiences on the outdoor development course when they had tried to put the behaviours into practice themselves.

A series of complementary change initiatives were implemented to support RATIO. First, a Values Statement was issued, drawing attention to the values that should underpin the behaviours Glaxo was trying to achieve in RATIO. The values were identified as:

We value:

- Our contribution to the health and wellbeing of the nation
- Our relationship with our partners in the delivery of healthcare
- Honesty in everything we do
- The contribution of all individuals and their personal development
- The learning which comes from listening
- The effective use of all resources, particularly people's time, energy and commitment
- The taking of responsibility for decisions and actions
- Achievement

A further initiative was the creation of project groups and task forces. These were encouraged in order to break down the functional divisions that had been identified as problematic in the attitude survey, and through their implementation promote amoeba-like structures to emerge within the organisation.

Finally, the cultural change programme coincided with the relocation of Glaxo Pharma's head office to open plan offices in Stockley Park. This move was used as a further opportunity to reinforce the change programme and enabled the new ideas to permeate quickly through the organisation. A considerable sum of money was invested to create a design and architecture of the new building which would mirror the organisational changes that Glaxo were trying to embed. The senior management team ensured that maximum symbolic use was made of the interior open-plan design of the new building, in order to chip away the functional divides identified by the survey, through open and easy communication.

Results of RATIO

Interviews held with the staff revealed that the RATIO initiative had wide owner-ship. It was perceived as being devised by the staff rather than being developed and imposed by management, and as having been well communicated. Staff understood what RATIO meant and could relate the initiative to their work. Significantly it was felt to be an organisational strategy rather then a human resource strategy.

By comparison, the Values Statement was not widely recognised, and was less well regarded than the behavioural statements from RATIO. Furthermore the values were seen as an imposition from the top and consequently were less well remembered:

> *To be honest with you, the value side of things I think is very wishy-washy. To give you a classic example, we had a regional managers' meeting that looked at the values. Eight of us round the table went 'What? What's that?' We couldn't even remember seeing the memo that came out. Nobody had explained it to us ... Everybody knew RATIO and we all felt quite comfortable with that. We were all involved in that. We were all involved in the pulling together of RATIO. It was communicated very well to us. But the values have not been communicated out in the field at all well, I believe. They are just so wishy-washy.*   (Manager)

A factor that hampered the implementation of the new culture was the inability of some managers to live out and demonstrate the required behaviour. Although not a purposeful resistance to change this was a significant block on the cultural change process.

Overall though, the biggest source of resistance appeared to be from the trading companies, particularly the field staff and regional sales managers. There were signs of conflict between the long-term demands of the change programme, and more immediate pressures to continue to achieve sales targets. When under pressure managers reverted to command and control forms of management. This was interpreted as an illustration of the familiar divide between field sales staff and head office staff. The senior management team concluded that more fundamental change had to follow.

PART 2: 1994–98

Continued external problems

The NHS, Glaxo's prime customer, faced further fragmentation as hospitals changed to operate as semi-autonomous Trusts, in an attempt to make the health service more 'business-like'. This further increased the focus on cost control and value for money:

> *New people were influencing prescribing decisions and the medical representative's jobs became even more difficult. Not only did you have to present the total benefits of the product, but you had to find the right person in the first place.*   (Customer Focus: No. 4)

Additionally throughout the pharmaceuticals industry the cost of R&D rose because of developments in biotechnology.

Second change programme – re-engineering and mergers

Re-engineering

In late 1994 Glaxo introduced a re-engineering initiative called 'Customer Focus'. This was developed with the aim of creating a flexible organisation that would proactively seek new opportunities rather than reacting after the event. As part of this Glaxo started to market the idea of selling products and establishing complementary services such as asthma clinics in hospitals. This was accompanied by the adoption of a more customer relationship marketing approach to their main clients, the prescribers.

> *We had a sort of pause in which the organisation worked much better in terms of teamwork and things we wanted. But it wasn't until late 1994 that we were able to persuade the senior commercial people that a dramatic re-engineering initiative was necessary.*   (HR Director)

The re-engineering started with an analysis of customer needs, followed by process redesign, the identification of new competencies and a new organisational structure. Glaxo aimed to move away from a focus on individual products to one on the broader concept of disease management, and to embrace a more holistic conception of product and service. Marketing teams were asked to identify ways of becoming leaders in disease areas, not just concentrating on selling a drug, but by providing services that looked at all aspects of the disease. The shift towards disease management was supported by the use of cross-functional teams.

Further, because of spiralling R&D costs arising from developments in biotechnology, the programme also sought to promote alliances with universities and biotech companies in an attempt to spread its R&D costs, and bolster its profile.

As a result of the re-engineering exercise, five regional directorates, with each region divided into five to seven business areas, were set up, to replace the old hierarchical product silos. Previously the organisational structure was essentially a product–market structure rather than a customer–service structure, which made it increasingly out of touch with the large-scale changes occurring in the NHS. Glaxo changed to a structure based around process, to mirror that used by the NHS.

Internal merger

As part of the re-engineering and restructuring, internally Glaxo's two original trading companies, Allen and Hanburys and Glaxo Laboratories, were merged under the name Glaxo. The internal merger involved bringing together the two largest field sales forces in the UK, and presented the senior management team with a complex and difficult exercise. A particularly important aspect of this was due to the fact that the sales forces represented a highly educated and skilled workforce, which Glaxo did not want to lose through unnecessary alienation. The vast amount of knowledge, intellect and potential possessed by the workforce would not be easy to replace if any employee decided to leave:

> *It was like bringing together two groups who know each other well and there are all the differences between them, and they know what is good and what is bad about each other. That is far harder than bringing together groups where one doesn't know much about the other at all.*
>
> (HR Focus Group)

There were few redundancies from the merger (less than 20, and all were voluntary), but the restructuring led to a reduction of hierarchical layers from seven to four.

A massive communication exercise involving seminars, workshops, employee meetings, newsletters and other media was employed to put forward the merits of the merger. The extent of activity reflected the recognition that there was still anxiety at all levels in the organisation regarding the changes, as the new behaviours and practices required a major shift in employee mindset:

> *It was very traumatic. Some people just did not accept the changes.*
>
> (Senior management)

Furthermore employees were being empowered by being granted for the first time large budgets for regional and business areas. Yet there was still anxiety at all levels:

> *It is an experiment on our part. We do not know if it will succeed.*
>
> (HR staff)

External merger with Wellcome

In January 1995 during the implementation of the internal merger, Glaxo announced a £9.1 billion merger with one of its competitors, the British-based pharmaceuticals company Wellcome, to form Glaxo Wellcome. At the time this was the largest recorded merger in the UK. The decision to merge with Wellcome was made possible only by the arrival of Sir Richard Sykes as Glaxo's new CEO. (The previous chief executive had been vehemently opposed to a merger of any kind.) Sykes personally championed the merger in a bid to create a new structure for the organisation. His rationale was to undertake a horizontal merger with another drug manufacturer, rather than follow the preferred industry route of vertically integrating with drug-distribution companies.

His beliefs behind such a move was that a strong supplier with a sizeable chunk of the market would be able to exert leverage over distributors. The merger brought Glaxo Wellcome a 5.1 per cent share of the world market, where its strengths lay in specific areas rather than in the overall marketplace. As a result of the merger Glaxo Wellcome had 35 per cent of the gastrointestinal market, 25 per cent of the antibiotic market, 25 per cent of the respiratory market and up to 70 per cent of the anti-viral market.

Though announced as a merger, it was clear the process was perceived internally as a takeover, a view reinforced by the respective sizes of the two firms: Glaxo sales were nine times those of Wellcome, and Glaxo had eight times as many staff. The perception that it was a takeover helped to reduce to some extent employee anxiety over the changes, since many believed that Glaxo staff would 'win out' in the rationalisation of jobs.

Since Glaxo incorporated Wellcome's operations in the midst of the internal merger, it was felt that integrating Wellcome would be simple. Wellcome's head office was closed, with a generous severance package offered to those not wishing to relocate to Glaxo's headquarters. The Wellcome research site at Beckenham was also closed. This meant that the numbers joining the new company were relatively low. Worldwide there were 5,000 redundancies resulting from the merger; a fifth of research staff left and nearly 70 of 160 development projects were discontinued.

The initial groundwork for the new organisation was undertaken by teams and divisional directors, who met in the UK, the USA and other large markets. This was described as the 'information-gathering' phase. Joint task forces were then established in order to manage the merger process, with some teams focusing on geographic areas whilst others focused on functional processes. These teams were supported by central platform services such as HR, finance and law. Sitting above the task forces was a central co-ordination team of nine senior executives, initially all Glaxo managers, but later Wellcome colleagues joined them. It was the responsibility of task force teams to make integration proposals to the executive team.

In addition to the restructuring, different employee behaviours had to be aligned behind the new business strategy and structure. These included team-working competencies, increased customer-facing skills, the ability to work in a networked organisation, and taking greater business responsibility. Therefore, to support the internal and external mergers, a series of complementary initiatives were implemented.

Competency framework

A competency framework was established with the aim of integrating recruitment, appraisal, development and rewards. The competencies were divided into five core areas: personal qualities, planning to achieve, business and customer focus, supportive leadership and working with others. The competency framework described the skills, knowledge and behaviours required throughout the company which all levels had to achieve.

Appraisal

The old-style appraisal forms were abandoned because they were seen as too output-orientated. It was no longer seen as a formal one to one process between manager and subordinate, with a straight link to pay depending upon performance. The new approach relied on the individual to gather as much information about their performance from whoever they thought relevant including people external to the organisation, such as customers or business partners. They were encouraged to discuss their performance on an on-going basis. Extending the source of inputs into employee review was a reflection of the increased project working and the move away from working exclusively for one manager. For example, can one line manager alone judge the worth of an employee working with a variety of different groups, often not within the line manager's area?

Therefore this system of appraisal, in part, addressed the 'remote manager problem': the concern that with more people working on projects, if appraisal is carried out by a line manager they are too remote from the subordinate's perform-ance to be able to adequately judge value.

Rewards

The development of a new reward strategy was instigated to mesh with the new competency framework and replace the complex existing system which was func-tionally structured and heavily reliant on job families and external comparison. Reduction of complexity, movement across functional boundaries and greater dif-ferentiation in payment levels were the stated aims of the new system, together with a much stronger emphasis on development and continuous improvement.

The new system introduced a broadband grading structure of six main bands where roles were graded against the competency framework. The former focus on basic pay changed to include a greater mix of basic and bonus pay.

Training and development

To complement the organisational transition, much of the training and develop-ment moved away from formal provision towards coaching and counselling. In each regional directorate a coach was responsible for the training and develop-ment of the area team, and each business unit manager was assigned a mentor from a firm of external consultants:

> *We've done a tremendous amount of work in helping the coaches become true coaches, not just trainers or side-kicks for the business managers, but truly coaches who are there to help individuals and the team develop the skills they need for the job they are in now and to think more long term about where they are going.*   (Focus Group)

Development was used to assess fit against the competency framework. A 'devel-opment network' was created, a central resource which collated all information concerning development and put it into a resource guide. The resource guide and open-learning centre (with workpacks, videos, CBT, etc.) allowed employees to look at their development plan and decide where they needed to improve and how they could get help. 'Cascade' was a computer package which enabled indi-viduals to give and receive feedback from named individuals. It also allowed employees to choose their development areas against the competency framework and gave hints on how they could develop in their everyday job.

Results of the re-engineering and mergers

By 1996 Glaxo Wellcome (GW) was the world's largest pharmaceuticals company by sales and the third largest company in the UK. In the UK the Glaxo culture remained dominant after the merger with Wellcome, although this was less the case in the R&D divisions worldwide. However, despite all the change activities accompanying the restructuring and mergers, emphasising self-management and individual responsibility, there were still signs in Glaxo Pharma of what could be considered complacency. In a survey held immediately after the mergers, 71 per cent of Glaxo Wellcome employees agreed that the organisation was flexible enough to cope with change (69 per cent in 1993). Further, 85 per cent of staff believed the organisation would achieve its aims (62 per cent believed so in 1993), and the confidence in management's ability to cope with a crisis had actually risen, from 56 per cent in 1993 to 61 per cent by 1996. Risk taking had increased, but not radically – 37 per cent of employees felt people were still afraid of taking risks compared with 45 per cent in 1993.

There had been some resistance to the changes, as employees had questioned the adoption of the concept of disease management and the move away from a centralist organisation towards a flexible regionalised organisation. This was again reflected in the attitude survey where only 15 per cent of employees believed that morale was high, compared to 12 per cent in 1993, and 53 per cent feeling it had become worse in the last two years. Positively, however, 94 per cent of employees agreed that the organisation had a clear corporate strategy compared with 80 per cent in 1993, and 74 per cent felt they knew what management was trying to achieve (63 per cent in 1993).

The new appraisal process received a mixed reception: 53 per cent of employees were satisfied with the appraisal compared to 63 per cent in 1993, whilst 48 per cent believed their work goals were clearly defined, compared with 73 per cent previously. Seventy-three per cent stated they understood the basis on which their performance was appraised, against 81 per cent in 1993. There also seemed to be increased confusion over the link between effort and reward, as 38 per cent of employees thought the rewards were directly related to performance at work, compared to 50 per cent in 1993.

The new structure, however, appeared to offer greater opportunities for career progression through project work and secondments to other parts of the company. Seventy-three per cent of employees said the opportunities to develop new skills had increased, whilst employee perceptions of promotion prospects also increased: 41 per cent said career opportunities had increased over the last two years. Only 24 per cent of employees felt they did not have the opportunities they needed to be promoted, compared to 32 per cent in 1993.

The survey also showed that 88 per cent of employees agreed that there was more pressure at work resulting from the change programmes over the last two years, with 65 per cent agreeing this was also true of work hours. Seventy per cent of employees said that job security had diminished. In addition, it indicated only minor increases in individual responsibility for performance and team working, as some managers still harboured doubts over the new approach:

> *If you want an empowered environment you want people to take responsibility. How do you manage poor performance in an empowered environment where the teams haven't quite got to the stage where they can take over that function and take out poor performance?*
>
> (Line Manager)

PART 3: 1999–2000

Following the merger of Glaxo and Wellcome the new organisation performed steadily, although by this time Zantac and Zovirax, the blockbuster drugs of each organisation, were no longer on-patent.

Glaxo Wellcome's customer base was also beset with further changes stemming from the Labour Party's victory in the general election in 1997. This affected areas of funding, partnerships and the use of certain drugs, and was compounded by the fact that Glaxo Wellcome's reputation was no longer sufficient to guarantee sales. Therefore, GW shifted its focus to products in three main areas: respiratory, central nervous system and HIV.

In response to these pressures GW Pharma implemented a strategy of segmentation that pushed responsibility for profit and loss further down the organisation. It refocused on strategy from a regional perspective. Furthermore much of the internal activity was focused on retrenchment. Many of the business development programmes launched in the mid-1990s were cancelled, and the first of a number of small redundancy programmes saw the loss of 50 employees.

Emphasis was placed on sales targets, monitoring and moving away from self-managed teams. There was a feeling that the organisation would no longer 'suffer fools gladly'. This led to survey respondents commenting on increased work pressure, low morale, low job security, and having less identity with organisational values and loyalty to the organisation. However, some positive elements occurred as the staff were deemed to be less arrogant and complacent, and the management style was felt to be less controlling and more thoughtful.

The senior management team also changed, and became much younger. But despite their comparative youth, the team was criticised by low-level staff for being remote and inaccessible. The team set a 'work–life balance' policy in place to discourage working after 6pm. Yet there remained peer pressure from lower levels to work extra hours.

Performance management became embedded and quarterly formal appraisals were adopted. Each employee had a competency assessment and profile, personal development plan and career plan. Self-appraisal from colleagues and customers was encouraged and valued throughout the organisation. Seventy-four per cent of respondents said colleagues gave input to their appraisal, and 34 per cent had customers make informal feedback. However, low-level staff felt there was inadequate formal career planning provided for them. Training and development was rated highly with 69 per cent of respondents believing that coaching made a significant impact on their performance.

There were concerns that line managers had imposed targets which were felt to be unrealistic and demotivating, and, as a result of the new economic climate, the rewards received for attaining these targets were unfair. Furthermore Glaxo Wellcome was no longer perceived to be an industry top payer: base pay had not risen, and an emphasis was placed on performance-related pay. Many employees left for either competitors or particularly dot.com start-ups who were offering share options and rapid career progression at that time.

Although many low-level employees complained they had received no contact from HR personnel, the HR function was praised by senior staff for their speedy, fair and respectful handling of the redundancy and restructuring programmes throughout the 1990s.

This set the context for the subsequent merger with SmithKlineBeecham.

ASSIGNMENT QUESTIONS

1 What was the change context at Glaxo at the beginning of the 1990s?

2 What were the design choices taken and were they appropriate?

3 What was the change context like by the mid-1990s prior to the internal merger and associated changes?

4 Were the design choices taken in the mid-1990s an appropriate way to build on the earlier changes?

5 Given the situation at Glaxo in 1999–2000, what were the strengths and weaknesses of the change approach they adopted during the 1990s?

5

Designing the transition: the implementation path

5.1 INTRODUCTION

So far, this book has discussed the initial planning and design for change implementation. Chapter 2 introduced the range of design choices open to organisations implementing change. Chapters 3 and 4 discussed how to assess the key contextual features of the change situation, and how to use these factors to judge what change approach to take. As yet, little has been said about the design of the more detailed steps to achieve the implementation of the desired change approach or, for that matter, once change gets underway, how to manage the implementation. This is the focus of the next three chapters – the design and management of the actual transition:

- The notion of three change states, the *current* (where the organisation is now), the *future* (where the organisation wants to be), and the *transition* (how to get to the future state), is revisited.
- The concept of a change *vision* is introduced, and it is explained how this aspect of the future state needs to be considered before moving on to design the transition.
- The need to diagnose barriers to change that may be encountered during the transition is discussed. Barriers arise primarily from organisational culture and stakeholders.
- The notion of the transition state is expanded to explain how it encompasses three change phases – mobilise, move and sustain.
- The concept of the transition curve is explained to illustrate how the organisational transition process of mobilise, move and sustain is underpinned by the personal transitions of individuals within an organisation.
- Creating mobilisation, or developing readiness for change, is discussed along with a series of techniques for achieving this.
- Consideration is given to how to design a series of change interventions, and how to sequence their deployment, to achieve the chosen change approach, and move the organisation through the transition from mobilisation to ultimately sustaining the changes.

Chapter 6 extends the discussion of the range of *change interventions* that can be deployed during the transition state to achieve the desired end result. The special *management* and *resource requirements* of the transition state are discussed in Chapter 7.

5.2 THE THREE CHANGE STATES: THE CURRENT, THE FUTURE AND THE TRANSITION

Chapter 1 introduced the concept of three change states[1] (see Figure 5.1). Whilst we are assuming that readers of this text have already mastered the techniques to enable them to diagnose the current and future organisational states from other texts, before we move on to consider the detailed design of the transition, we do need to revisit the analysis of the start and end points of change. In particular, we need to give consideration to developing a vision or picture of the desired future organisational state, and to diagnosing the barriers to change that exist in the current state.

5.3 THE FUTURE STATE – DEVELOPING A VISION

Since the 1980s, there has been an increasing emphasis on the need for a powerful change 'vision', or picture of the future, if change is to be successful. Transformational change in particular usually consists of a number of projects and initiatives. Without a unifying vision, these initiatives can appear to be unrelated, confusing, and piecemeal (see Lendco, Illustration 4.3). Employees can struggle to understand what they are trying to achieve and what the future organisation looks like. A vision gives change recipients a target to aim for, and the incentive and energy for change. It should also generate commitment to change.

A vision is usually a qualitative expression of the desired future state. There are

---

Figure 5.1   Three change states

To achieve change it is necessary to:

1 Assess the current organisational situation.
2 Define the desired future organisational state.
3 Determine how to get there.

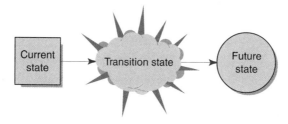

various descriptions of what constitutes a good vision, but generally three aspects are mentioned. A vision encapsulates what the organisation is trying to achieve; a rationale for the changes to be undertaken; and a picture of what the future organisation will 'look like', which incorporates something about the values of the new organisation and what is expected of employees. In addition, visions need to appeal to the majority of an organisation's stakeholders, and comprise realistic and attainable goals.[2] For many organisations, since a vision is about explaining to people where the organisation is going, having a vision means having a vision statement. However, in reality, communicating a vision requires a consistency of actions and words.

5.3.1 Vision statements

A vision should be expressed in such a way that it can be communicated effectively to employees in a way that is memorable. Employees will find it difficult to remember overly long and complex messages. Few individuals are able to remember even a page of detail, so a memorable vision statement is likely to be short and to the point. If a vision cannot stimulate interest and some degree of understanding in a short space of time, there is still more work to be done. A good vision statement should also be exciting and challenging. Furthermore, employees need to understand how they can help make the vision happen – they need to be able to link what they do on an everyday basis to the achievement of the vision.[3]

Some of the most famous vision statements include that of Komatsu, the Japanese earth-moving equipment manufacturers, who wanted to 'Encircle Caterpillar'. Caterpillar were the industry leader in Komatsu's sector at the time. Similarly, Honda wanted to become a second Ford, a pioneer in the automotive industry. These statements show that using examples, metaphors or analogies can help to succinctly express what is required to employees without using jargon. Other vision statements may be addressed more specifically to a particular change initiative, rather than longer-term evolution. Cummins Engines, the manufacturer of diesel engines and power generation systems, needed to tap into the innovative ideas and energies of its employees to remain successful. It started with the development of a vision, 'Making people's lives better by unleashing the Power of Cummins'.[4]

Giving employees a vision is a critical part of the change process. How can people change if they don't understand what they have got to change to? Yet many people are cynical about vision statements despite their popularity. Vision statements can be woolly and generic. Employees often feel that they are a PR exercise rather than a genuine attempt to communicate the goals of change. In addition, words are open to differing interpretations. What matters is a common understanding of what the vision is about, rather than the words used. In fact, the process used to develop a vision can be as important as the vision itself. A more participative process in which employees are involved, and in which two-way dialogue and discussion is used to foster a shared understanding of what the vision is about, may lead to a more effective vision. The words of the agreed vision statement may be no less woolly, but there should be more clarity about the expectations of employees and the changes the company is embarking on.

This was the approach taken by British Airways World Cargo (BAWC), the freight arm of British Airways, in the mid-1990s.[5] BAWC was experiencing tough competition with new competitors entering the market and more demanding customers. In addition, BAWC was perceived by its stakeholders to be a company who over-promised and under-delivered, had high costs with out-of-date working practices, low productivity, and employees who paid little attention to standards. However, BA decided to invest £250 million in a new World Cargo Centre at Heathrow and in new technology, but this had to be accompanied by organisational change. The leadership team prepared a new vision for the organisation, but it was shared with staff through a series of half-day sessions, at which groups of 20 people from different parts of the business engaged in facilitated discussions with two senior managers, aided by video, posters and debate. There was no simple one-line statement, instead the vision was based on a conversation around the big picture elements of the BAWC future, such as what the future BAWC would look like, the types of jobs available (workforce reductions at Heathrow from 1,500 to 1,100), and how this future was generated.

5.3.2 Aligning actions and words: using the web to help formulate a vision

Vision statements are only one way of expressing the change goals and aspirations of an organisation. Visions can be communicated through pictures. One technique is the 'strategy canvas', where a one-page picture showing both the current and future states is developed and used to share the vision with an organisation's employees.[6] But visions can also be communicated through behaviours as well as words, particularly the behaviours of the senior managers and other role models in an organisation. Indeed, behaviours may be a more effective way of communicating a vision. If actions and words are not aligned vision statements are quickly discredited. It is therefore important to understand, as part of the vision process, what new behaviours are required from managers to support the vision, and also what old behaviours, events and actions need to be discarded if employees are not to receive conflicting messages about what is now acceptable behaviour. This means it is important to understand how to develop actions to support and reinforce the vision, and how to identify barriers. In the example given above of BAWC, senior managers were shadowed by consultants to ensure they were engaging in agreed behaviours supportive of the vision.

A picture of the future organisation can be developed by drawing a new cultural web. This is a useful way of building a picture of the future organisation since the web incorporates not just new structures, but also what symbols, routines and control systems are needed.[7] It forces a consideration of some specifics about change. Illustration 5.1 shows the current and future webs developed by an organisation referred to here as Metto, the European division of a chemicals business. This illustration shows how the web can capture the key elements of change required. Metto wishes to undertake a fundamental change from an internally focused, manufacturing and product-oriented organisation, to one which puts customer needs first, and offers excellent service on a pan-European basis. Power and organisational structures, routines, rituals, stories, symbols and so on all need to change to support this. We discuss the role of symbolism throughout the transition in more detail in Chapter 6, but as the Metto web shows, completing the web helps to identify new symbols, symbolic behaviour, routines, and systems that can be used to reinforce the espoused vision.

Developing an outline of a new cultural web is an important exercise early on in the design of the change process, even if there is as yet no vision statement. Questions considered in Chapters 3 and 4, such as the scope of the changes to be undertaken by an organisation, cannot be answered unless there is at least an outline of the desired future state.

Obviously not all the *levers* and *interventions* for change identified in the future web can be put in place on day one of the change process to support the vision statement. This is why this chapter is devoted to a consideration of how to phase the different change levers and interventions through the transition state. Furthermore, the cultural web cannot be used to capture all levers and mechanisms by any means. In particular, interventions to do with communication and personal development, in order to achieve an employee awareness of the need for change, or an ability to manage and undertake change, have to be considered separately, and are given due consideration in Chapter 6.

5.3.3 Linking vision development to design choices

The change approach selected affects the way a vision for the change process should be developed. For example:

- If the change approach selected is *top-down* and *directive*, as may be the case for a reconstruction or a revolution such as that undertaken by Scottish and Newcastle Retail (see Chapter 2, Illustration 2.2) then a vision statement and a future cultural web can be developed by one person, such as the chief executive or the managing director, particularly if this individual is in the change role of *leadership*. Alternatively, the web and vision statement can be developed by the senior management team.

- If the change approach and style is to be more *bottom-up* and *collaborative*, then a wider range of employees can be involved in the process of vision and cultural web development. Vision statements do not necessarily 'appear' from an individual's sudden burst of inspiration, they may have to evolve gradually through a lot of hard work. Organisations may choose to use external facilitators to help

Illustration 5.1

Metto cultural web

(a) **Current organisation**

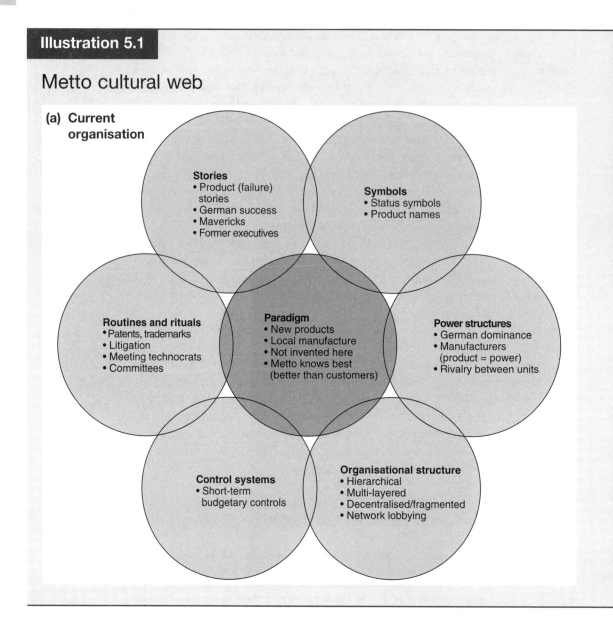

Stories
- Product (failure) stories
- German success
- Mavericks
- Former executives

Symbols
- Status symbols
- Product names

Routines and rituals
- Patents, trademarks
- Litigation
- Meeting technocrats
- Committees

Paradigm
- New products
- Local manufacture
- Not invented here
- Metto knows best (better than customers)

Power structures
- German dominance
- Manufacturers (product = power)
- Rivalry between units

Control systems
- Short-term budgetary controls

Organisational structure
- Hierarchical
- Multi-layered
- Decentralised/fragmented
- Network lobbying

achieve widespread employee participation, or use senior managers to lead the process.[8] This is likely to depend on decisions already made about the *change roles*, (leadership, team, external facilitation), which in turn should be based on contextual circumstances to do with capability and capacity for change.

- In circumstances where a more *participative* change approach has been selected, a combination of the above two approaches to vision development may be selected, whereby the senior managers, or change team, design an initial web and vision statement, and then consult staff.

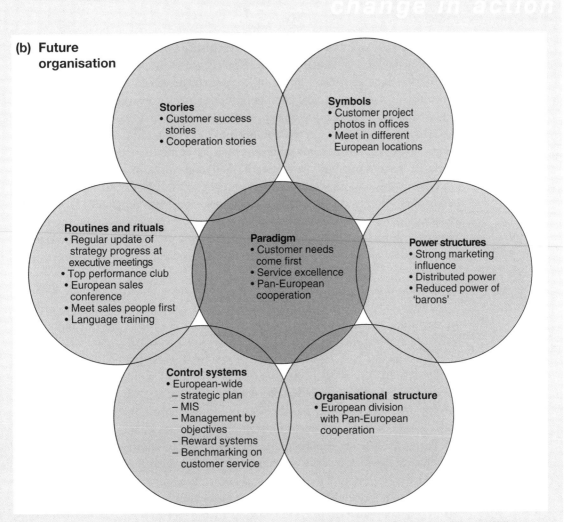

change in action

(b) Future organisation

Stories
• Customer success stories
• Cooperation stories

Symbols
• Customer project photos in offices
• Meet in different European locations

Routines and rituals
• Regular update of strategy progress at executive meetings
• Top performance club
• European sales conference
• Meet sales people first
• Language training

Paradigm
• Customer needs come first
• Service excellence
• Pan-European cooperation

Power structures
• Strong marketing influence
• Distributed power
• Reduced power of 'barons'

Control systems
• European-wide
  – strategic plan
  – MIS
  – Management by objectives
  – Reward systems
  – Benchmarking on customer service

Organisational structure
• European division with Pan-European cooperation

Source: G. Johnson, 'Mapping and re-mapping organisational culture', in V. Ambrosini, G. Johnson and K. Scholes (1998) *Exploring Techniques of Analysis and Evaluation in Strategic Management*, Hemel Hempstead: Prentice Hall.

5.4 BARRIERS TO CHANGE

Once the future state for the organisation is understood it is possible to diagnose the barriers to change. Most barriers to change arise from the old *organisational culture* and *organisational stakeholders*.

5.4.1 Identifying barriers to change and levers to overcome them

Any *vision* developed of the future will encapsulate new structures, systems, and ways of behaving that have to be put in place, but without consideration of existing barriers it is possible, almost by default, to leave old systems and ways of behaving in place, and these can subsequently prove obstructive. For example, one organisation undergoing change wanted to move to a structure of profit centres in a move to devolve responsibility and increase middle manager empowerment. However, old control systems, such as centralised decision making on levels of resourcing and recruitment, and authorisation of certain types of expense claims and expenditure were initially left in place. Old senior manager behaviours, such as countermanding local decisions, also remained, symbolically challenging the espoused move to devolved responsibility. As a result the middle managers perceived little increase in their scope for discretion or autonomy. Interventions needed to be put in place to address these barriers if change was to progress.

This example illustrates that existing *organisation cultures* provide some of the strongest barriers to the implementation of change. If the existing organisation culture and the potential barriers to change it creates are not understood from a technique such as cultural web analysis, the way the organisation and its members operate may continue to be driven by the existing culture, rather than by the desired new ways of behaving. A web analysis would have revealed that the existing control systems and old symbolic and routine ways of behaving were barriers to successful implementation of profit centres in the example given above. In the Metto example in Illustration 5.1, the existing culture presents several barriers to the desired integrated European organisation, and the aim to offer high-quality customer service. These include the historical emphasis on new product development from a technical point of view, and rivalry between business units to develop different products. The symbols were all to do with technical excellence, such as the CEO talking to the 'technocrats' rather than sales people, and the technical literature and photographs on the office walls. For change to be successful, the range of levers deployed need to address these issues. More specifically, the identified barriers, including old behaviours, need to be removed or destroyed.

However, as emphasised in Chapter 3 when discussing the need for preservation, change does need to avoid throwing out *positive aspects* of an organisation alongside the negative aspects. Therefore, when examining the cultural web, attention should be paid to not just the barriers to change, but also those aspects of the organisation that are either an asset or a facilitator of change and need to be retained.

Powerful stakeholders can also provide significant barriers to change. The way such stakeholders are likely to react to the proposed changes should have already been built into the design choices made from the consideration of power as one of the contextual features. However, it is also important to understand the way different stakeholders will respond to change as implementation progresses, and then consider how this is to be tackled. This is to do with issues of resistance management, which is discussed in Chapter 7.

5.5 DESIGNING THE TRANSITION STATE: THE ORGANISATIONAL LEVEL

Once the design of the future state has been completed, and it is known what barriers to change have to be overcome, it is then necessary to design an implementation path to deliver the future state. This involves thinking about which change levers to deploy and in what order. Of course, many levers and interventions will already have been identified. The future cultural web will contain details of new structures, systems, routines and symbols needed. The consideration of barriers to change should have led to some decisions about old structures, systems and ways of behaving that need to be dismantled or discouraged, and the mechanisms that can be deployed to achieve this and facilitate change.

To provide more shape to the way the identified levers and interventions should be sequenced, and what additional interventions may be needed, it is helpful to subdivide the transition state itself into three other phases – mobilise, move and sustain (see Figure 5.2).

This model is based on the one devised by Lewin.[9] The original model referred to unfreezing, moving and refreezing:

- *Unfreezing* is about making people within an organisation ready for change by making them aware of the need for change and dissatisfied with the existing ways of working. It is about creating the *readiness for change* among the workforce, at all levels from senior managers downwards, discussed as part of the change kaleidoscope in Chapters 3 and 4. Change is a painful, difficult experience for both organisations and the individuals within them. To

Figure 5.2   **Three phases of transition**

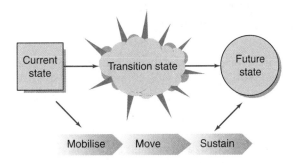

undertake change people need to feel that the problems and the pain change will cause are outweighed by the need to change.

- *Moving* is the implementation of the needed changes through the selected range of levers and mechanisms.

- *Refreezing* involves embedding the changes throughout the organisation to ensure members do not relapse into patterns of old behaviour.

There are many criticisms of this model. One is that it is too linear and simplistic. Whilst such criticisms are true, the principle of *unfreezing* is still widely acknowledged as an important part of any change. Managers introduced to this model will often comment that on reflection they can see that the change process within their organisation stumbled along rather than acquiring momentum, because the staff within the organisation were never 'unfrozen' and made ready for change. Similarly, the concept of refreezing is still recognised as having some merit, as it seems that without efforts to indicate that change is over, change drift can set in. A common comment from managers is that the change processes within their organisations have been left unfinished, since no real attempt has been made to institutionalise the required behavioural and attitudinal changes throughout the organisation. The result is a continual backsliding of staff into old ways of behaving and a confusion over where the change process has got to. As such, the concepts of unfreezing and refreezing are still important.

On the other hand, it is also often commented that unfreezing and refreezing are inappropriate terms to use in modern organisations. Many organisations move from a period of on-going adaptation, to a radical change, and then back into adaptation through continuous improvement. This is why it is becoming more common for the unfreeze phase to be referred to as mobilisation and the refreeze phase to be referred to as sustain or institutionalise. Mobilisation is about mobilising people behind the latest change initiative. The term conveys better the sense of redirecting energies and efforts into a new project. Similarly terms such as sustain and institutionalise embody the need to instil the new behaviours and attitudes throughout the organisation and signal the end to major change, while avoiding the implication that there will be no more change.

5.6 FACILITATING PERSONAL TRANSITIONS: THE INDIVIDUAL LEVEL

Organisations only change if the individuals within that organisation change. To an external customer, the behaviour of the people that the customer encounters summarises what the organisation stands for. If an organisation wants to change the way its customers see it, it has to change the behaviour of its people. Strategic change has to be driven down throughout the organisation. Yet, as Chapter 1 explains, all too often, change management is viewed as something that is 'done'

Figure 5.3	**Dual leadership responsibilities – managing the organisational and individual change paths**

to people. Employees of the organisation are treated as passive on-lookers who will comply with the directives and objectives issued from the top.

Therefore, to achieve change, a change agent needs to understand how individuals change, and build this into the mobilise, move and sustain model. Change leaders need to recognise that they have two parallel sets of tasks: (1) leading the organisation through change, and (2) leading the individual organisational members through that change, (see Figure 5.3). This is why change capability, as discussed in Chapters 3 and 4, is so important because part of change capability is having the ability to lead staff through change.

Individual transitions can be likened to the bereavement and mourning process. It is a psychological process that research shows all individuals go through. Individuals will experience feelings of loss, and will have to work through those feelings of loss and come to terms with life afterwards.[10] This takes time, although varying degrees of time for different individuals. This text uses the concept of the *transition curve* to explain how individuals pass through change.

5.6.1 The transition curve

The *transition curve*[11] describes the process individuals go through during change, and is depicted in Figure 5.4. The transition curve suggests individuals undergoing change pass through seven stages:

- In *stage 1*, individuals initially experience *shock* when they encounter the need for change, and a dip in their self-confidence due to the need for them to undertake personal change and to do things differently.

- *Stage 2, denial*, is a stage when individuals may try to rationalise the changes as not really involving a significant change for themselves. Individuals may try to tell themselves that working in a new role will involve nothing different from their current role. As a result their self-confidence goes back up again, but this denial can also prevent them from moving forwards. Trying to fulfil a new job in the same way as they did their old one may mean they do not perform well.

Figure 5.4	The transition curve

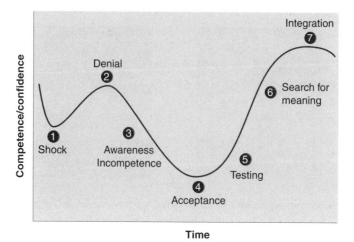

Source: Based on Adams, J., Hayes, J. and Hopson, C. (1976) *Transition: Understanding and Managing Personal Change*, London: Martin Robertson & Company

- To move on to *stage 3, awareness,* individuals need to develop a recognition of the need for personal change. However, acquiring this awareness, which may be prompted by discussion with others, or a recognition that old ways of doing things no longer work, also brings with it a *drop in confidence* as individuals become aware of their inadequacy to fulfil their new role.

- Individuals will be able to move forward to *stage 4, acceptance,* when they can accept the need to let go of the past – to let go of old attitudes and behaviours and adopt new ones.

- *Stage 5, testing,* is to do with identifying and testing out new behaviours, maybe as a result of training. As new behaviours start to enable individuals to perform more adequately in their new role, confidence starts to build again.

- By *stage 6, search,* the individual is assimilating learning from their successes and failures, and starting to understand why some behaviours work and others do not.

- *Stage 7, integration,* is marked by an integration of new behaviours into the everyday way of working by individuals. There ceases to be a gap between an individual's perceived ability to perform and the expectations placed on that individual.

5.6.2 Experiencing the transition curve

Illustrations 5.2 and 5.3 are illustrations of change journeys experienced by individuals. Illustration 5.2 describes the journey undertaken by an individual who quickly adapted to a transition to a new job role, whereas Illustration 5.3 shows an individual who adapted, but found the process far more traumatic than the first. Both examples illustrate well the emotional nature of the individual transitions, and the second powerfully shows how an individual can need a lot of help to get through a personal transition. Some individuals never complete the transition. They get stuck half-way through, and never really recover from feelings of loss and that things used to be better in the old days.

The headings 'sensing', 'shock' and 'despair' in Illustration 5.3 demonstrate how hard it can be for an individual to let go of the past and come to terms with the need for change. Similarly, the headings 'disorganization', 'realization', 'steadying', 'testing' and 'acceptance' in Illustrations 5.2 and 5.3 reveal the feelings of loss and inadequacy that individuals can experience as they try to understand what is expected of them and what they need to do, but also how there is a gradual acceptance that change is necessary. 'Moving on' in Illustrations 5.2 and 5.3 is about the individuals emerging on the other side of change, feeling competent to perform in their new roles.

Illustrations 5.2 and 5.3 also show that all individuals pass through the transition curve at a different rate and in a different way. The curve depicts a typical pattern or response rather than a prescriptive route that all individuals adhere to. It shows that resistance to change is a natural phenomenon associated, like grieving, with a reluctance to give up possessions, people, status and expectations.[12]

Illustration 5.2   *change in action*

A rapid adaptation

JOURNEY	REACTION
Shock	'I was offered the job in the morning and started in the afternoon. I knew what the job was, but there was an awful lot to learn.'
Acceptance	'It wasn't planned and it meant a significant change of life, but I welcomed it – I wouldn't have liked to have stayed in my previous job.'
Testing	'I learnt very quickly, I asked a lot of questions, read a lot and quickly got on top of the job. I gave the appearance of being in control within days – though, of course, there were many months of learning.'
Moving on	'I'm in control.'

Source: Adapted from Stuart, R. (1995) 'Experiencing organisational change: triggers, processes and outcomes of change journeys', *Personnel Review*, 24, 2.

Illustration 5.3

change in action

A painful adaptation

JOURNEY	REACTION
Sensing	'I'd been getting all sorts of messages.'
Shock	'It was totally contrary to everything that I'd been told.'
Despair	'I felt very criticised, not understood and totally incompetent.'
Disorganisation	'I felt totally confused. I thought that I must be going nuts. Had I the right perception? Paranoid? I'd lost all sense of judgement. I felt out of control. Doubt. Am I dreaming this?'
Yearning	'I had vivid dreams, replaying the events leading up to . . . replaying them in different ways. It was like a dreadful nightmare.'
Despair	'I felt isolated but was unable to talk to other people. I had a real feeling of desperation. At one stage, I didn't think I'd survive. It was a desperate time.'
Realisation	'I realised I had no alternative. I had to get my self-esteem and credibility back into shape sufficiently to carry on. I had to own up and take responsibility for what I'd done; I felt betrayed, cheapened and scapegoated. I was very angry with the organisation for blaming me. I am responsible but look what you made me do.'
Steadying	'I moved (within the organisation). I spent a long time wilfully forgetting. I started to feel better – a sense of more stability. I was defensive – fearful that things could get out of control again.'
Testing	'I was continuously building anew. I attended courses, some things went well; it took a long time to feel better about myself.'
Meaning	'Getting a clear view of what I'm good and not good at. Developing my understanding of the reality and limits of my relationship with the organisation.'
Sharing	'It was important to talk about it.'
Moving on	'I feel powerful. I've put things into perspective and learned from them. It is okay to be me and to trust my perception – and that it's not the only one.'

Source: Adapted from Stuart, R. (1995) 'Experiencing organisational change: triggers, processes and outcomes of change journeys', *Personnel Review*, 24, 2.

5.7 LINKING INDIVIDUAL AND ORGANISATIONAL TRANSITIONS

The concept of the transition curve can be combined with the mobilise, move and sustain model, as shown in Figure 5.5, to help remind designers of change what interventions in these phases are trying to achieve for the individual recipients:

● The stages of *shock* and *denial,* moving into *awareness,* accompanied by feelings of loss, fits with the *mobilisation.* Interventions aimed at helping individuals to come to terms with the need for change and to let go of the past would, therefore, be built into the mobilisation phase through the types of mobilisation tactics discussed below. The mobilisation tactic(s) adopted would still need to match the context and the selected design choices.

● The experience of individuals as they move through *awareness* to *acceptance, testing* and *search* will underpin the *move* phase. Thus interventions such as education and training, personal development, new work procedures and systems, and new management styles, which help individuals through these stages should all be included in the move phase. Coaching and counselling, from either internal or external facilitators, for staff who are having problems adapting may also be necessary here.

Figure 5.5   **Linking organisational and individual change**

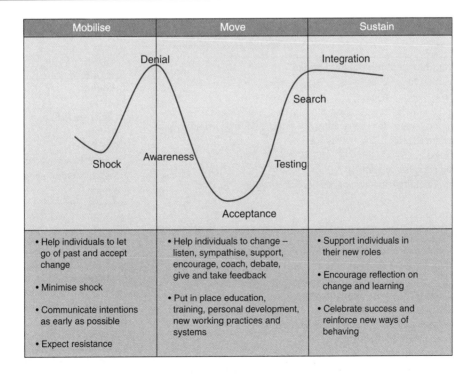

Illustration 5.4

change in action

An exercise on the transition curve

Helps through shock and denial
Finding a coach/mentor to off-load feelings on
Knowing from discussions with others you are not alone
Identifying +ves and −ves
Having friends/trusted people: emotional support
Communications enabling mental preparation – what is to happen, what it will be like
Getting information in advance, and involvement
Understanding the transition process

Hinders
Disinformation
Lack of information
Isolation
Only seeing the negatives
Guilt – others worse off

Helps through awareness phase
Letting go of the past
Identifying new goals
Receiving information: options, facts versus rumour and speculation
Understanding alternatives – receiving options, information
Putting things in perspective
Addressing real fears (new tools, for example)
Creating an enemy
Allowing expression:
    OK to be angry/sad
    Empathy with feelings
    Listening
    Conflict not suppressed
Anticipating falling output and standards

Hinders
Opinions not allowed
Uncertainty
Lack of forums for expression
Blame
Negativity

Helps through acceptance/testing phase
Finding support for yourself
Those who are negative leave
Maintaining focus; first steps; short-term goals
Learning encouraged: new behaviours rewarded (informally), coaching, mistakes allowed, risk taking encouraged
Training
Reinforcing success/celebrating it
Forging new identity/relationships: social activities, peer support groups
Leadership

Hinders
Blame
Punishing failure
Jealousy
Resistance
Keep celebrating the past
Negative attitudes from others

Helps through search for meaning/integration phase
Rewarding/celebrating success
Continuing to emphasise plans/goals
Providing long-term goals – Work starts here
Role models who live the vision
Giving feedback and encouraging reflection/learning
On-going team/network building
Providing on-going development opportunities

Hinders
Moving on to next change initiative and forgetting current
No new goals/targets

- The range of *levers* deployed in the *move* phase will need to fit the design choices selected. In circumstances where there is little *time* or *money*, it may prove difficult to provide support via counselling or coaching to staff members who are struggling. There may have to be a trade-off between what is ideal and what is possible. The emphasis may need to be on changes to structures and systems, with imposed changes to roles and responsibilities, and new service and quality targets. If the required change is *transformational* in nature, it will be necessary to drive in value change and not just behavioural change. The levers will need to reflect this with a greater emphasis on personal development, communication, counselling and coaching rather than just skills-based training. Similarly, if a *participative* or *bottom-up* change approach is selected, it will be necessary to utilise levers that encourage staff participation and enable staff to have some say in the way change develops. This may mean greater investment in workshops and cross-functional teams to develop new working practices and procedures.

- The *sustain* phase is about helping the *integration* process. Again the levers and interventions used will need to match the design choices of change target and change levers. Interventions that can be particularly helpful in this phase when the *change target* is *behaviours* or *values* include reward mechanisms to reinforce and support behavioural change undertaken by staff. If the *change target* is *outputs*, such levers may have been used in the move phase. Symbolic interventions can also be helpful here to reinforce change. Since both human resource systems and symbolic interventions as levers of change are discussed in more detail in Chapter 6, this point will be revisited there.

An exercise on the transition curve which asks people to consider a change process they have been through and what helped and hindered them at each stage of the personal transition (see Illustration 5.4) reveals that the interventions that help individuals move through the curve are mostly interpersonal and symbolic. The interventions are to do with communication, coaching, training, support, and encouraging appropriate new ways of working through symbolic means such as celebrating successes and achievements. This emphasises the importance of the interpersonal subsystem of change interventions discussed in Chapter 2 as one of the design choices, and reinforces the need to put interventions in place in all four subsystems (technical, political, cultural and interpersonal) for significant change to take root in an organisation.

Whilst we therefore need to spend time considering how the design choices are put together with our knowledge of the current and future states, and our understanding of how individuals go through change, we first need to consider the important phase of mobilisation.

5.8 MOBILISING FOR CHANGE

Mobilising an organisation sounds simple enough in theory, but is far more difficult in practice because it is about making *individuals* ready for change. The use of logic and rational argument will not necessarily be enough to convince individuals who may stand to lose a lot by change, or who may have to undertake personal change themselves, or have to invest considerable effort into the change process, that there is a strong need to change.

Mobilisation may occur because a significant change in the environment has led to a decline in the organisational performance that is tangible to all employees, such as the arrival of new competitors leading to a sharp decline in market share, or a take-over or sell-off. This may lead to a felt need for change that can be capitalised on, or maybe even a crisis. But this is not always, and is in fact rarely, the case. What creates a crisis for managers may leave the rest of the workforce relatively untouched. After all, that is what managers are paid to do – sort out problems. If no crisis or felt need for change is evident, then mobilisation has to be managed in some way. The change equation is a useful way of thinking about how to achieve this.

5.8.1 The change equation

The change equation, shown in Figure 5.6, states there are three components that need to be present for individuals to be prepared to undertake change. For individuals to feel that the problems and pain of change are outweighed by the advantages of need to change, it is necessary for people to be:

1 dissatisfied with the status quo;

2 convinced the proposed changes are a viable way of resolving current problems;

3 believe the proposed changes are achievable.

This equation is particularly helpful when considering mobilisation. It also ties into the discussion in the previous two chapters on readiness for change. Mobilising individuals is about getting individuals to recognise that change is necessary, and that they have to let go of the past, but also that the proposed changes are desirable because they will solve the problems the organisation is facing, and that they are achievable.

Consideration of the three components of the change equation gives us insights into how we can generate readiness for change. There are a variety of different means that can be used and the following lists only some of them.

| Figure 5.6 | The change equation |

$$C = (A \times B \times D) > X$$

When

C = Change

A = Level of dissatisfaction with the status quo

B = Desirability of proposed change

D = Practicality (risk of disruption) of change

X = Personal cost of changing

Source: Adapted from *Organizational Transitions: Managing Complex Change*, 2nd edn, by Beckhard, R., and Harris, R.T., © 1987. Reprinted by permission of Pearson Education, Inc., Upper Saddle River, NJ.

5.8.2 Questioning and challenging of the status quo

There are a variety of techniques that can be used to encourage staff to question the appropriateness of the existing way of doing things for the organisation's longer-term survival, creating dissatisfaction with the status quo:

- Encourage debate about the appropriateness of the current way of operating. This was the technique used to mobilise the partners and senior managers in KPMG. Illustration 2.6 in Chapter 2 reveals that workshops were run to encourage the KPMG partners to debate the need for change. The senior management conference was used to encourage debate among senior managers about the need for change and what type of change. However, as Chapter 2 also points out, not all levels of staff were involved in these sorts of initiatives, and therefore it could be argued that an awareness and acceptance of the need for change was not generated throughout the organisation.

- Disseminate information showing how the organisation compares poorly with the organisations with which it competes. This could be done through the use of internal communication media, or it could involve the chief executive of an organisation using the business press to tell his staff that the organisation is performing poorly.[13] The fact that the chief executive is talking openly about the organisation's performance legitimises debate.

- Introducing techniques such as 360-degree appraisal, whereby subordinates are given the opportunity to appraise their managers, as well as being appraised themselves by those managers. This can legitimise debate about existing management styles and barriers to change within the organisation.

- Questioning and challenging may also be achieved by the symbolic means discussed next.

Illustration 5.5

change in action

Encouraging questioning and challenging at Whites

Whites is a medium-sized car dealership. When the new MD took over, herself a symbol of change in a macho business, she first needed to convince her senior managers and staff that she was serious about changing from a pushy, sales-driven culture to one more customer-focused. First she looked at staff and customer attitudes. She had 15 hours of video testimony from clients who were not satisfied with their experiences which she showed to her managers and staff. She also challenged traditional ways of working in the organisation by announcing that she was happy to see a drop in revenue during the change process – whereas the previous emphasis had always been to think of the bottom line first and everything else second. As proof of this statement, she closed the dealership for an afternoon to launch the change programme.

However, staff not only needed to be convinced of the need for change, but also to understand what was to change. They didn't like the current autocratic management style,

but were also resistant to change. The organisation did not have a culture in which people were empowered or would take initiative. The MD adopted a style of persuasion. She employed a training consultancy and asked for volunteers to train as change champions. Fifty showed an interest, and 20 of these became continuous-improvement facilitators. Staff were put into groups and asked to identify their issues. Working groups were set up to look at the issues identified. Meetings started slowly as employees felt managers didn't want to listen to them. Teams were given £500 to spend on anything they thought would benefit the business, but early on had to be pushed to use this money.

These early change initiatives have led to a series of change initiatives that have radically changed the way the organisation operates, the relationship between different parts of the organisation, such as technicians, sales and after-sales, and the way the organisation works with the customer.

Source: Adapted from Littlefield, D. (29 July 1999) 'Real change dealer', *People Management*, pp. 44–6.

Illustration 5.5 discusses an example of mobilisation achieved primarily through encouraging questioning and challenging. The managing director of Whites, a car dealer, relied on a variety of techniques, such as videos of customers saying they were dissatisfied, challenging existing preconceptions, such as saying she was prepared to let revenue drop whilst change took place, but also, for more junior staff, getting them involved in identifying their issues and possible solutions. This illustration also shows how one of the mobilisation techniques on its own is unlikely to be enough. Some things done by the MD represented symbolic breaks with the past. Furthermore, to make staff feel the changes were viable and achievable they also needed training in techniques such as continuous improvement.

5.8.3 Symbolic breaks with the past

Making symbolic breaks with the past is about doing things differently to indicate that things are changing. This may then also legitimise questioning and challenging of the status quo. There are many different ways of achieving this.

- Senior managers can indicate by their behaviour, or the way they dress, that things are different. Sir John Browne, Chief Executive of British Petroleum, wanted to foster a culture of teamwork and accessibility at BP when he first took up his position, so he positioned his office on a middle floor of the company's head office in London, rather than on the top floor. The office has no door, and is next to an open-plan area occupied by Browne's fellow executives. Instead of a door, the office has a sliding panel which Browne can close if he requires privacy.[14] Later he wanted to show BP's commitment to taking care of the natural environment, despite the apparent contradiction between this and the company's gas and oil exploration activities. He first made a very public speech in which he acknowledged that global climate change was a problem that BP could no longer ignore and outlined BP's plans to address the issue, and then he withdrew BP from the Global Climate Coalition, a Washington-based lobbying organisation which opposes government intervention on climate change.[15]

- Changes can be made to the way things are done. Older staff due for promotion may be passed over in favour of outsiders with a different skill-set, and other types of staff may even be made redundant. This is a particularly powerful mobilisation mechanism in any organisations where jobs were always for life and promotion was often linked to length of service rather than performance, although there are not many such organisations left these days. An example would be the move by many of the large UK accounting firms in the 1990s to make non-performing partners redundant for the first time ever.

- Changes may be subtle. If there is to be more of an emphasis on customer service and less on technical product aspects, then this can be supported by indications of a power shift from production to marketing, maybe by giving marketing a larger budget for marketing, or by moving senior marketing people to more prestigious offices closer to the MD and therefore the central seat of power. At Hoechst, the German pharmaceuticals company now part of Aventis, early changes were led by Jurgen Dormann. His appointment as CEO represented a break from the past since he was the first 'Mr' – the first CEO not to be a Dr or Professor. He was selected for his business acumen rather than his reputation in the research laboratories.[16]

- Symbolic breaks with the past may be more direct and challenging. Whatman, the paper maker since the eighteenth century, has a site reminiscent of its past – a warren of Victorian buildings, with old-fashioned clocks, quaint signs and four papermaking machines. These machines have now been adapted to make all kinds of paper other than the artist's paper the company originally made.

However, Whatman's membership of the federation of Papermaking Industries has only recently been cancelled by the new Chief Executive, and the paper-maker's trade union simultaneously de-recognised, at the start of a transform-ation process to retrieve the fortunes of this ailing company. Many of the 1,000 staff will be lost in the coming months as they are replaced by technology. All this is part of a shift to give up the 'black art' of papermaking and recognise that this is only one part of the business. More shocking, staff have been told that if papermaking doesn't prove competitive, it will all be outsourced, as some has already on certain grades of paper.[17]

5.8.4 Drastic measures and shock tactics

Some symbolic changes may be quite ruthless, verging on shock tactics. Such shock symbolic moves could involve wholesale closures or sell-offs of parts of the business that used to be core to the identity of the organisation but are no longer. The outsourcing of all paper making at Whatman would, therefore, be a shock tactic. Such moves are common in take-over and turnaround situations. These moves can challenge the very essence of an organisation's beliefs about its ident-ity. Other measures may also equate to shock tactics:

● In November 2001 BT, the British telecommunications company, was de-merged into a number of stand-alone companies. BT Cellnet, the UK and European mobile phone business, was floated off to become mmO2. There were many significant breaks with the past that occurred as part of the de-merger process for the mmO2 staff. This mobilised them for the more substan-tial culture change required to turn mmO2 into a leaner and more dynamic company. First, the employees experienced a change of employer from a large, stable blue-chip company to a much smaller entity. Second, the old BT brand was dropped and replaced internally and externally in all promotional activity with the brand O2, which has been designed to have a more youthful appeal. Other complementary changes were also made. The Pay and Go tariff, for example, was supplemented with a youth tariff 'Pay and Go Wild'. Furthermore, all mmO2 employees had to leave the BT buildings in which they currently worked. Staff were relocated to a new office where there were no BT staff. In addition, there was a need to rationalise the workforce. In January 2002 a discretionary leavers scheme was announced. The first wave of redun-dancies was announced shortly after that. Those staff remaining had to be allo-cated to the new structure. Some were allocated to similar job roles, albeit with expansion of responsibilities. However, other positions had changed substan-tially in terms of the job role, and were advertised for any unassigned staff to apply for. Finally, new performance measures were put in place for staff. The de-merger process was also accompanied by much communication through briefings, newsletters, videos and training.

● An international engineering and contracting company used several shock tactics to mobilise staff within one of their UK industrial business units for change. At the beginning of January 2002 a new senior director arrived from another division to take the position of Managing Director. His arrival was accompanied by e-mail and intranet notices announcing the restructuring of the UK business to support a broader corporate shift towards a service-orientated business and reducing business costs. By the end of his first week the new Managing Director had dismissed the previously two most senior directors. In the following three months a new senior management team was appointed, staff were made redundant, and the remaining senior management were moved to open-plan offices.

5.8.5 Communication, education and training

The above three approaches are all useful for generating dissatisfaction with the status quo. Whilst symbolic gestures can also be used to illustrate what the new organisations is to be about, it is normally this approach, communication, education and training, that is used to create an understanding of how the proposed changes will help the organisation and that the proposed changes are achievable. Various communication and training interventions can be used to help get across to people why change is needed, what changes are needed, and to provide them with the skills they need to make change happen. Such interventions are becoming increasingly popular, as it is realised that genuine change requires considerable investment in mobilising the workforce. The woes of Marks and Spencer have been well documented, and undoubtedly by 2000 most staff recognised that change was necessary – but change to what? As part of the recovery significant investment has been made in culture change. The new HR Director, following her appointment in 2000, started the process with a two-day workshop for senior HR people, which led into a communications event to launch the change process to all 500 personnel and training staff at Lord's Cricket Ground. The event included not only presentations on the change programme but also actors who played M&S as it was, and as it would be. In addition there was an interactive exhibition, with stands representing the different aspects of the change programme such as games based on TV programmes and sports.[18] Bill Grimsey, the Chief Executive of Iceland, the frozen foods chain, tried something similar to launch his transformation process in 2001. He brought in consultants to organise a one-day high-energy, participative event designed to get across the key change messages – what is changing and why – to the managers and to win their commitment to Iceland's new goals. The managers went through a series of activities that involved listening, questioning and presenting back their own summaries of what they were being told and their own ideas. These activities were all stage managed to resemble some other event, like a TV show.[19]

However, both these examples only reached limited staff groups – the rest of the workforce still had to be mobilised. Illustration 5.6 describes how education

Illustration 5.6

Launching change at Glenbrook Steel Mill

Glenbrook Steel Mill in New Zealand was acquired by BHP, the Australian minerals company, in 1991 when they were expanding their steel division. Although the mill was contributing revenue for BHP, in October 1996 a programme of voluntary redundancies was put in place to reduce the 1,600 workforce by 400 in response to pressure from BHP to cut costs by $50 million (New Zealand dollars). Glenbrook were operating in a competitive market with a small, declining domestic market and a high exchange rate. In addition, the mill's machinery was getting older. Replacement technology was expensive requiring significant capital investment.

If things didn't improve, the mill faced closure, and such negative stories were being reported in the newspapers. There were also a lot of negative stories circulating in the mill, to do with the company closing, and the Australian office not valuing the New Zealand office. The MD, who was close to retirement, was prepared to put his head on the chopping block with Australia and say yes, we can continue to be profitable. He told the workforce he would stay and help them through the difficult period ahead. He put a big commitment into the mill and encouraged everyone else to do the same.

First, it was necessary to make the company more dynamic, to speed up decision making to enable faster reactions to the market and other changes. The redundancies had already flattened the old hierarchical structure. Now it was necessary to make the flatter structure work by pushing decision making down the organisation. Kepner Tregoe decision-making tools were introduced through training to enable staff at all levels to make decisions. The training was started in 1997, but Kepner Tregoe consultants remained on-site for over 2 years to help individuals put their training into practice.

At the same time a course, 'Leadership for Inventing the Future', was launched. The aim was to destroy a lot of the negative gossip and stories circulating in the organisation, whilst at the same time creating energy and motivation to work for the future – to 'ditch the past' and create a clean slate to move forwards with. The course was designed to encourage employees to acknowledge the reality of the competitive market, but recognise that this didn't have to be the end. If the staff worked as a team it would be possible to turn things round. Every single employee, and their family, was invited to attend. The course lasted 3 days with the entire company going though it in a 2-week period. It included sessions on breakthrough technologies, leaving the past behind, looking at what actually happened as opposed to rumours and gossip, and getting rid of personal and work-related emotional baggage that created constraints to doing other things. By the end of the course everyone was feeling more positive about where the Glenbrook was, and people were doing things like writing letters to others who they felt they had tensions with saying sorry, let's get on with things from now on. The course was an emotional experience for many attendees – some people were reduced to tears.

Source: Adapted from Riordan, D. (4 May 1997) 'Working through trouble at mill', *The Sunday Star-Times* (Auckland), and interview with employee of BHP, 1997.

and training was used to mobilise the workforce at Glenbrook Steel Mill, part of the Australian resources company, BHP, following the shock of redundancies. There were two aspects to the training. The redundancies and press coverage had already created a level of dissatisfaction – if not despondency – with the status quo. Closure was a definite possibility. The leadership course was aimed at getting the employees to believe they could move forwards together as a team. It was an intensive personal development intervention aimed at altering the employee's attitudes to their situation. The decision-making training was about enabling them to move forwards.

5.8.6 Earlier reconstruction or adaptation

The notion of mobilisation also connects back to the discussion in Chapter 2 on change paths. Sometimes, the mobilisation for an evolutionary or revolutionary change is an earlier change. The examples of this given in Chapter 2 include General Electric, Asda, and Scottish and Newcastle Retail. In all these instances, the initial turnarounds were effected through much 'slashing and burning', which acted in part to mobilise the organisations for the more fundamental and transformational culture changes that had to follow. Harsh reconstructions often contain many shock tactics. However, it must be realised that earlier change may not on its own be sufficient as a mobilisation mechanism. Illustration 5.7 shows how Belgacom, the Belgian Telecommunications Company, went through a period of adaptation from 1991 to 1995, but then moved into a rapid reconstruction at the end of 1995 as the first step on the path to more fundamental cultural evolution. The reconstruction involved many shock tactics, such as the redundancies and the 200 vacancies created at the top, and many symbolic breaks with the past, such as the new structure which in diagrams symbolically indicated the importance of customers by putting them at the top of the organisation structure chart. The retraining of staff subsequently played a key role in enabling individual change. The S&N Retail example in Chapter 2, Illustration 2.2, similarly describes the additional effort put into the education and communication initiatives used to launch the culture change process at the new head office, following the restructuring and the relocation. As suggested by the change equation, people need to understand that the past has gone, but also to understand what is expected of them in the future.

5.8.7 Linking mobilisation to design choices

As with all change interventions, the mobilisation tactics need to be context-specific. What works in one context will not work in another. A key aspect of any successful mobilisation tactic is likely to be novelty, which means doing things differently from the way they have been done in the past. An understanding of an

Illustration 5.7

change in action

Mobilising change at Belgacom

In the mid to late 1990s the newly appointed CEO of Belgacom, the Belgium telecommunications company, initiated and led a change project to transform the company into a customer-oriented, outward-looking organisation. The company had been publicly owned, bureaucratic and insular with a technical focus and offering a job for life. Although the company became independent in 1991, it was not given managerial autonomy until the mid-1990s. By this time, external pressure in the form of deregulation of the telecommunications industry, the entrance of foreign competitors into national markets and technological innovation provided the impetus for the CEO's change programme called TURBO (Transforming, Upgrading, Making Responsible, Belgacom's Organisation).

The programme started on 1 January 1996 with the implementation of a new customer-oriented structure that replaced the old geographic regions with three customer-oriented divisions and several support divisions such as finance. The CEO announced the new structure in May 1995 and that the top 200 positions would become vacant from October. They were then filled between October and December through a competitive application process open to everyone. In other words, the old top 200 managers had to apply for the new jobs along with other applicants. To complete the implementation of the new structure from January, a similar process was cascaded down to the lower levels. In addition, new objectives

to do with customer satisfaction, quality and cost reduction were put in place. Finally, projects were requested from all levels of the organisation to aid the objectives. The CEO likened the old structure to a 'gigantic aircraft carrier' and the new to a 'fleet of smaller ships' with decentralised yet co-ordinated communication and decision making.

However, TURBO was also about a cultural change. This second step was based on the PTS (People, Team, Skills) early retirement and retraining plan. Early retirement was offered to 6,300 employees (those older than 50 or with more than 20 year's service), while a further 6,800 employees were each offered a personalised training programme to help them prepare for their new job in Belgacom. These plans were based on new descriptions developed within each division. 'Job Centres' were set up to assess individual employees, make training plans, and make job role recommendations. A learning Development Academy was established to carry out the training.

Belgacom's CEO had a successful professional background as a change initiator in other organisations which gave him a change leader image. The departure through retirement of long-time staff minimised resistance to top-down change whilst the implementation of the retraining plans boosted its acceptance. The individual approach provided support for employees going through change.

Source: Adapted from Vas, A. (2001) 'Top management skills in a context of endemic organisational change: The case of Belgacom', *Journal of General Management*, 27 (1), pp. 71–89.

---

organisation's *administrative heritage* may, therefore, be helpful here, especially if an organisation wants to communicate a real commitment to change.

Administrative heritage is to do with the organisation's history and particularly its change history. It is about the types of events and traditions that are remembered by the members of the organisation. For instance, previous change attempts may have been initiated the same way, perhaps by the appointment of new managers, and the announcement in memos and meetings that changes and some restructuring are to take place. If following these past change initiatives, staff have then seen little change, this would not be a good way to launch a new attempt at change. The approach taken needs to be visibly different. Otherwise, staff will assume that the message of change equals no change, as it has done in the past. Alternatively it might be that previous change attempts have been very successful, but the changes have been incremental in nature, whereas now the organisation needs to undertake radical and more fundamental change. Again, it would be unwise to initiate the latest changes in the same way as previous changes. The Marks and Spencer, Iceland and Glenbrook examples given above are all attempts at mobilisation which are novel and a break with the past. Similarly, when Cummins launched their vision statement (see section 5.3.1 above) they used presentations that were novel for the organisation, involving the use of music, fun activities, audience participation and group break-out sessions. The aim was to use the new behaviours required, such as encouraging staff to contribute and put forward new ideas, as part of the workshops.

The key contextual features will also affect the decision on which sort of mobilisation interventions to use. For example:

- An organisation with *little time* to deliver change, and a *low readiness* for change, in which the change agent has the *power* and need to impose change via a type of *reconstruction* or *revolution*, will need to achieve mobilisation quickly. More dramatic and directive means, such as symbolic breaks with the past and shock tactics, may be necessary. See the examples of O2 and Whatman given above. This would also be consistent with a change approach in which the intent is to *target behavioural* change.

- An organisation with *more time* to deliver change, whether via *adaptation* or *evolution*, can utilise techniques such as encouraging a questioning and challenging of the status quo, or communication, education and training. This was the approach taken by Whites (Illustration 5.5). Use could also be made of symbolic breaks with the past, particularly if there is a low readiness for change and time could become a factor if change is not initiated.

- When there is more time, the choice of mobilisation tactic(s) may also depend on whether the change agent has selected a *participative* or *directive* change approach, and the degree of power of the change agent. A change agent with little power can possibly do little other than to encourage questioning and debate to build support. Change agents with more power can utilise a broader range of tactics. The *change target* should also be considered. For example, if the aim is to achieve *value change*, then communication and education, or even personal development interventions, are more likely to be needed as at Glenbrook Steel Mill, if staff are to understand the new values the organisation is trying to develop.

- If the aim is to deliver change in a bottom-up fashion, then the change agent may need to establish initial communication and workshop seminars to stimulate debate and encourage staff to take ownership for moving the change agenda forwards.

- If an organisation ultimately wants to deliver *transformation*, but is either in *crisis*, or for some reason such as a lack of capability or lack of change agent power, is unable to embark on a transformation immediately, then the earlier reconstruction or adaptation will contribute to a readiness for future more fundamental change.

5.9 DESIGNING AND SEQUENCING CHANGE LEVERS

This chapter has argued so far that to move an organisation from the current to the future state, it is necessary to mobilise the members of the organisation behind the change, then to move the organisation by putting in place a series of interventions that will lead to the desired changes, and then finally to sustain the changes to prevent individuals backsliding into old ways of behaving. This chapter has also suggested that many of the change levers should already have been identified, by developing a new web with new systems, structures, routines and symbols, and by considering the barriers to change and how to overcome them. Mobilisation tactics have also been discussed. What now needs to be done is to put the mobilisation, move and sustain phases together with the identified levers and mechanisms to determine when to do what. However, it must be recognised that there is still additional work to be done on designing change levers and interventions, some of which are discussed in more detail in Chapter 6.

5.9.1 Four subsystems of change

It has already been pointed out above that, particularly if the change is transformational in nature, many communication, education and development interventions may be necessary to help individuals through the transition process. These interventions will be in addition to the levers that can be identified from something such as a web analysis, but they are important for facilitating the process of individual transitions. As shown above, most of the interventions that help people through the transition process are to do with what Chapter 2 identifies as interpersonal change levers. Therefore, we simply use the four subsystems identified in Chapter 2 – the technical, the political, the cultural and the interpersonal – in conjunction with the Lewin model to help us complete the detailed design. These subsystems map onto the web analysis since the technical subsystem is about structures and systems, the political subsystem is about the power structures and networks, and the cultural subsystem is about symbols, rituals, routines and stories. (See Figure 5.7.)

Exactly how to use the model given in Figure 5.7 is easier to explain with reference to an example. Illustration 5.8 maps out the mobilise, move and sustain

Figure 5.7	Four levels of levers

	MOBILISE ⟶ MOVE ⟶ SUSTAIN
Technical	Changing all formal and informal structures and systems
Political	Changing all formal and informal networks and power systems
Cultural	Changing all routines, symbols and stories
Interpersonal	Changing communication, training, management development and education

the process put in place at KPMG by Colin Sharman, the UK senior partner, through the 1990s.[20] The range of change interventions used to facilitate this transition was extensive.

Illustration 5.8

change in action

Change at KPMG

	Mobilise	Move	Sustain
Technical	New structure • client focused • co-location • new office (end 1992/93)	• Recruitment assessment centres • Identification of competencies • HR – appraisal/ development/bonuses/ five bands for pay • Continual shift to industry- based units	• New structure (Oct 1996)
Political	• Partner strategy workshops • Workshop feedback • Briefing sessions (Partners and Senior Managers)	• Lead partners and engagement partners	
Cultural	• 'Popart' • Partner redundancies (early 1990s) • Consultants and Auditors as industry-based unit heads • No use of committees • Colin Sharman	• Development centres • Assessment centres for partner promotion • Rejection of partnership applications • Removal of dining room • Performance not time served for promotion	• Upward appraisal • Client surveys • Values initiative/Values Charter (1998) followed by Dilemma Workshop and other related events
Interpersonal	• Senior management conference • Partners' conference (with J. Dimbleby) • 20/20 vision – Senior and Junior Manager conferences – Press releases (in company) – Videos	• Announcement of new HR systems • More open communication • Leadership project • Industry unit development • Feedback from staff at Partners' conference • Reports on Partners' conference to staff • Staff opinion surveys	• Partners' conference to launch Values Charter

Source: Adapted from the cases on KPMG in Johnson, G. and Scholes, K. (1999) *Exploring Corporate Strategy*, 5th edn, Hemel Hempstead: Prentice Hall; and Thornsberry, J. (1999) 'KPMG: Revitalising culture through values', *Business Strategy Review*, 10(4), pp. 1–15.

- *Mobilisation.* Chapter 2 explains the launch of the change process with the partner workshops and the launch of 20:20 vision. The next step was to make the firm customer orientated. In one weekend the firm was restructured. Audit, tax and consultancy staff moved from their discipline-based groups into industry-based units. Staff and partners were physically relocated in the KPMG offices to sit within industry groups. (Some argue that the co-location was a move intervention, rather than mobilisation since it *moved* the organisation. However, Sharman subsequently acknowledged that the reorganisation itself had little impact. It made individuals realise that change was coming, but it did not on its own require *individuals* to change their behaviours and their attitudes, or show them what changes were personally required of them.) In terms of the change equation, the workshops and conference discussions, and the launch of the '20-20 Vision' followed by the restructuring, were all about creating a dissatisfaction with the status quo and a belief in the suitability of the proposed changes, and then enabling staff to change.

- *Move.* A series of change initiatives were then put in place, many stemming from the leadership project, which aimed to position KPMG as the leading advisory firm. Much was done to develop fair and open means of developing staff and partners with the right competencies. Pay structures were simplified, appraisal systems and development centres were developed to trigger a move from time served to performance, and the promotion path to partner was changed from hang on to your current partners coat tails and move up with him (a patronage system), to one where prospective partners had to go through assessment centres. This led to the rejection of some partnership applications – a first for a firm in which existing partners could normally bully through their nominees for new partners. Attempts were also made to develop a culture of more open, two-way communication with feedback from staff to partners and feedback to staff on partner activities.

- *Sustain.* By the late 1990s, there was still some way to go with changing values. The firm was restructured in the UK in late 1996 to consolidate and build on the earlier structural changes. More fundamental, an international values initiative was put in place to further required behavioural changes. Whilst there were many initiatives put in place on an international basis with a lot of work with partners, in the UK it led to the Values Charter, launched at the UK Partners Conference in 1998. Values were translated into behaviours. Workshops, such as dilemma workshops, were run for partners and staff.

5.9.2 Linking the sequencing of levers and mechanisms to the design choices

Some managers question whether it is really possible to plan out in advance an entire organisational transition as described in this chapter. The answer is no, but the degree to which it should be planned is also affected by the design choices. For example:

- If the change process is to be more *directive* and imposed, particularly within a *tight timescale*, it may be both possible and desirable to be more precise about what changes are to occur when.

- Even in change processes designed to be more *evolutionary* and *emergent* over time, it is useful to give careful thought to how the status quo is to be challenged to achieve mobilisation. Furthermore, some of the early choices that need to be made, such as whether reward and selection systems are to be used to sustain the changes or as part of the move phase, do need to be given consideration. One difference between more *collaborative* and more *directive* change processes may be more to do with who is involved in, or consulted on, the design of the process, rather than the mobilise, move and sustain path selected.

- *Timescales* have an impact. It is possible that in a *big-bang* change process the different interventions that need to be put in place occur so rapidly that it is hard to distinguish between mobilise, move and sustain interventions. When rapid reconstruction is a precursor to more fundamental change, all the reconstruction initiatives will become a series of shock interventions that in part mobilise the organisation for the next step of more fundamental evolutionary change.

- Whatever the design choices, considerable thought should be given to the mobilisation phase.

The strength of a model such as mobilise, move and sustain is not to do with the answers it gives, but the questions it forces change agents to ask. Without such a model, it is all too easy to put in place a series of interventions which have little effect because the members of the organisation are not ready for change and do not understand what the changes are all about. It is also possible to leave the changes unfinished, because steps are not taken to institutionalise the changes. Similarly, without the connection of the organisational change process to the individual change process through the transition curve, particularly when attempting to undertake more fundamental change, it is possible to underestimate the range of interventions needed to achieve the required individual changes. However, it is necessary to remember that different levels of the organisation may be at different stages at different times. Senior managers may have progressed to the move phase whilst interventions aimed at mobilising lower-level staff are still being put in place.

5.10 KEY QUESTIONS TO CONSIDER WHEN DESIGNING MOBILISE, MOVE AND SUSTAIN

Working out exactly what to do to achieve change, even with the outline mobilise, move and sustain model presented above, is still complex. No wonder change agents resort to off-the-shelf recipes or call in consultants. Furthermore, whereas it is assumed that readers will have a knowledge of how to design new structures and systems from *Exploring Corporate Strategy*, there are many other interventions mentioned above that they need to know more about, such as communication, education, management development, and symbolic activity, to name just a few. These cannot all be covered in this chapter.

Figure 5.8, therefore, details eight key questions to consider when developing an outline of a transition process and the sequence in which the change levers and interventions should be deployed. It should be noted, as explained extensively above, that the order in which these questions are considered and dealt with may differ from context to context. The eight questions are not meant to be a prescriptive step-by-step list.

1 Is there a coherent strategy understood and shared throughout the organisation?

The overall strategy needs not just to be translated into a clear vision that can be shared and understood throughout the organisation, but also broken up into actionable pieces. Any change initiative is likely to consist of a number of major projects, such as redesigning work processes and procedures, office and depot relocations, designing and installing new equipment and technology, job redesign, the introduction of total quality and/or continuous improvement techniques, and possibly business process re-engineering. Furthermore, even a restructuring may involve intermediate steps. It is therefore necessary to create

Figure 5.8   **The eight key questions to consider when planning a transition**

1	Is there a coherent strategy understood and shared throughout the organisation?
2	Are supporting structures and systems under development?
3	Is there a trigger for change or has one been manufactured?
4	Are there visible 'early wins' designed into the change process?
5	Are day-to-day activities aligned to get required outputs?
6	Are the identified barriers to change being removed/dealt with?
7	Are changes supported with symbolic activity?
8	Is communication built into the change process?

coherence from all these projects, not just in terms of a unifying vision, but also to understand dependencies between projects. The way these projects are to be managed and run will be determined by the change start-point and management style selected.

This is a very important step. It is the major projects that will determine most of the resource requirements for the change process in addition to the resources needed to keep the business going during the transition. The projects, their links and interdependencies, and their resource requirements, will form the basis of the change plan. This text does not have space to discuss project management as such, but obviously, in any major change project, project management has a key role to play. At some point a plan, or maybe multiple plans by business division, detailing what is to be done, when and by whom, has to be put together. Progress has to be monitored against this plan.

2 Are supporting structures and systems under development?

Consideration must be given to change levers to do with formal and informal organisation structures and power structures, information systems, management systems, measurement systems and HR systems. Systems extend from the way budgets are developed to how quickly phones are answered. Some of the needed changes to structures and systems should have been identified by a detailed cultural web analysis, discussed above in section 5.3.2, but more work is likely to be needed.

At this point it is now necessary to consider when to implement what. Is the new structure to be put in place to enable changes as part of the mobilisation, or are interrelationships and responsibilities within the new structure to be allowed to evolve and then be institutionalised through formal systems and reporting relationships in the sustain phase? Is the new structure to be put in place immediately, or are there to be some sort of interim structure and management mechanisms? Similar questions need to be asked about the new systems. Which are to be used to challenge the status quo, and which to sustain the changes? New measurement systems on, for example, customer service levels, may be used to challenge, and new reward mechanisms may be used to sustain the changes.

3 Is there a trigger for change or has one been manufactured?

This is about designing the mobilisation process as much as anything else. It has been discussed in some length above, particularly in terms of mobilisation tactics.

4 Are there visible 'early wins' designed into the change process?

Mobilising can be helped by making demonstrably successful changes early on, which is sometimes referred to as making 'early wins' or 'picking the low-hanging fruit'. AID analysis, assessing *attractiveness* versus *implementation*

Illustration 5.9   *change in action*

Attractiveness versus implementation difficulty

Position projects and change initiatives according to the degree to which they are difficult to implement, and how attractive they are in terms of the benefits they deliver with respect to the costs. When considering difficulty of implementation think about the number of barriers, and likely stakeholder responses to the initiatives. In the above example, project A may be a good project for early wins. The viability of initiative C given its low benefits should be questioned, and project D needs further consideration of what can be done to ease its implementation.

Source: Reprinted from *Journal of Project Management*, 16 (1), Tony Grundy, 'Strategy Implementation and Project Management', pp. 34–50, Copyright (1998), with permission from Elsevier Science.

difficulty, shown in Illustration 5.9, can be used to help identify which projects should be tackled first to give demonstrable early wins that symbolically indicate that change is (a) achievable, and (b) going to happen whether individuals like it or not. However, this step may not just be about identifying projects to put in place early on. This step may also include things such as system changes which remove old ways of doing things that staff have consistently identified as a barrier to change. It involves any interventions that the recipients of change can identify as a positive step on the way to change, and that can be used as an example of progress and success.

5 Are day-to-day activities aligned to get required outputs?

This is about understanding which routines to change or remove, and which new routines to put into place, and when. However, it also includes the design of HR systems (rewards, appraisals, selection, training and management development), and giving further consideration to additional control systems that may be needed. As such, it overlaps with step 2. Since HR systems can play a very important role in shaping an individual's behaviour, they are also discussed in more detail in the next chapter.

Routines can be hard to diagnose. Some routines may encapsulate the overall way staff operate. For example, in many service organisations that are not customer-focused, and are traditionally risk averse, staff may follow a general routine of 'process before sales', which means that when faced with a form and a customer, a member of staff will first worry about filling the form in correctly, and the customer and their concerns second. Such routines are likely to be identified as part of the web analysis.

However, managers may not know what all the daily routines followed by their staff are, even though some of these routines may create inefficiencies and blockages to change. Such routines will only be identified when projects examining existing working practices are undertaken, and will have to be tackled at that time. An alternative way of gaining an understanding of routines and ways of working that are blocking change is through much wider participation in the change process by employees. Arguably, the General Motors Go-Fast scheme discussed in Chapter 2 is a technique for identifying organisational routines that are blocking change.[21]

6 Are the identified barriers to change being removed/dealt with?

If interventions have not already been developed to deal with structures, networks, cliques, stakeholders, routines, control systems and symbols that have been explicitly identified as barriers to change, this must be built into the change process. It also needs to be decided when these barriers should be removed. Some of the old symbols and ways of operating may be removed as part of the mobilisation tactics; other routine ways of behaving may be harder to change and require additional interventions in the move phase.

7 Are changes supported with symbolic activity?

Symbolic activity can be built into all three change phases, with a particular impact on the individual level and the climate, in order to support the changes taking place. This is a very important topic and will be developed further in the next chapter. A particularly important aspect of symbolic activity is senior manager behaviour. As we stress above when discussing visions, senior managers must behave in a way that supports the message of change they are trying to put across.

8 Is communication built into the change process?

Again, this is an area of critical importance during change, which can be broadened to include education and personal development. It will also be developed further in the next chapter. Broadly, a communications strategy needs to be developed which underpins all the three phases of change, to help individuals to both understand and achieve what is expected of them, and to keep them informed of progress and developments.

5.11 SUMMARY

This chapter has explained the concept of the transition state as an intermediate state between where an organisation is now and where it wants to be in the future. The transition state requires explicit consideration of how it is to be designed and managed:

- The transition state can be conceived of in terms of three change phases – mobilise, move and sustain. However, it must be recognised that in any organisational transition these three phases are underpinned by the process of individual change and the transition curve. Organisations can only change what they do if the people within them change.

- To be able to design the change levers and interventions, it is necessary to ensure that there is a vision of the desired future state. The understanding of the desired future state can also be used to diagnose potential barriers to change.

- Some of the levers and interventions to be deployed will be identified when the cultural web is used to formulate the picture of the desired future organisation. Others will be identified by a consideration of how to deal with the barriers to change and how to achieve readiness for change. Others may have been identified as part of the original change lever design choices (technical, political, cultural and interpersonal). However, additional interventions, particularly in terms of communication, education, training, personal development, human resource systems and resistance management, also require consideration.

- To help complete the design of the levers and interventions, and decide how to sequence the chosen interventions, it is useful to use the four organisational subsystems that are part of the design choices within the mobilise, move and sustain phases. These four subsystems help to focus attention on the additional levers and interventions needed to help individuals through change and facilitate the development of the appropriate organisational changes.

An additional design complexity is to ensure that there is a match between the selected change approach and the design of the transition state. The next two chapters build on this chapter, by extending consideration of critical change interventions such as communication, symbolic activity, human resource systems, and politics, and by considering how change agents should actually manage the transition once it is underway.

REFERENCES

1. The concept of change as three states, the present, the future and the transition, is advanced by Beckhard, R. and Harris, R.T. (1987) *Organizational Transitions: Managing Complex Change,* 2nd edn, Reading, MA: Addison-Wesley.

2. The development of vision statements is discussed by Kotter, J. (1996) *Leading Change,* Boston, MA: Harvard Business School Press; by Nadler, D.A. and Tushman, M.L. (1990) 'Organizational frame bending: Principles for managing reorientation', *The Academy of Management Executive,* 3 (3), pp. 194–204; and also by Jick, T. (1989) *The Vision Thing (A),* Harvard Business School, Case number N9-490-019.

3. See reference 2 above.

4. Cummins: Powering forward with a new vision, *The Times 100 Case Studies,* www.thetimes100.co.uk

5. Speight, R. (2000) 'Changing the way we manage: Managing the soft strands of change at British Airways World Cargo', *Journal of Change Management,* 1 (1), pp. 91–9.

6. Chan Kim, W. and Mauborgne, R. (2000) 'Charting your company's future', *Harvard Business Review,* 80 (6), pp. 76–83; Chan Kim, W. and Mauborgne, R. (6 August 2002) 'Pursuing the holy grail of clear vision', *Financial Times.*

7. Re-webbing, along with designing new structures, control systems and routines as change levers, is not discussed in detail in this text, as it is covered in *Exploring Corporate Strategy,* 6th edition, Chapter 11. See also Johnson, G. (1997) 'Mapping and re-mapping organisational culture', in Ambrosini, V., Johnson, G. and Scholes, K. (eds) *Exploring Techniques of Analysis and Evaluation in Strategic Management,* Hemel Hempstead: Prentice Hall.

8. See reference 2 above.

9. The unfreeze, move and refreeze model of change developed by Lewin, K. ('Group decision and social change', in Maccoby, E.E., Newcomb, T.M. and Hartley, E.L. (eds) (1958) *Readings in Social Psychology,* pp. 197–211, New York: Holt, Reinhart and Winston) remains one of the most widely used change models.

10. For additional information on how individuals experience change, and what helps individuals through the change process, see Bridges, W. (1991) *Managing Transitions: Making the Most of Change,* Reading, MA: Addison-Wesley.

11. The transition curve is based on the ideas presented by Adams, J., Hayes, J. and Hopson, B. (1976) *Transition: Understanding and Managing Personal Change,* London: Martin Robertson and Company. Others identify similar, but compatible, models of stages in individual transitions. See Elrod, P.D. and Tippett, D.D. (2002) 'The "death valley" of change', *Journal of Change Management,* 15 (3), pp. 273–91.

12. This can be seen from texts such as Parkes, C.M. (1986) *Bereavement Studies of Grief in Adult Life,* London: Penguin.

13. Spector, B. (1989) discusses unfreezing mechanisms in 'From bogged down to fired up: Inspiring organizational change', *Sloan Management Review,* 30 (4), pp. 29–34.

14. See Lorenz, A. (26 April 1998) 'BP boss drives change through the pipeline', *The Sunday Times,* p. 9 for a full account.

15. Rogan, M., Gratton, L. and Ghoshal, S. (2002) 'The transformation of BP', London Business School Case LBS-CS02-002.

16. Antal, A. (2001) 'The transformation of Hoechst into Aventis Case B', ECCH Collection, 302-032-1.

17. (21 May 2002) 'Paper chase leaves Whatman torn between past and future', *Financial Times.*

18. Crabb, S. (10 January 2002) 'Thrill of the purchase', *People Management* pp. 26–31.
19. Maitland, A. (31 October 2001) 'A new and unusual way of breaking the ice', *Financial Times*, p. 16.
20. Johnson, G. (2002) 'KPMG (A): Strategic change in the 1990s', in Johnson, G. and Scholes, K. (eds) *Exploring Corporate Strategy*, 6th edn, Harlow: Financial Times Prentice Hall.
21. Examples of similar interventions are discussed in Pascale, R., Millemann, M. and Gioja, L. (1997) 'Changing the way we change', *Harvard Business Review*, 75 (6), pp. 126–39.

WORK ASSIGNMENTS

5.1 Develop a vision for an organisation with which you are familiar and which needs to undergo change, drawing on all the different mechanisms suggested in this chapter (action versus words versus pictures). Where possible also draw up a present and future culture web for this organisation. Consider the blockages for change that need to be removed if the vision is to be delivered.

5.2 Consider a work or project assignment team you have worked with that needed to be reorganised in some way to work more effectively. What were the blockages for change? How could you have overcome them?

5.3 Think about a personal and significant change you have been through. Track your experiences at different phases of this change using the transition curve. Consider what was helpful/unhelpful during each phase, and what you have learned from this process to enhance your future personal change capability.

5.4 Track a change process you have experienced against the mobilise, move and sustain model. How well was each phase managed and what could have been done better?

6

Designing the transition:
change levers and interventions

6.1 INTRODUCTION

The previous chapter explained how to conceive the actual change implementation, the transition state, as having three phases – mobilise, move and sustain.
Chapter 5 also discussed how to diagnose barriers to change, how to mobilise an
organisation behind a change initiative, and how to sequence the selected levers
and interventions through the transition. This chapter builds on this, by focusing
on the design of some additional levers and interventions required to effect
change during the transition period. It considers:

- Using communication, both verbal and symbolic, as a lever to facilitate the
  change process, and help individuals through the transition.
- Building new human resource management systems, including the way staff
  are selected, appraised and rewarded, as levers to support change.
- Using personal development and training to facilitate change.

The chapter also discusses how these interventions can be used to help mobilise
and move an organisation, and ultimately sustain the changes put in place.

6.2 COMMUNICATION DURING CHANGE

One of the key things to remember when communicating with other people is
that what the speaker thinks they have said, and what the listener hears, may not
be the same thing. Communication does not necessarily lead to the transfer of
meaning,[1] *since it is the listener who creates the meaning for themselves.*
Everyone knows the game of Chinese whispers. Someone whispers a message to
their neighbour, who then whispers that message to their neighbour and so on.
The message that the last person in the line receives, when recited back, is usually
nothing like the message the first person communicated to their neighbour. In
reality, even when messages are not communicated by whispers, they still change
as they are conveyed from one person to another. This is not just due to an

imperfect memory for things that have been heard and read. Listeners absorb more than the words used by a person communicating, because individuals communicate in many different ways. They communicate not just by the words and language they use, but also through their body language, the words and phrases they emphasise, and the degree of emotion used. In addition, listeners make assessments about the validity of what a communicator is saying, based on their knowledge about the communicator's track record of delivering against promises, and the communicator's perceived levels of integrity and credibility.

This is problematic in change situations as the message that counts for change recipients is, of course, the one they have received. And the one they receive may not be the same as the one the communicator intended. The recipients then act on the basis of their interpretations. Communication during change has to be designed to take this into account. One of the advocated techniques for overcoming differences in interpretations is to provide *message repetition*. This is the provision of the same information several times, by repeating the same message in a different way, or by conveying the same message by different means of communication, throughout the change process. Techniques such as verbal and written communication, but also non-verbal and symbolic means of communication, such as changing artefacts or using ritual, behaviour, language and stories, can be used to convey certain messages and implications about change. Effective change agents need to understand the many different means by which they are communicating with their staff, so that they can be conscious of what they may be communicating both intentionally and unintentionally, but also so that they can utilise the *different communication mechanisms* to help get their message across.

6.3 VERBAL COMMUNICATION

Verbal communication includes both written and spoken communication. There are four issues to consider for each key stakeholder group/audience – timing, communication channels, message content, and message presenter.

6.3.1 Stakeholder needs

The stakeholder groups will differ from organisation to organisation. The primary target for communication may always be the employees, but other external stakeholders, such as the unions, the customers, the suppliers, and the shareholders, must not be forgotten. When Exel was created from the merger of the National Freight Corporation and Ocean Group in May 2000, for example, it was necessary to communicate with investors and customers as well as employees. A team was used to ensure that the messages sent to the three audiences were identical, although through different communications media and expressed in different ways.[2] Even staff within one organisation may have differ-

Figure 6.1 **Stakeholder communication requirement**

	LEVEL OF KNOWLEDGE OF CHANGE				
	Awareness	Understanding	Support	Involvement	Commitment
Senior managers					
Middle managers					
Supervisors					
Staff					
Customers					
Suppliers					
Shareholders					

Timing

Channel

Content

Presenter

ent information requirements, due to the different ways they are affected by the changes. If change is being implemented by the use of pilot sites and then extended, for example, even staff as yet not having to undergo change will still need information on what the changes are about, how they are being managed, and progress to date.

The starting point for any communication strategy should be to identify all internal and external stakeholder groups affected. This should then be supplemented by a consideration of the needs of each stakeholder group. Do they need just to be aware of the changes, or does communication need to lead to their commitment to the changes? (See Figure 6.1.) The differing levels of understanding required affects when people need to be told and which channels to use. Furthermore, whilst a consistent core message may be needed, different stakeholder groups may need to be told different levels of detail, or informed about different aspects of the change process, or have different needs that have to be addressed. Therefore message content may vary by stakeholder group. Finally, different message presenters may also be necessary.

Illustration 6.1

change in action

Communication during closure of a call centre

STAKEHOLDER GROUP	CHANNEL	PRESENTER	TIMING
Senior managers	Copy of briefing	(Issued by HR)	Prior to briefing
Call centre location: managers	Face-to-face with Q&A session	Quality Manager	Day 1 (9.00)
Call centre location: staff to be retained	Face-to-face with Q&A session	Customer Services Director HR, Quality Manager	Day 1 (10.15)
Call centre location: call centre staff to be made redundant	Face-to-face with Q&A session	Customer Services Director HR, Quality Manager	Day 1 (10.30)
	1–2–1s if required	Customer Services Director	Day 1
	1–2–1s if required Individual employee letters Question and Answer Sheet	Team leaders (Issued by HR) (Issued by HR with individual letters)	On-going Following briefing
	Closure Party Handover of Oscar the Goldfish	Staff Staff	Before staff leave Before staff leave
Call centre location: staff to be relocated	Face-to-face with Q&A session	Head of Service Delivery	Day 1 (10.15)
Other call centre locations: call centre staff	Face-to-face with Q&A session	Team Leaders	Day 1 (10.30)
All staff	Intranet/Notice board bulletins Open Door policy for questions	(Issued by HR) Senior Managers	Day 1 (10.30)

Source: Adapted from a report by Sarah Ramsden, James Cheyne and Linus Gregoriadis.

Even what may seem like a relatively small change within a much larger organisation can need to be communicated sensitively and carefully, with attention to consistency of message and use of multiple channels for the sake of both those directly affected by the changes and the survivors. A British utility took the decision to close one of its three call centres in line with business needs to maintain costs and improve service following poor performance against key performance indicators. This meant the redundancy of 20 people. The announcement of the call centre closure in October was made in July. Care was taken to develop a number of different briefings for different stakeholder groups (such as staff to be made redundant, staff to be retained, unions, etc.) containing a consistent and carefully scripted message, yet also tailored to the audience. Senior managers were sent a copy of the brief in advance and thought was given to the questions and issues that might be raised during the briefings and suitable answers. A variety of channels were used to communicate the message both verbally and in written form (see Illustration 6.1), including face-to-face meetings between managers and staff, 1-2-1s, and use of intranet and notice boards. Since the changes involved redundancies there were certain legal requirements to be met, such as the presence of a union rep when staff were briefed. The Customer Services Director was selected as the person to communicate the briefings to (1) meet the requirements for a legal right of appeal to a more senior person (in this case the MD), and (2) because the immediate call centre manager, the Head of Service Delivery, had previously made a commitment to keep the site going, raising credibility issues. Symbolic issues also had to be dealt with. The call centre staff had clubbed together to purchase a call centre goldfish, Oscar, who had achieved company-wide fame in the company newsletter, and had become an object of certain ritualistic behaviour, such as all staff and managers saying hello and goodbye to him as they arrived at/left the call centre. Oscar was to be cared for by remaining non-call centre staff. A closure party was also arranged for those affected.

6.3.2 Timing of communication

When to communicate *what* is a serious issue. *There is no ideal time*. Employees will always want as much information as soon as possible, whereas the designers of the changes may want to give as little information as possible, until they are completely clear about what is to be done. The designers may also be concerned about issues of confidentiality; openness may not be possible. However, change agents need to be aware that:

● Employees resent hearing of change from sources other than management, such as the press,[3] and there is a need to control potentially harmful rumours.

● The later the communication, the less the time and opportunity for employees to absorb, understand and adjust to what they are being told. Readiness for change helps to reduce resistance.

| Figure 6.2 | Communication during change |

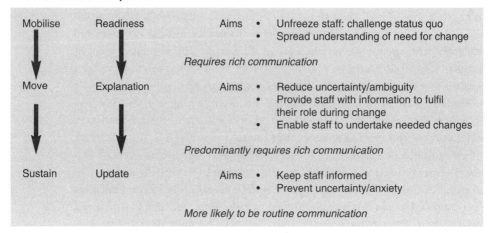

Three communication phases:

Mobilise   Readiness   Aims • Unfreeze staff: challenge status quo
                               • Spread understanding of need for change

Requires rich communication

Move   Explanation Aims • Reduce uncertainty/ambiguity
                               • Provide staff with information to fulfil
                                  their role during change
                               • Enable staff to undertake needed changes

Predominantly requires rich communication

Sustain   Update   Aims • Keep staff informed
                               • Prevent uncertainty/anxiety

More likely to be routine communication

- Incomplete announcements and honesty are better than cover-ups.[4] If managers are not honest early on, they will lose their credibility. Even if in the early stages of change it is not possible to explain all the details, it may be possible to inform staff of options being considered, or the change scenarios under consideration and the organisational implications of these, and provide timetables of when staff should be informed of what decisions.

- Details will always leak out, even if those leading the change have adopted a policy of silence on the changes under consideration.[5]

For employees who actually have to change as a result of the change process, the types of communication needed during a transition can be mapped against the mobilise, move and sustain model introduced in the previous chapter (see Figure 6.2):

- In the early days of change, communication should be timed to achieve a *readiness* for change, an understanding and commitment, as part of *mobilisation*.

- As change progresses towards the *move* phase, the communication should start to focus more on giving individuals the *information* and *support* they need to undertake the changes being asked of them, and also on *reducing* the *uncertainty* and *ambiguity* individuals will be experiencing as they attempt to understand 'what this all means for me'.

- *Update* information on the progress of change and what is to happen next is required throughout the change process, but more so as the momentum of change picks up.

An overall proviso is to remember that the planned communication will *never* be enough. Communication is the responsibility of not just those appointed to run communication seminars and workshops, but also all managers and supervisors throughout the organisation who have teams of people that they need to help through the change process. This also has implications for what should be communicated and to whom.

6.3.3 Communication channels

Figure 6.3 shows the wide variety of communication channels available during change. There are also a variety of informal and *ad-hoc* channels of communication such as conversations over lunch or at the coffee machine. The key to choosing a communication channel is to match it to the audience needs and the communication aims (see Figure 6.1). For example, HBOS, the UK banking group, like many other organisations, uses in-house TV to communicate important information to many staff spread across different sites and companies simultaneously. However, such a mechanism can only generate *awareness* of change.

Figure 6.3   Communication channels

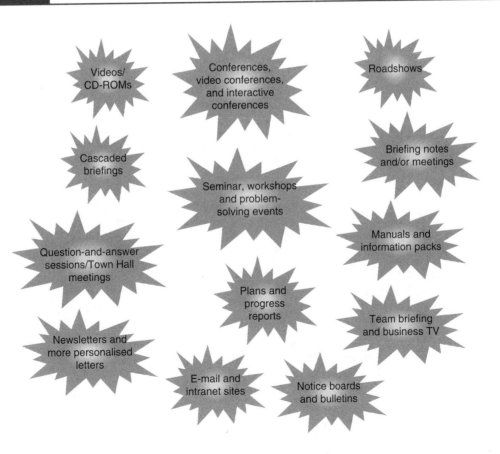

Figure 6.4   Effective versus non-effective change communication

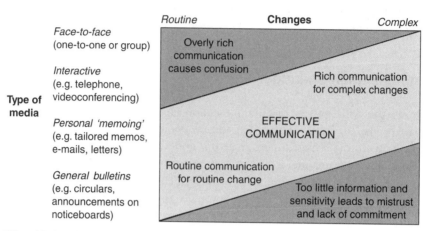

Source: Lengel, R.H. and Daft, R.C., 'The selection of communication media as an effective skill' (1988) vol. 2(3).

By comparison, when ICL started a knowledge management project called Project Vik (Valuing ICL Knowledge), its first initiative was Café Vik, a global information service as a website on ICL's intranet. It needed people to not only be aware of the service, but also to use it. To introduce the service the team invested in some café tables and chairs, and with six PCs established a 'Café Vik' in standard conference rooms at ICL sites. Using different briefings for managers and employees based on their different needs, small groups of staff were briefed and then given the opportunity for a hands-on session in the café environment created by the props.[6]

Figure 6.4 gives some guidelines on how to match audience needs to channel. As a general rule, in non-routine, complex situations, such as change, where staff need to develop a deep understanding of how they personally need to change, richer forms of communication media, such as face-to-face, are best. Less rich forms of communication, such as written and electronic means, are more suited to routine, non-change situations or for update information and generating awareness.

Since rich communication channels are two-way and face-to-face, such as work-shops, they provide an abundance of communication cues. They allow for the expression of concerns, answers to questions, the sharing of interpretations and experiences, and the sharing of problems and solutions. Research consistently suggests that this is the most effective form of communication during change, preferably through small groups, which affords the participants the opportunity to ask questions and air concerns. This approach also enables the message to be targeted to the needs of that particular group of individuals. This is why cascaded communication is popular in many organisations, with the senior managers briefing their managers, and these managers then briefing their staff and so on. However, unless the managers doing the communication are good presenters, well trained in the details of what they are communicating, enthusiastic about the message they are delivering, and sufficiently knowledgeable to answer questions, this mechanism can lead to poorly briefed information about change, and therefore a poorly informed and cynical workforce. A specially trained group of communicators may, therefore, be a better alternative.

Lufthansa recognised the need to utilise two-way face-to-face means of communicating for all groups of staff during the transformation of the airline (see Illustration 2.9). However, they also recognised the different needs of different groups of staff. They ran strategic communication forums for top management, such as the Top 50 Conference and the Top Forum. Then there were more mass communication means for other levels of staff, such as town meetings. Board members and top managers regularly went on-site to talk directly to employees about change initiatives. There were also open-space events and 'learning maps', which involved thousands of employees working in groups of 10 to bring up hot issues in a structured one-day event. In addition, there were trainer conferences and TQM workshops.

If individuals involved in change are to achieve an understanding of the behavioural and attitudinal implications of change, rich means of communication may need to be more than just face-to-face question-and-answer sessions. They may include workshops, or even personal development interventions with role play, to achieve *experiential learning*. Developing such management development interventions is discussed later in this chapter. Something that is now popular in many organisations is the use of actors to role-play situations. Actors run workshops at which they act out particular scenarios, halting at certain points to ask the workshop participants how they should proceed. In this way, without directly exposing themselves to the role-play situation, organisational members can learn to deal with novel situations and new required ways of behaving when interacting with, for example, customers.

Illustration 6.2 summarises the approach to communication at Ford's Halewood plant in the late 1990s and into 2000 as it was transformed from an out-of-date production facility for the Ford Escort into a modern factory for the production of the X-type Jaguar. This required a cultural shift for the organisation. The illustration reveals the value of intensive and rich forms of communication targeted at those who actually need to undertake personal change. These channels of communication can be supplemented by more symbolic means of communication, such as letters of thanks, certificates and awards, discussed in more detail in the next section. When SEEBORD Energy, an energy company in southeast England, wanted to promote their newly developed customer-focused vision to their staff they utilised a mix of verbal, written and symbolic communication. They used typical communication forums such as 'leaders' workshops', staff briefing sessions, and a quarterly magazine. In addition, they put in place an awards scheme for staff demonstrating the sorts of behaviours required by the new vision, ran a 'values artwork' competition which encouraged staff to submit artwork visually representing the vision's values that could then be used to promote the values throughout the business, and subsequently launched an ideas

Illustration 6.2

Creating a high-performance factory – Ford and Jaguar

Ford chose their Halewood plant, Liverpool, UK in 1998 to produce the X-type Jaguar. Production of the X-type at the factory was to replace production of the Ford Escort at Halewood from July 2000. Halewood was not an obvious choice for production of the X-type with its history of poor labour relations, shopfloor militancy, productivity and quality. The plant needed to undergo a transformation from a volume-driven, productivity and cost-first culture to a quality-first culture built on flexible working patterns.

Once a new Operations Director was installed at Halewood and he had appointed a new management team, the first step was to get the workers to sign to the 'Halewood Charter', an agreement to flexibility, mobility and new working practices. The Halewood Charter, or the Gateway Agreement, was based on Ford's product development 'Gateway Process'. Five hundred jobs had to go. Early retirement and redundancy were on offer to those who didn't want to sign. All employees were appraised for their ability to cope with change, and those who couldn't cope received voluntary redundancy, and in some cases were replaced by new recruits. The change process subsequently put in place to deliver the Gateway Agreement had three pillars to it – centres of excellence, quality and culture change.

Centres of excellence were established to implement the new working practices contained within the Gateway Agreement and improve quality, with each centre representing a part of the assembly process. Initially in March 1999 only four centres were established, but 31 had been created by July 2000. In each centre, new processes were introduced with shopfloor workers participating in the design and continuous improvement. Line-side 'cardboard cities' were cleared away and replaced with new racking and packaging to ease component delivery and picking. New managers for the centres were selected through assessment centres. Other initiatives included the introduction of the Japanese-Style Ford Production System and Six Sigma quality system. The workers have learned new approaches that involve empowerment and flexibility. More responsibility has been given to the operators. The plant won QS 9000 certification in June 1999.

The culture change programme was run in parallel to the centres of excellence initiative. Prior to July 2000 a consultancy organisation was brought in to do a culture profile of the plant and develop new values and behaviours. They ran a series of two-day workshops for the senior management team and workforce volunteers at the beginning of 1999. The workshop volunteers then became facilitators delivering the programme to the 3,000 employees between March 1999 and Summer 2000.

In July 2000, assembly of the Escort finished and the line was stopped from August to December 2000. During this time the factory refit took place to transform Halewood into a modern factory capable of manufacturing the X-type Jaguar.

The communications utilized during the change programme included:

Vision cards: Issued to all employees in October 1998 to communicate the new Halewood Vision and required behaviours.

Benchmarking: Union members, shift leaders and supervisors taken on a week-long visit to Jaguar's West Midlands plants during negotiations for the Halewood Charter to convince unions of the merits of the proposals for new working practices.

Green book: This contained the details of the operating principles of the new business and a copy was sent to every employee's home in March 1999 with a request for them to sign their agreement to it.

Quarterly communication sessions: Between Operations Director and workforce to inform workforce of progress and forthcoming changes. Extended to daily, weekly and monthly sessions for different categories of employees.

Newsletter: Glossy newsletter produced periodically called *Vision.* First edition in February 2000.

Employee letters: From the Operating Director to the workforce requesting their continued support and co-operation in March 1999.

Training and workshops: Culture workshops for all employees in 1999 and into 2000 aimed at changing attitudes, values and behaviours. Five hundred employees sent to West Midlands plants for training in 1999 to become change champions back at Halewood. During the shutdown many training events took place. Production workers were trained in IT, numeracy and literary skills. Community projects were run with the local council to facilitate the development of the new production teams. All supervisors and group leaders, along with selected operators, went to visit another Jaguar plant to acquire skills in their part of the production chain. There was training in lean manufacturing. There was also a brand-awareness workshop on Jaguar and an on-going series of team-building workshops.

Creating unity: Employees and families taken to the British Grand Prix in April 2000. Family Day on 21 July 2000 when the last Escort was built and the factory closed for the refit. Employees and families taken to see *Disney on Ice* in October 2000.

Symbolism: many early initiatives, such as the new management team, were symbolic in their own right. In addition, the old factory was dark, dirty and cluttered. The belief the plant would close led to little investment or maintenance in the 1990s. Some operators ate their sandwiches in the cars as they were more comfortable once the seats were in than other options such as the benches beside the line. Today the factory has silver metallic cladding on the outside at the front to present a smarter image. The inside of the factory has been completely refitted with wide aisles, glossy flooring, brighter lighting and modern equipment with parts delivered just-in-time. It is painted in Jaguar's corporate colours. An orange cord runs through the factory which any worker can pull to stop the line at any time to deal with quality issues. It is clean and designed to maximise safety with separately marked pedestrian and forklift lanes. There are screens showing statistics and announcements, café-like rest areas, a canteen, and management areas with many performance reports produced by both team leaders and production workers on noticeboards.

Sources: Adapted from Samii, R. and Van Wassenhove, L.N. (2002) 'Jaguar comes to Halewood: The story of a turnaround', INSEAD, Case number 602–013–1; Pickard, J. (18 April 2002) 'Top gear', *People Management*, pp. 36–42; 'Jaguar: Creating world class performance in a Jaguar assembly plant', *The Times 100 Case Studies*, 7th edn, **www.thetimes200.co.uk**.

competition. They also had other original events such as 'Energyzone' discussions led by senior managers, which focused on elements of staff cynicism, such as 'Here we go again'.[7]

Most communications strategies will utilise many different types of communication, including written communication. To return to Figure 6.2, the richer forms of communication used to achieve mobilisation and explanation may need to be supported by less rich forms of communication. Participants will never remember everything they are told at briefings or workshops. Written documentation can provide useful back-up and reference material. Update information, which is about supplying regular information on change progress, can also be provided by less rich channels of communication. Written communication, in the form of newsletters or noticeboard bulletins, for example, can be used to provide updates on progress and plans. However, written communication is often used inappropriately. In times of change, people are busy, stressed and concerned. They are unlikely to sit down and read large amounts of written material. The main content of any substantial booklets or manuals may be better covered in some form of seminar, workshop or training, with the manuals issued as reference material.

An increasingly popular type of written communication is e-mail. Many organisations also set up intranet sites to provide information on their change initiative and give progress information. Whilst these are temptingly simple channels for direct communication with all employees, and a good means of briefing back-up information and progress, there are drawbacks. Employees can't be forced to read the messages, and e-mails may simply become lost among all the other e-mails employees receive. There is heavy competition for employee air space. As a result, organisations are investing in communication management systems, which prioritise and package communications, ensuring that important messages get priority and are not mixed in with trivia.[8] Staff based out of the office can also miss out on such communication mechanisms. SEEBORD Energy utilised SMS text messaging to reach field sales employees with the real-time messages placed on the intranet site set up to support their communication programme. New communications technology is constantly being created to make it possible to deliver more sophisticated communication packages in novel ways.

6.3.4 Message content

Again, the key issue with the message content is to match the detail to the audience needs:

- If the message provides information that is personally relevant, and is couched in language the recipients can relate to and understand, the more likely it is that the message will be understood and retained.[9]

- Employees do not just need an organisational vision, they also need a personal

| Figure 6.5 | The communication collision |

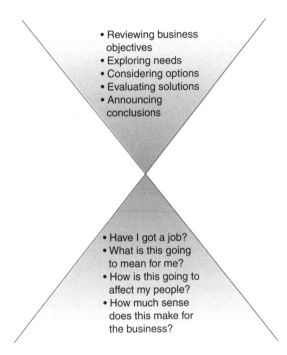

- Reviewing business objectives
- Exploring needs
- Considering options
- Evaluating solutions
- Announcing conclusions

- Have I got a job?
- What is this going to mean for me?
- How is this going to affect my people?
- How much sense does this make for the business?

Funnelling information down the hierarchical pyramid means the greatest number of people get the least context and the lower down the organisation you are, the less sense information makes.

Source: Bill Quirke, Communicating Change, 1995, McGraw-Hill Publishing Company.
Copyright holder: Bill Quirke, Synopsis Communication Consulting, 113 Farringdon Road, London EC1R 3BX.

vision. In a change situation, the question everyone wants an answer to is, what is going to happen to me? Until individuals know if they will have a job, or where they will have to relocate to, or how their terms and conditions will change, they are unlikely to take in much else.[10]

- For the change agents and people who have worked with them on designing the change process, it is too easy to announce just the conclusions and not explain the thinking that has gone into the decision-making process. This can lead to people asking questions about why particular options have not been considered, when they may have been, and questioning the feasibility and suitability of the proposals (see Figure 6.5).

6.3.5 Who should communicate the change?

In situations of dramatic change, the obvious answer to the question of who should communicate the change would appear to be the senior managers, and preferably the MD or CEO. If senior managers do not personally deliver bad news or news of dramatic change, this can be interpreted as a lack of concern for the welfare of staff, or maybe even a reluctance to give bad news personally. The size of the organisation, or the geographic spread, can make it impossible for one or two people to lead all presentations, particularly if there is a need for all staff to hear certain information at a similar time to contain unhelpful rumours, or to avoid the symbolic implication that certain groups of staff are more important to the company than others. Many organisations overcome this by using videos, which are then shown by managers to staff and accompanied by a question-and-answer session. This may work, but like cascaded communication, the communicators need to be well trained and motivated. Resourcing communication is, therefore, a serious issue – particularly since it can be a time-consuming activity.

In some instances the use of the line supervisor may be more appropriate[11] as they are more likely to be able to translate change into language and terminology that is relevant to their staff. It may also be appropriate to involve managers and supervisors in the second wave of communication, when more detail pertinent to particular groups of staff is being communicated. Update and progress information can also be given by line managers and supervisors. However, if line managers are to be responsible for communication, this should be built into their performance management in some way. All managers are overwhelmed during change, and if communication is not made a priority it may not happen.

Anyone who has to communicate change to others needs to have as much information as possible. If managers are asked to brief their staff, but cannot answer their questions, and have no means of feeding the questions upwards to obtain answers for their staff, they are unlikely to generate much commitment for change. Furthermore, when change is to be communicated by individuals who have not been involved in the planning, some thought needs to be given to the issues that might arise, and how these issues should be dealt with. This can be enhanced by collating all questions asked and then issuing answers. Organisations may use something like an advisory board or focus group composed of employees from all parts of the organisation to review communications for content and delivery, and raise questions that may be asked.

6.4 SYMBOLIC ACTIVITY

6.4.1 Symbolism and symbolic activity

Exploring Corporate Strategy, Chapters 5 and 11, already discusses symbolism and symbolic activity in some depth. The points made include the following:

- Symbolic activity includes a wide variety of message-sending events, activities and behaviours, as well as the manipulation of organisational artefacts such as status symbols, uniforms, language and logos. It can include *rituals* (see below), *physical* organisational aspects, *behaviours and language,* particularly of change agents and of those in positions of authority, *stories,* and *systems* such as reward and measurement systems.

- Symbolic activity is anything that conveys something about an organisation to the individuals within it. For example, organisations that see themselves as being very successful often have impressive head offices located in prime

---

Illustration 6.3   *change in action*

Change in an NHS Trust

A new Chief Executive was appointed at GH Hospital to lead a change programme aimed at gaining support from the hospital's consultants, for the change in status of the hospital to a self-managing trust, as part of the wider-ranging NHS reforms. The hospital acquired Trust status in the mid-1990s. However, the changes put in place also involved a turnaround of the hospital.

The CEO adopted a range of interventions. Many hard interventions were put in place including restructuring to clinical directorates, and the update of financial, planning and administration systems. The CEO also utilised political interventions. He used a collaborative change style with much discussion early on with key stakeholder groups, including the lead consultants, and used imposed external changes, such as the arrival of the NHS internal market, to legitimise the change process. There were on-going discussions with senior and middle managers throughout the change process, and senior management/consultant away-days were held to design a mission for the hospital.

However, a key aspect of the change process was the emphasis the CEO placed on symbolic activity:

- *Behaviour:* The CEO wore jeans and T-shirts and played loud pop music at middle manager away-days to emphasise that the process was also about having fun and experimenting.
- *Rewards:* The CEO sent gifts, such as baskets of fruit, to parts of the hospital which had made particular progress.
- *Ritual:* There were many away-days for all levels of staff. These became both rites of sensemaking used to help staff understand the need for and implications of change; and rites of challenge legitimising questions about the current way of doing things.
- *Language:* Hospital porters, cleaners and catering staff were given the new title of ward assistants. In the early days of change the CEO used crisis language, such as 'go under' and 'not survive' to encourage recognition of the need for change.
- *Stories:* Stories were not consciously used by the CEO himself, but they did play a role. Stories were told by others about the CEO and his energetic style, since it symbolised to them that there was a new openness and that ideas were welcomed.
- *Structures:* The 12 lead consultants from each directorate were made the majority group on the senior management executive to indicate that the consultants would continue to carry weight. A group of 12 staff drawn from across levels was used to aid communication between staff and the executive, but this also indicated that managers wanted to hear staff views.

Source: Adapted from Brooks, I. (1996) 'Leadership of a cultural change process', *Leadership and Organization Development Journal*, 17(5), pp. 31–7.

commercial locations, with smart reception areas and polite, uniformed receptionists, and panelled opulent boardrooms. This symbolism becomes a shorthand representation of what the organisation stands for, and attaches importance to.

● Symbolic activity is powerful because it has an impact on the way individuals interpret things. The prescription commonly encountered in texts on change for senior managers to 'walk the talk' is key, because if all the non-verbal cues about what change means do not support the verbal and espoused messages about change, individuals will interpret the espoused messages as meaningless. If senior managers preach empowerment and greater accountability, but continue to issue orders and countermand decisions made by their staff, then the staff will not believe in the espoused messages of change. It is important to ensure consistency through time of all actions and words.

The intent here is to emphasise how symbolic activity can support verbal messages of change, and help individuals through the mobilise, move and sustain process. Illustration 6.3 describes the change process undertaken at an NHS hospital. It describes the range of symbolic interventions used by the CEO to underpin the changes occurring and gain the support needed. The illustration reveals how symbolic interventions can be used alongside the more commonly encountered structural and political interventions, particularly in situations which involve the need for a culture change. Similarly, the Ford and Jaguar example above shows how substantial change needs to be accompanied by changes to the symbolic environment in which employees operate if employees are to believe the rhetoric of change. Illustration 6.2 describes the Halewood plant's transformation from dark, dirty, and cluttered to clean, modern, staff-friendly and efficient in support of the move to a quality culture.

Illustration 6.3 also reveals that it is not just behaviour that has impact, but also language. Some organisations do explicitly use language to help foster change. When David Neeleman set up JetBlue, the low-cost US airline, he used different language to foster a functional, family culture of greater equality. Flight attendants are 'crew members', the HR department is 'people', and the uniform group is called the 'appearance standards department'.[12] Disney is famous for its use of language to create the image of theatrics and the stage for its theme parks. Personnel are 'central casting'; employees are players in a live performance and they are cast for a role or are a host or a hostess; employees work on-stage and go back-stage for a rest; they wear costumes not uniforms; customers are guests and form an audience; and rides are attractions.[13]

There is a warning that needs to be attached to the use of symbolic interventions. Just as verbal messages can be interpreted differently from the way they were intended by the recipients of the messages, symbolic communication can similarly be interpreted differently from the way it was intended. Chapter 7 returns to this point when discussing the need for monitoring mechanisms during change to understand how recipients are responding to the change initiatives put

| Table 6.1 | Organisational rituals and culture change |

TYPES OF RITUAL (RITE)	ROLE	EXAMPLES
Rites of passage	Consolidate and promote social roles and interaction Confirm transition	Induction programmes Training programmes New offices/logos
Rites of enhancement	Recognise effort benefiting organisation Similarly motivate others	Award ceremonies Promotions Published successes
Rites of renewal	Reassure that something is being done Focus attention on issues	Appointment of consultants Project teams/task forces
Rites of integration	Encourage commitment to shared identity Reassert norms	Christmas parties Uniforms Lunchtime drinks
Rites of conflict reduction	Reduce conflict and aggression	Negotiating committees
Rites of degradation	Publicly acknowledge problems Dissolve/weaken social or political roles	Firing top executives Demotion or 'passing over' Limit scope of previously powerful groups
Rites of sensemaking	Sharing of interpretations of, and making sense of, what is happening	Rumours Stories Gossip Surveys to evaluate new practices
Rites of challenge	'Throwing down the gauntlet' Indicate old way no longer the best	New executives' different behaviour/dress Deteriorating company performance Removal of old ways of doing things Redundancies
Rites of counter challenge	Resistance to new ways of doing things	Grumbling, anti-change graffiti Working to rule, sabotage, absence from change meetings

Source: Adapted from Johnson, G. and Scholes, K. (1999) *Exploring Corporate Strategy*, 5th edn, Hemel Hempstead: Prentice Hall.

in place. Symbolic interventions are less likely to be successful if they are used as one-off interventions, and more likely to be effective if there is a consistent and on-going use of many different symbolic levers throughout the transition. Attention also needs to be paid to the removal of behaviours, events and language that symbolically suggest no change to the way of doing things within the organisation. The key here is consistent communication of the same message through multiple communication vehicles.

6.4.2 Symbolic activity and transition management

To consider how symbolic activity can help individuals through the transition curve, and therefore to mobilise, move and sustain the change process, it is necessary to consider:

- How symbolic activity can be used to *challenge* the status quo to achieve a realisation of the need for change.
- How symbolic activity can be used to legitimise *questioning*.
- How symbolic activity can be used to indicate what is *expected* of employees in the changed environment.
- How symbolic activity can be used to help employees develop a new and united *identity*.

Chapter 5 has already discussed the use of symbolism during mobilisation. Symbolic breaks with the past, through senior manager behaviours, or events, or the removal of status symbols, can be used to indicate that things are to be done differently in the future, and to legitimise questioning and challenging of the status quo. The use of ritual can also be particularly helpful here – see Table 6.1 for a list of the different types of rituals.

Rituals (rites) can be defined as 'a formal action normally repeated in a standardised way',[14] that have become embedded into the way of life in an organisation. It is possible to encourage people to challenge and question, and also to indicate new desired ways of working, by removing or changing the emphasis of old rituals, and putting in place new rituals. Rites of passage, degradation, enhancement, renewal, conflict reduction and integration help, to varying degrees, to mobilise, move and sustain organisations.[15] As such, different rituals may have different impacts throughout the mobilise, move and sustain process (see Figure 6.6).

During the *mobilise* phase :

- *Challenge* rituals, such as the publication of declining performance or increasing competition, can be important as they can be used to trigger a recognition of the need for change. They can also be used to create and mandate dissatisfaction with the current way of doing things, be it by new executives doing things in a different way, or competitive benchmarking. Chapter 5 (section 5.8.3) describes how the papermaker Whatman cancelled membership of the

Figure 6.6	Linking change and symbolism

CHANGE PROCESS	SYMBOLIC ACTS	EFFECT
Mobilise: Shock/denial awareness	*Challenge* *Degradation* *Sensemaking*	Legitimise questioning Show old ways gone
Move: Acceptance Testing Search	Decreasing: *Challenge* Increasing: *Degradation* *Counter-Challenge* *Conflict-Reduction* Increasing: *Enhancement* *Integration* *Renewal*	Legitimise questioning Provide role models and new identity Tackle resistance
Sustain: Integration	*Enhancement* *Integration* *Renewal*	Reinforce new identify and new ways of doing things Assess progress

federation of Papermaking Industries and de-recognised the papermaker's trade union as part of a move to position papermaking as only one part of the business rather than the core business. These were rites of challenge. One organisation used a wall-smashing ceremony to initiate the start of an open-plan shopfloor, followed by the creation of administration rooms on the shopfloor to replace the previously separate administration offices to enhance communication flows between blue- and white-collar workers.[16]

- *Degradation* rituals, such as removing and replacing top executives, or discontinuing old practices, can be used to generate questioning about the validity of the old ways of doing things. Clerical Medical, the life insurance provider, made many changes from the mid-1990s, including demutualisation and changing the way they sell their products to independent financial advisors from product push to customer relationship selling. Senior staff that did not support these changes were asked to leave.

- Since challenge and degradation will also create a lot of uncertainty, it is likely that there will be many *sensemaking* rituals, much speculation, gossip, sharing of information and rumours, during the mobilisation phase.

During the *move* phase:

- *Challenge* and *degradation* rituals are likely to continue to be important as individuals are continually encouraged to discontinue old ways of doing things and adopt new ways of behaving.

- The greatest levels of resistance, and therefore rites of *counter-challenge*, may be encountered in this phase as individuals have to actually undertake change. It may, therefore, be necessary to use on-going *degradation* rituals to diminish old social identities, maybe via shock tactics such as redundancies and demotions in crisis-driven change.

- Rites of *conflict reduction*, including consultations and negotiations with unions or staff groups, and dealing with staff grievances, may be necessary to overcome resistance.

- Rites of *enhancement*, *passage*, and *integration* are likely to become important, as it becomes necessary to establish new role models of how things should be done, and to foster a new organisational identity. This is the time when individuals will be testing out new behaviours and searching for new meanings.

- Rites of *enhancement* could involve the giving of public rewards for individuals performing well according to the terms of new organisational performance criteria, or the public praise of such individuals in newsletters. In Glaxo SmithKline UK Pharma, the sales division of GSK, they award bronze, silver and gold pins to staff who exhibit the new desired behaviours for the merged organisation following the merger between Glaxo and SmithKline Beecham. Staff are encouraged to wear their pins 'with pride'.

- Rites of *integration* encourage a common organisational identity, and could include a wide variety of social events or meetings. Siemens utilised many rites of integration when taking over Westinghouse of the USA. Football matches were organised between blue-collar operatives from plants on both sides of the Atlantic, and there were also ice-hockey tournaments and kart-racing sessions between teams from Germany, the USA and Canada. At the Siemens gas turbine factory in Berlin, staff have had intensive English lessons to enable regular discussions between themselves and workers at the Westinghouse gas turbine factory in Canada, and there have been regular exchanges of staff visits between the two factories.[17]

The *sustain* phase is about reinforcing change, as such, the rituals likely to be of use being those to do with *enhancement*, *integration* and *renewal*. The rites of integration and enhancement may be a continuation of those introduced during the move phase. These rituals may become part of the new organisational culture. McDonald's Restaurants has a number of rites of integration and enhancement in place to ensure its consistency of operation whilst maintaining the team culture of the organisation. Senior managers regularly go on formal restaurant visits that give the managers a chance to meet restaurant staff and managers, and to reward and recognise high achievers. The visits also allow senior management the opportunity to refocus the efforts of restaurant managers on new strategic or operational initiatives. 'Founder's Day' is celebrated each year on the anniversary of the birth of Ray Kroc (McDonald's founder). On Founder's Day, all office support staff, senior managers and representatives from company suppliers and agencies work in a restaurant for the day, both as a tribute to Ray Kroc and also to reaffirm that every employee is an important part of the team when it comes to maintaining the company's high operational standards. There are also many staff incentives, such as the Employee of the Month Award in each restaurant. This competition escalates through the various regional structures, culminating in a national Employee of the Year Award. The Sponsorship Awards are held annually for hourly-paid staff who are either in further or higher education, or following a continuous pursuit in the sports or arts (including music). Up to 100 Awards of £1,000 each are made to the successful employees to help them invest in their own future. The President's Award is made annually to a select group of salaried employees nominated by their Regional Vice President, with the winners being personally selected by the Company Chairman. Nominated employees will have achieved outstanding results through their vision, inspiration and leadership, and act as role models to their colleagues, displaying McDonald's key leadership behaviours and core values. Recipients of the award receive an enhanced bonus of one-third of their annual salary and a special recognition award, presented at a gala celebration dinner. Service Awards are made at various employment milestones and are awarded to employees at regional gala dinners. Gifts carrying the McDonald's logo are often given out at staff conferences.

6.5 LINKING COMMUNICATION TO DESIGN CHOICES

The above sections detail some of the different ways of communicating, and some of the issues to take into account when designing a communication strategy as part of any transition. In general, in any change process, the more communication with staff by a variety of different means, the better. Furthermore, there is always a need for certain types of communication like progress information. However, there is a need to match the communication strategy to the context of the changes and the design choices already made. The key issue here is to understand the role of communication in the design choices made so far. For example:

- If the *change style* selected is *education* and *delegation*, then the communication strategy needs to be designed to have many seminars and/or training and education interventions upfront that are about creating an awareness of the need for change, an understanding of what needs to change, and providing staff with the skills to undertake change.

- If the *change style* is to be more *directive* or *coercive*, particularly since these change styles by their nature are top-down, and may be associated with a lack of time, then much of the communication may be more one-way with less of an emphasis on participation. Dramatic symbolic gestures are more likely to be used to support directive and coercive change styles.

- If the change *levers* selected include *communication, education* and *personal development*, maybe to effect a value change, then such activity needs to be built into both the mobilise stage and the move stage to help staff understand what is expected of them, and to enable them to change.

- If the *change levers* selected include *symbolic activity*, as they should if there is an intent to effect either behavioural change or ultimately value change, then those communicating the changes, and those in a prominent managerial role, need to be seen to support the espoused messages of change by their behaviours, actions and language. Conscious thought should also be given to how symbolic activity can be built into the communication strategy at all stages of the transition process.

● All *mobilising tactics* (see Chapter 5) involve communication in one form or another, be it verbal, written or symbolic. Decisions about the mobilising tactics will need to be built into a communication strategy.

● *Time* and *capacity*, particularly money and managerial resources, can affect the communication strategy. It may be that these factors mitigate against an extensive communication strategy. This is likely to be true for organisations in crisis. In such situations communication may be primarily by decisive symbolic actions, such as those undertaken at mmO2 (Chapter 5, section 5.6.4, Drastic measures and shock tactics). Face-to-face communication is likely to be limited and more tell than sell.

Figure 6.7   Components of a human resource system

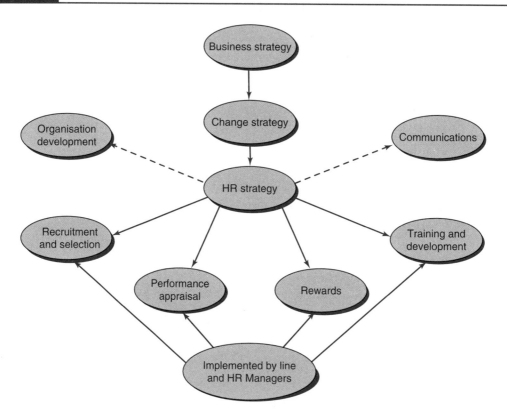

6.6 BUILDING NEW HUMAN RESOURCE MANAGEMENT SYSTEMS

6.6.1 The human resource system

Human resource management (HRM) policies and processes are one influence on individual and group behaviour within an organisation. They can be used both to move the organisation through change and also to reinforce and sustain the newly formed organisation once the change is over. Although frequently ignored by change agents, changes in human resource policies or procedures are in fact powerful communicators and can reinforce a new strategic direction. Figure 6.7 shows that the main components of a human resource system[18] include:

- *Recruitment and selection*: designing jobs, and attracting, selecting and appointing staff into the organisation. *Recruitment* is concerned with looking for people whom the organisation might wish to employ. It is to do with advertising vacancies and attracting people to apply to the organisation. *Selection* is the process by which an individual or individuals are chosen for appointment from the pool of individuals who have either applied through the recruitment process or been recommended for a position. Recruitment is the process that produces candidates. Selection is the sorting of the candidates, maybe through interviewing and profiling questionnaires, to identify the final appointments.

- *Appraisal*: measuring, monitoring and assessing staff performance, often against previously set objectives; assessing staff for either rewards / bonuses or future training or development; and defining future performance objectives.

- *Reward*: rewarding individuals or teams for contribution, and motivating them to stay and/or perform. This includes both monetary and non-monetary forms of reward.

- *Development*: training and developing staff for either improved future performance or as part of general career development.

- *The HR function*: the role and structure of the HR function may need to be redesigned to fit the needs of the change process.

The case study on Kraft Jacob Suchard in Illustration 6.4 describes how the company used its HR systems to support a change in business strategy. The case study is used to illustrate how the linkages between the different HRM components are important, and can be used to support the transition process.

For the components of the HR system to work effectively as change levers the organisation has to ensure three forms of linkage[19] – *temporal, vertical and horizontal*:

- *Temporal linkages* ensure that the human resource policies and processes change over time as the business strategy evolves.

- *Vertical linkages* ensure that the human resource policies and processes are

Illustration 6.4

From acquisition to innovation at Kraft Jacob Suchard

Kraft Jacob Suchard, now known as Kraft Foods, was the European division of the Philip Morris food business. This illustration looks at the head office of KJS UK, the fourth largest business within the European region. Growth used to be achieved through acquisition. The culture was based on the concept of continuous improvement, providing clear objectives and strategies and supporting a strong results-oriented approach to business. Clear financial targets detailing growth figures in turnover and profit were agreed by KJS in Zurich, the European HQ, and each company devised its own broad strategy to fulfil them. The severity of the targets, together with a strong emphasis on driving costs out of the business, had brought a culture that stressed short-term payback. Recruitment and selection policies had reinforced the results-oriented approach, hiring employees who could 'deliver the objectives in the right way' and who were 'high calibre people capable of progressing throughout the organisation'. A large investment in training and development workshops had established the culture from the top down and had instilled a common set of values. There were also strong performance-appraisal procedures.

A short-term horizon had developed within the majority of managers, particularly as the emphasis was on the specification of behaviour, and promotion was on results and fast payback on investment. The rigorous objectives had also produced a culture which was risk averse. In 1995 a more determined shift in business strategy was announced with a declared intention of KJS becoming a company that grows organically through innovation.

Innovation

In 1995 KJS Europe was restructured. The salesforce shifted from a geographic approach to a customer relationship marketing approach. The strategic focus shifted from growth through acquisition to developing what is known as power brands such as Kenco coffee or Philadelphia cheese. This new focus was intended to emphasise innovation and has led to new product introductions such as Carte Noire coffee. Four clusters of HRM initiatives supported this shift in business strategy: the introduction of a new vision and values; the refining of the performance management system; the development of new leadership talent and the restructuring of the HR department.

Vision and values

The vision and values intervention attempted to free up managerial entrepreneurial initiative and encourage creative and innovative behaviours. The core values were identified as: 'delivering results; openness, integrity and respect for others; a passion for ideas; continuous improvement; development and recognition of our people.' The vision included 'growth through innovation'. Line managers gave feedback on the appropriateness of the senior management's development of the vision and values in a series of workshops, and the entire package was shown to staff at a set piece event at Cheltenham race-course.

change in action

Performance management

The aim of the Managing and Appraising Performance process (MAP) was to link the company's strategic objective to the goals of each employee. The major change in the process was the introduction of the new values, with the Philip Morris Leadership Profiles, into the evaluation and development needs analysis process. The amended profiles stressed teamwork, empowerment, innovation and creativity. MAP was also made more future orientated rather than being centred solely around the evaluation of past performance. In addition, more attention was given to coaching and counselling, with middle to senior managers going through an extensive coaching programme. However, surveys revealed that staff saw rewards and recognition as a major block to the achievement of a more creative culture. Furthermore, the persisting short-term demands of the business caused a degree of conflict, with some staff questioning whether managers could give sufficient time to coaching.

Developing leadership

The new Philip Morris Leadership Profiles were meant to help identify high-potential staff. New profiles have been incorporated into the career development process. Yet there remained concern about the 'first bounce' strategy for recruitment. This means the company hires its staff from the pool who have been already trained by its excellent marketing competitors.

There is no graduate entry scheme. Clearly the emphasis on innovation and risk taking requires the company to encourage high-talent individuals in the first instance.

The HR function

The HR function has moved away from providing what was essentially a support role to one which stresses business partnerships. The speed and efficiency required of an HR department supporting a business strategy of acquisition earned the HR function in KJS a reputation as a tough department. A climate of innovation and risk taking put different demands on the function. A new HR director was appointed who reappraised the purpose of the function with its business customers. Six areas were identified as important including, for the first time, organisational effectiveness and climate as well as the traditional areas such as recruitment and selection. The statement which launched the newly vamped department stressed its role in managing change, working with employee potential and being a business partner. The function appointed HR client managers to each business unit and function, and removed much of the administrative personnel management burden from these new posts by establishing two speciality centres for recruitment and HR administration to add to the existing two for training and development and compensation and benefits.

Source: Adapted from Hope Hailey, V. (2001) 'Breaking the mould? Innovation as a strategy for corporate renewal', *International Journal of HRM*, November, pp. 1126–40.

congruent and reflective of the business strategy and the business goals within that strategy. There is little point in having a business strategy which can only be achieved through the development of a team culture if the compensation and benefits system rewards individual performance rather than team perform-ance. At the beginning of the Kraft Jacob Suchard case there are strong verti-cal links between the business strategy of acquisition and the HR policies on appraisal and performance management.

● *Horizontal linkages* ensure that the human resource policies and processes are congruent with each other. Do the criteria by which people are selected bear some resemblance to the criteria by which they are appraised for perform-ance? To extend the example given above, if the business strategy needs a team-based culture, then the criteria used in selecting staff, and appraising staff and rewarding staff, should all be linked into team performance so that each activity complements the others. This is illustrated in the second part of the Kraft Jacob Suchard case where the failure to align the reward and bonus system behind the new vision and values, and other aspects of performance management, acted as a barrier to change. Employees soon become cynical about change if one policy appears to contradict another.

6.6.2 HRM and transition management

Recruitment and selection

There are several ways that recruitment and selection can be used to support change interventions. During the *mobilise* phase one of the most common mech-anisms used to indicate the need for change is redundancy. However, tactics can be more subtle. For instance, organisations can change the *selection criteria.* Selection criteria may include past experience, personal skills, qualifications, knowledge areas, attitudes, and so on. If the organisation is seeking to achieve a cul-tural change, for example, these criteria can be altered to reflect the new norms and values that an organisation is hoping to embrace. Kraft, by changing its Leadership Profiles, sent a strong message that the management behaviours required by future leaders were going to be substantially different from those used in the past. New selection criteria also enable the use of degradation and challenge rituals. For example, setting new selection criteria for certain positions may mean that staff with appropriate qualifications need to be brought in from outside the organisation to fill vacancies previously filled through internal promotion. This also indicates to existing staff that they no longer have the appropriate skills.

Staff can also be made to *re-apply* to the organisation for a job as at BELGACOM (see Chapter 5, Illustration 5.7). If selection criteria have also been changed, or fewer jobs made available in the new structure, this may mean that some staff are offered redundancy rather than a job (see Illustration 6.2 above). Organisations can also change the *type* of people recruited. They may decide to start to *recruit* and/or *promote* from a pool of potential candidates previously ignored. In Kraft they began to question their recruitment strategy of 'first bounce' as they felt they needed to attract the highest potential new graduates in order to foster their new climate of innovation. Challenging existing perceptions of who fills which jobs can both symbolically and practically aid a change process.

During the *move* phase, the tactics may be similar to the mobilise phase. Selection criteria may be altered to allow for an on-going reduction of staff by identification of those staff not able to perform against the competencies now required by the organisation. Job redesign, changing the actual structure of job roles, may also be used. This was a key part of the changes at the Ford's Halewood plant (see Illustration 6.2) where significant changes were made to the way cars were assembled to enable production of the X-type Jaguar. The UK high street retail banks (cf. Lendco in Chapter 4) have also deployed this tactic for existing posts within their branch networks. The job descriptions of bank cashiers have been changed to reflect the new emphasis on selling of services and products. Such changes may in turn affect the number of staff needed and the sort of people required. The changes may also lead to the introduction of more flexible working, or annualised hours, where staff work more hours at one time of the year than at others to meet the fluctuating level of customer orders.

During the *sustain* phase, the recruitment and selection interventions are likely to be aimed at longer-term change within the make-up of a workforce, rather than short-term change to the staff an organisation already has. Organisations may change the *way* people are recruited. For years life insurance companies recruited from among the best 'A' level school leavers. The life insurance industry ran a strong internal labour market, with good internal training processes, which enabled the school leavers to rise to the top managerial levels within an organisation. As the industry changed, with new entrants coming into the marketplace and the advent of new technology, the internal labour market broke down, and the majority of staff recruited in as clerical workers were much more likely to stay within the clerical ranks for much of their lives. It was then necessary for the industry to change its recruitment practices. It could not continue to take the brightest and the best from the school leavers whilst being unable to fulfil their career expectations. Equally, it made more sense economically to seek to recruit less qualified people who would cost less for the clerical jobs.

Organisations may change the *selection mechanisms* (interviews, assessment centres, psychometric tests) for both new recruits and for the promotion of existing staff, although some organisations may choose to do this in the move phase. Such moves can also be symbolic, sending messages about which practices are now valued in comparison to the old ways of doing things. In the 1990s many accountancy firms changed the way future partners were selected. Managers were traditionally promoted to partner through the patronage and recommendation of an existing partner. Means such as assessment centres were introduced to determine which of the prospective candidates for partnership had the appropriate profile, and who would therefore be put forward for partnership.

Appraisal

The most common way of using appraisal systems to help deliver change is to alter either the criteria or the objectives against which staff are assessed. Criteria may be changed by reshaping the skills, competencies or behaviours against which staff are assessed, and objectives may be changed by reshaping what staff have to achieve. For example, to aid a shift in priorities for lecturers at a university from teaching to research, the objectives in the appraisal system leading to promotion, pay rises or bonuses may be altered to include getting research published in academic journals.

However, there are other *symbolic* changes that can be made to an appraisal mechanism to aid *mobilisation* and *movement*. 360-degree appraisals can be introduced whereby staff also appraise their managers as well as the other way round. This was done at WH Smith (Chapter 4, Illustration 4.2) to help mobilise the deferential culture. Other aspects of appraisal can also be changed to aid *move* and *sustain*. The frequency with which managers have to appraise their staff could be changed. It may be specified that managers are expected to *informally* keep in touch with their staff throughout the year to assess how they are coping with change, so that the *formal* annual appraisal is merely a summary of what is already known. This suggests a change in role for the manager, to one more to do with coaching and counselling. This happened within Kraft Jacob Suchard where coaching and counselling became mainstream management activities. It was an attempt to move away from the formal appraisal system which reinforced the short-term results and output culture. A shift towards more coaching and counselling may also help to support staff through the awareness, acceptance and testing parts of the transition curve (see Chapter 5) when staff may feel incompetent, anxious and angry about the change they are undertaking.

If changes are made to the appraisal system, it is essential that during the *sustain* stage of transition they are followed up by changes in promotion criteria and career management decisions. If the appraisal emphasises innovation yet all the more risk-averse members of staff continue to rise to the top of the organisation, there is a danger that the organisation will revert to its original character under crisis conditions. In the sustain stage it is essential to embed the new forms of performance evaluation within the enduring routines and rituals within the organisation.

Reward

Reward covers the whole compensation and benefits area and is a common change lever to help obtain changes in staff behaviour and performance. Reward is concerned with both rewarding people for past performance and motivating them for future performance. It also acts as a means of retaining staff. However, reward is a very broad category and people can be rewarded in many different ways. Reward can encompass being sent on training courses as a bonus for particular performance. It might include extra holidays, payment for college fees, access to childcare, and company cars. All of these forms of reward can be used to help recruit and retain staff with a range of different needs, but also be used to motivate people to embrace change. Given the links between reward and motivation, it is easy to see how compensation and benefits can promote change, both through the transition phase and beyond.

To understand how to use a reward system effectively within an organisation, and when, a change agent needs to understand the different motivations of staff groups. For some groups, such as sales representatives or investment bankers, financial rewards are a critical motivator and immediately changing the bonuses to *mobilise* staff may guarantee a rapid response even in the first stage of transition. The criteria against which bonuses are paid, for example, could be altered. If, previously, performance-related pay was determined by how many individual sales were achieved over a short period of time, a shift towards relationship marketing might suggest that the reward system should be altered to reflect the ability to sustain longer-term customer relationships. This is as true for senior managers as it is for more junior staff.

More negatively, pay freezes or cuts, or the non-payment of the usual annual bonuses, send strong signals that change is really happening. Alteration of non-financial rewards, such as subsidies for canteens or health clubs, can also be used. Cancellation of such rewards could be introduced to bring home to staff the seriousness of a financial crisis.

For others, however, financial reward is not a primary motivator. Nurses, many academics and people working within the not-for-profit sector may well be motivated more by an appeal to their personal or occupational values in the first instance rather than an immediate change to a reward system. Yet even in value-driven organisations, in the *move* and *sustain* stages, commitment to the desired future values will need to be illustrated by changes in the reward systems. Kraft Jacob Suchard failed to realign their rewards system behind their new vision and values statement which made their staff query the senior management's commitment to innovation and risk taking in the longer term. Furthermore, if, in earlier stages of the transition, the recruitment policies have been changed to start attracting different types of staff, such as mothers returning to work or semi-retired people, then a different range of rewards may need to be offered to retain these staff. Such employees may value flexibility over financial reward.

As in the mobilise phase rewards may be symbolic, giving messages to staff about what they have to do to help with the change process – or maybe even keep their job. Staff may be rewarded for simply supporting the changes. For instance, line managers can be given bonuses for spending time counselling their staff through change or implementing change-related initiatives. Other rewards may include writing about staff who are deemed to be doing the right things in newsletters, to portray them as role models to others, or publicly giving staff who make the sorts of change wanted recognition through the use of rites of enhancement as discussed above. Staff could also be rewarded by other means, such as training and development courses. Those staff who are doing the right things may receive sponsorship for something like an MBA course, or be sent on a high-profile management development programme at a top business school.

Sustaining change is more to do with maintaining and retaining changed behaviours into the longer term. Changes to reward systems in this phase of change are more likely to be permanent changes to the overall framework of rewards. It is at this point that an organisation may implement, for example, a new cafeteria benefits system, or embed symbolic rewards into the permanent way of working in an organisation. At Kraft Jacob Suchard, when the changes in values are written into the reward system permanently then the staff will see that innovation is not a passing phase.

Development

Change may involve staff acquiring new skills, new knowledge, new working practices, or new behaviours, attitudes or values. Development and training is the mechanism used to help achieve this. Training seeks a specific outcome in terms of skills or behaviours. Development is more challenging and broader in remit. It may include experiential learning, which can encompass outdoor development courses, or it can be classroom based. Education is even broader in its aim, seeking to open a delegate's or student's mind to new ways of thinking. The key to success is to choose the right delivery channel for the type of change design chosen, and the level of people who are the recipients of the learning process. Senior management react less well to training and better to education, whereas staff requiring new skills need training.

There are many mechanisms for delivering development and training. For example:

- *Off-site interventions*: this can involve courses on specific skills or knowledge areas such as IT, or qualifications in banking.

- *General management programmes*: either in the form of degree-based courses such as MBAs, or executive development courses that examine all the management functions. Organisations can also have customised general management programmes designed to suit their own needs. For example, in the early 1990s, the NHS decided to fund a number of hospital consultants to attend management development programmes at business schools, to improve the level of management within the NHS. However, some regional health authorities chose to devise their own tailor-made programmes.

- *In-house training*: this can take the form of courses or job-based learning.

- *In-house computer-based/intranet training*: employees can have direct access to new knowledge and skills through programmes offered by the company on the office intranet. Such programmes are becoming increasingly sophisticated.

These different interventions can be used to different effect to help *mobilise*, *move* and *sustain* an organisation. Personal development is very powerful during the *mobilise* phase, since it is concerned with helping an individual to grow and change at an individual level. It is about challenging the way individuals see things. As such, it is a type of intervention that is valuable in circumstances where value change is required of individuals. Illustration 5.6 in Chapter 5 discusses such an intervention at Glenbrook Steel Mill. Personal development can also be used to aid mobilisation when a type of behavioural change is needed which in turn requires individuals to recognise the degree of change this requires from them personally.

Personal development programmes designed to aid mobilisation are likely to be in-house programmes designed with the intent of putting many staff through them simultaneously to achieve a critical mass of support for change. However, if the need is to mobilise particular senior managers, then these people may be sent on open management development programmes. Of course, if the mobilisation style selected is education and delegation, then the mobilisation interventions may be more about education than personal development.

During the *move* phase, both training and development will be needed to help staff develop either new skills, behaviours or attitudes. If change is about delivering new skills, the interventions will be more to do with training whereas if the emphasis is on value-based change, more personal development interventions will be needed. Again, courses are likely to be designed specifically for the organisation if a critical mass of people needs to attend. However, coaching and counselling by outside facilitators, a more intensive form of private, individual personal development, may be provided for more senior managers to help them develop the new attitudes or behaviours required of them *or* to provide them with the change skills they need to help their staff through change. This approach was used by British Airways World Cargo, the freight arm of British Airways, in the mid-1990s to help their senior managers to achieve the required changes in their behaviours (see Chapter 5, section 5.3.1).

If training and development initiatives are to be used as change levers they must be chosen with the change outcomes in mind. So, for example, if an organisation decides that for it to succeed at change all its senior and middle managers need to understand the change process and how to help their staff through change, then the course designed would need to fit this objective. This means that the contractor of the course for the organisation needs to be able to evaluate the objectives of every available course and assess their fit with the requirement. It also means that the participants need to be able to link the content of any change related training to the desired outcomes of the organisational change programme.

During the *sustain* phase, interventions will be more to do with putting in place training to ensure the on-going development by staff at all levels, of the sorts of competencies the organisation requires for it to remain competitive in the longer term. Things such as new induction courses for new recruits could also be put in place at this point. Training and development initiatives will need to be supported by corresponding changes to the appraisal system. That way, people can be put on appropriate training courses and assessed against whether or not they are able to use the skills and competencies they are supposed to have acquired.

Another important sustain intervention is career development. Any organisation undertaking change needs to make suitable adjustments to its career-planning processes, to build the organisational leaders and competencies required for the future. It is very shortsighted for the current senior managers to anticipate that the behaviours or knowledge that got them to the top should also apply to the next generation of leaders. Career development may be delivered by a series of planned project assignments or job promotions aimed at giving the individual the range of experiences deemed necessary for future leaders, and/or management development programmes such as MBA courses. It may also incorporate activities such as coaching and mentoring, whereby more junior managers are assigned a more senior manager to act as their mentor on personal and career development.

In contrast to the above, senior managers may need to consider stopping some of the development activities that were more concerned with the process of change rather than the essential requirements for the future. Whilst this appears obvious, many interventions that were designed in order to change or move an organisation forward are continued beyond their useful life. It is as important to cease an activity once it is redundant as it is to start it in the first place. This can send powerful signals that the change is embedded within the organisation and is a success.

The HR function

The Kraft case illustrates the need to ensure that the HR function itself is aligned with the nature of the change. There are four main roles for HR: strategic partner to the business, administrative expert, employee champion and change agent.[20] For the HR interventions to make a full contribution to the change process, the business needs to understand the potential roles that HR can fulfil.

In Kraft Jacob Suchard the senior management realised that they needed to change the profile of the HR function if they were to be seen as credible as role models for the change. This did not simply involve a restructuring of the department but also a change in its director. The person brought in was seen to be able to fulfil the role of change agent and displayed the personal behaviours and competencies that represented the innovation and creativity they were trying to encourage.

6.7 LINKING HRM SYSTEMS AND DESIGN CHOICES

As with all other levers and mechanisms it is important to link the use of the HRM interventions to the design choices already made. For example:

- If the *change target* is *outputs*, then changes to rewards and performance objectives within the appraisal system are likely to be particularly helpful.

- If the *change target* is *behaviours,* as at Kraft Jacob Suchard, then a range of HRM interventions will be needed including training and development to help effect the changes to skills and behaviours, and changes to appraisal criteria and rewards to support the new behaviour.

- If the *change target* is *values*, then as the discussion on training and development makes clear, many longer-term development-related initiatives will be required aimed at altering the way individuals think about their work and their customers.

- If the *change start-point* is to be *bottom-up*, rewards and promotion could be used to encourage participation on *ad-hoc* basis. This would also be a symbolic intervention, indicating that those staff that get on and are valued are those that are contributing to the change process. More permanent changes to reward systems would only be instituted in the longer term to sustain the changes that had evolved.

- If the *change start-point* is *top-down*, then things such as performance objectives and rewards may be imposed to force in change, particularly when accompanied by a focus on behaviours to force change in quickly.

Other factors may also influence the decisions about which HRM interventions to use. Capacity, in terms of cash and employee time for change, is an issue as Chapters 3 and 4 have already explained. Organisations can be so overstretched because of the changes they are trying to implement that they cannot release staff, or allow them the time for the training that has been set up. There is little point in investing in an initiative while having no capacity to deliver it. Training and development programmes can also involve significant investment in terms of time and finance. Again, there is little point in designing a change process that requires these types of interventions, or extensive and expensive personal development interventions, if there is not the money for it.

6.8 SUMMARY

The purpose of this chapter has been to describe in some detail the use of particular levers and mechanisms to aid the transition process and help effect the required changes:

- Communication is particularly important during all phases of the transition.

During the mobilise phase, communication needs to be designed to create readiness; during the move phase communication needs to provide explanation; and as change progresses, communication also needs to provide update information for staff. It is always necessary to focus on matching the communication to the needs of the audience.

- Symbolic activity is important as an alternative form of communication during change. Rituals can be used to help facilitate the mobilise, move and sustain change process by legitimising questioning and challenging in the early stages of change, and promoting new role models and social identities as change progresses.

- Last, but by no means least, human resource management systems are a key change lever. Recruitment and selection, reward systems, appraisal mechanisms, and training and development are all interventions that need to be used to encourage individuals to adopt the new skills, behaviours, attitudes or values required as part of the changes.

This chapter completes the analysis of how to design the transition process, although it also starts to address considerations of how to manage the transition. As Chapter 7 will explain, given the dynamic and at times unexpected nature of the transition state, communication and political skills are key attributes required of change agents if they are to successfully negotiate the rocky terrain of change implementation.

REFERENCES

1. For a discussion of some of the principles of communication see Axley, S.R. (1984) 'Managerial and organizational communication in terms of the conduit metaphor', *Academy of Management Review*, 9 (3), pp. 428–37.
2. Johnson, R. (30 August 2001) 'On message', *People Management,* pp. 24–30.
3. For an examination of some of the factors that contribute to effective communication see Smeltzer, L.R. (1991) 'An analysis of strategies for announcing organization-wide change', *Group and Organization Studies,* 16 (1), pp. 5–24.
4. See reference 3 above.
5. See Duck, J.D. (1993) 'Managing change: The art of balancing', *Harvard Business Review*, 71 (6), pp. 109–18.
6. Lank, E. (19 February 1998) 'Café society', *People Management*, pp. 40–3.
7. Davies, E. (October 2002) 'Where does it all come from?' *Internal Communication*, 79, pp. 6–9.
8. Maitland, A. (2 August 2002) 'Positive messages from air traffic control', *Financial Times*.
9. Various authors discuss the need for communication to be relevant to the needs of the audience. See, for example, Klein, S.M. (1993) 'A communication strategy for the implementation of participative work systems', *International Journal of Management*, 10 (3), pp. 392–401; also Bertsch, B. and Williams, R. (1994) 'How multinational CEOs make change programmes stick', *Long Range Planning*, 27 (5), pp. 12–24.
10. For a discussion of the need for personal visions see Downing, S. and Hunt, J.W. (1990) 'Mergers, acquisitions and human resource management', *International Journal of Human Resource Management*, 1 (2), pp.195–209.

11. See Klein as in 9 above for the role of supervisors in communication.

12. Daniel, C. (26 August 2002) 'Inside track: Start of a longer haul into the JetBlue yonder', *Financial Times*, p. 8.

13. Peters, T. (1987) 'In search of Excellence', video - comments on Disney World, London: Video Arts.

14. For more information on organisational rituals and the use of ritual in change see Sims, D., Fineman, S. and Gabriel, Y. (1993) *Organizing and Organizations: An Introduction*, London: Sage. Trice, H.M. and Beyer, J. (1984) 'Studying organizational cultures through rites and ceremonies', *Academy of Management Review*, 9 (4), pp. 653-69. Brown, A.D. (1994) 'Transformational leadership in tackling technical change', *Journal of General Management*, 19 (4), pp. 1-12.

15. For more information see the same sources in reference 14 above.

16. Hwee, C.C., Demeester, L. and Pich, M. (2002) 'AlliedSignal Aerospace Repair and Overhaul (Singapore) (C)', INSEAD, ECCH case 602-036-1.

17. Marsh, P. (5 July 2002) 'Siemens generates goodwill in North America', *Financial Times*.

18. For a fuller discussion of the different components of a human resource system see Devanna, M.A., Fombrun, C.J. and Tichy, N.M. (1984) 'A framework for Strategic Human Resource Management', in Tichy, N.M. and Devanna, M.A. (eds), *Strategic Human Resource Management*, New York: John Wiley.

19. See Gratton, L., Hope Hailey, V., Stiles, P. and Truss, C. (1999) *Strategic Human Resource Management*, Oxford: Oxford University Press.

20. Ulrich, D. (1997) *Human resource champions: The next agenda for adding value and delivering results*, Boston, MA: Harvard Business School.

WORK ASSIGNMENTS

6.1 Consider the different ways that your university/business school or employer communicates with you – particularly at times of change. Why are these means of communication effective or ineffective? How could they be improved?

6.2 Consider somewhere you have worked, what rituals did you observe? How could their removal/shift in emphasis be used to aid change? What new rituals could be introduced?

6.3 Using practitioner journals or newspapers, find two examples of use of HR interventions to deliver change. Evaluate their success.

6.4 Identify the socio-economic groups that organisations may employ, such as single young people, working mothers, contract workers. How might the reward mechanisms, both formal and informal, be used to incentivise these people to undertake change and reinforce change behaviours?

Managing the transition: monitoring and resourcing

7.1 INTRODUCTION

The previous two chapters explained how to design the actual change implementation and the transition state, and also discussed how to sequence the selected change levers and interventions throughout the transition. This chapter builds on this, by focusing on the management of the transition state. It considers:

- The design of change outcomes and monitoring mechanisms to evaluate the progress and success of the change process.
- The different roles that need to be managed during the transition state and the issues to be considered for the individuals who fulfil them, with a focus on change agency, middle managers and change recipients.

The chapter opens with a consideration of the nature of the transition period itself. An understanding of what change is like once implementation gets underway is important for a greater appreciation of the types of monitoring mechanisms and skills required by those responsible for managing the transition.

7.2 MANAGING THE TRANSITION

It would be all too easy to assume from what has been said so far that the key to managing any transition is good upfront planning. It is true that the more planning and forethought given to the transition state, the better the chances of success, which is why the previous chapters devote so much attention to it. However, as Chapter 1 pointed out, it would be wrong to believe that implementation will unfold neatly in a linear fashion in accordance with carefully laid plans. The transition is better characterised as an emergent process full of surprises, with unpredictable and uncertain outcomes. Words like 'frustrating', 'chaotic', and 'difficult' are often used by managers to describe their experiences.

A good analogy is to think of the old slot machines that used to be found in entertainment arcades for children. A penny dropped in a slot at the top could take many routes. The 'prize' a child would get out of the machine would depend on the route the penny took. Leading change is a similar experience. Managers can drop interventions in at the top of the organisation, but the resulting outcome, in terms of the changes in behaviours or attitudes it produces, can be surprising and disappointing. Outcomes achieved are not always as intended. Change is about managing individual expectations and interpretations, not just structures and systems. Change agents need to work to align the interpretations of individuals with their change vision. This involves not just the use of verbal and written communication, but also the use of symbolic activity, education, training, and maybe personal development, all discussed in the previous chapter.

The nature of the implementation process also has implications for its management, one of which is that some type of specific transition management is needed to resolve problems as they arise, and keep the change process on track. It also involves recognising that the very nature of change, and the way individuals react to change, makes misinterpretation and unexpected outcomes not only likely to happen but very probable. It is therefore necessary to attempt to monitor change progress from the recipients' perspective. These issues are discussed in more detail in the rest of the chapter.

7.3 DESIGNING CHANGE OUTCOMES AND MONITORING MECHANISMS

7.3.1 Designing change outcomes and measures

As with any management intervention it is wise to establish some measures of success for the change process based on the desired change outcomes. Change outcomes describe the behaviours required of people and the types of outputs they are expected to produce in the future. They spell out how the behaviours of staff need to change on a day-to-day basis. Change outcomes are also measurable aspects of change. They are, therefore, important because they enable the change agent to devise ways to communicate to staff what is required of them, develop suitable training interventions and assess whether the desired behaviours and outputs are occurring.

Illustration 7.1 describes two examples of setting change outcomes – one in an organisation needing to grow by internal product development rather than by acquisition, and the other in an organisation wanting to introduce better customer services. Both these examples are of organisations that require their staff to undertake behavioural change. Therefore the outcomes set are more qualitative. In some circumstances, like the telesales organisation, these qualitative measures may need to be supported by more prescriptive outcomes, such as staff answering the phone more promptly, customer-satisfaction indices, or throughput indices for daily work activity.

The results from the performance management systems or staff appraisals can be used to assess the achievement of change outcomes. Other techniques for

Illustration 7.1   *change in action*

Setting outcomes

From growth by acquisition to growth by internal product and service development

An organisation with a policy of growth by acquisition realised that it was no longer viable to maintain the organisation's growth rate in this way. A policy of growth by internal development of new products and services was introduced. This required an overall outcome of more innovative staff behaviour. Changes introduced to help achieve this included job role flexibility with much less job demarcation, restructuring around teams, and experimentation. To assess whether the overall desired outcome was being achieved, additional behavioural outcomes set included team as opposed to individual working, a tolerance of mistakes, more risk taking, the generation of new product ideas, and new patterns of selling to push new products and services. The degree to which all of these behaviours were developing could be assessed through staff surveys.

Introducing better customer service into a telesales organisation

A telesales organisation wished to achieve an overall change outcome of a better level of customer service. This required a number of behaviour changes from staff, such as being more polite and friendly to customers, showing more initiative in the way they tackled customer problems, and taking more responsibility for resolving problems. Interventions put in place included training courses, newsletters circulating examples of good customer service and staff initiatives, and forums which allowed staff to exchange ideas on the ways to resolve common problems. Whether or not the new behaviours were occurring could be assessed by both staff and customer surveys. However, the softer measures were supported by some prescribed outputs that could be measured directly such as standards for rapidity of response to phone calls, letters and faxes.

assessing progress against outcomes include attitude surveys, customer surveys, interviews and questionnaires, as well as data on control measures such as how quickly the phone is answered.[1]

If an organisation is in *crisis*, however, and needs to effect a rapid reconstruction, then the desired change outcomes are more likely to be financial measures, such as profitability, levels of debt or stock levels. The desired outcomes might also include hard measures to do with internal efficiency, such as cost reduction, which in turn may be associated with targets such as staff reductions, levels of waste, and cycle times. Such task-based measures were used to improve turnaround time at AlliedSignal Aerospace Repair and Overhaul in Singapore (Chapter 2, section 2.5.1).

The emphasis so far placed on softer measures is not meant to imply that other harder and more quantifiable measures are not also needed. There is evidence that results-driven programmes, which focus on achieving specific, measurable, operational improvements within a short timeframe, in order to help achieve specific organisational goals, can yield considerable benefits.[2] The achievement of such goals will also provide visible early wins (see Chapter 5) in the change process. Furthermore, it is important that any set of measures put in place support the change process by encouraging staff to work towards the company's change vision and goals, as well as providing an overall view of business performance. When the Danish bank, BG Bank, needed to undergo change to stem its losses, a measurement system was put in place that measured each branch within its network on growth, profitability and customer satisfaction. In addition, a 360-degree feedback mechanism was put in place so that each manager could measure and improve their leadership against an agreed set of 15 categories of leadership.[3]

The need for a mutually supportive set of measures that align behaviours with an organisation's strategy, without creating a focus on one area of activity at the expense of another, has led to a technique, the balanced scorecard,[4] becoming popular throughout the 1990s. The balanced scorecard uses four sets of measures:

- Financial measures to assess how the company looks to shareholders.

- Customer performance measures to assess how the company is performing in the eyes of the customer.

- Internal operational measures to assess how well the company is doing on the business processes that impact on customer service.

- Measures of innovation and learning to assess if the company is continuing to improve.

The emphasis here has been placed on more qualitative measures because, as this text has already stressed, unless individuals change, then the organisation will not achieve its new strategy. Furthermore, simplistic measures such as levels of absence may be measuring levels of fear rather than levels of motivation, and may be masking problems.

7.3.2 Monitoring progress

Transition management is about ensuring that what is planned happens, but also about detecting and managing the unexpected. There are many well-known project management techniques that can help with developing detailed plans and schedules, monitoring progress against the plans, and developing resource requirements and implications.[5] Similarly, budgeting techniques will be required to prepare budgets and monitor costs. However, as described above through the slot machine analogy, many change processes are affected by unexpected outcomes (see Figure 7.1). Some of these may be positive, such as staff showing less resistance than anticipated, or being prepared to work very long hours to make the changes work. Many others are typically negative (unintended consequences), slowing down the pace of change.

Some researchers have made efforts to categorise different types of unintended consequences. Harris and Ogbonna[6] identify several such outcomes of culture change initiatives:

| Figure 7.1 | Interrelationships between components of the change process |

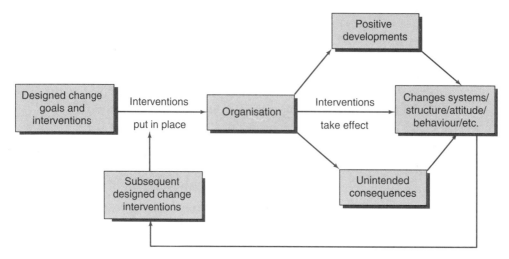

- *Ritualisation of culture change*: reducing culture change to periodic planned initiatives which become an annual ritual.

- *Hijacked process*: others hijack the culture change process as a vehicle to promote their own (maybe orthogonal) projects.

- *Cultural erosion*: other goals and objectives become more of a priority than reinforcement of the culture change.

- *Cultural reinvention*: the espousal of new attitudes and behaviours which camouflage the continuation of the old culture.

- *Ivory tower culture change*: planners create change plans in a vacuum which cannot be implemented in any meaningful way.

- *Inattention to symbolism*: not walking the talk. Old symbols, routines and rewards are left in place that contradict the new espoused culture.

- *Behavioural compliance*: employees follow the new rules and procedures (particularly when managers are around) without ever actually changing their beliefs.

Some of these unintended consequences can be laid at the door of change leaders – although they may not do these things deliberately. Other unexpected outcomes frequently arise because of the way change participants are interpreting the change interventions and communications they receive. For example, a manufacturing organisation introduced a new subsidised staff canteen as part of a change programme which also aimed to improve the work life of the employees. Despite the value for money offered, the workers continued to bring sandwiches and didn't use the canteen. Why? Sandwiches came out of the family housekeeping money, the canteen would have to come out of their 'beer' money (the money retained for personal spending out of their wages).

To understand the origins of unexpected change outcomes and why they are happening, it is necessary to understand how people are interpreting things and why. It is necessary to understand which planned (and unplanned) events and activities are having an impact, how these events and activities are being interpreted, and how this in turn is impacting behaviour. Since it is not possible to 'manage' or 'control' the interpretations of others, managing implementation becomes more of a process of aligning interpretations. Thus the attention devoted to different forms of communication vehicles in the previous chapter. However, it also means that to monitor change it is necessary to get at and understand why change recipients are reacting the way they are. This requires communication with people – talking to people. If, despite the best efforts of the change agent(s), staff do not understand what is expected of them, appropriate new behaviours and beliefs will not develop. Even worse, new and inappropriate ones may develop instead.

Furthermore, the senior managers, the ones leading change, may be the last to find out about the things that are not progressing according to plan. Bad news

---

Figure 7.2   **Techniques for monitoring and evaluating change progress**

- **Focus groups and workshops.** Groups of people from across different organisational levels, departments and functions can be drawn together to discuss the change process. Participants can be asked to discuss both what is going well and why, and what is going badly and why. They may also be able to contribute ideas on how problems can be solved, and maybe help each other with problems they are encountering. Workshops can become a way of sharing learning as well as monitoring change.

- **Management by walking about and open-door policies.** Senior managers can make a point of being visible, and available for staff to talk to. They can visit departments and offices and discuss the progress of change with staff.

- **Team briefing.** Many organisations use team briefing to keep staff appraised of progress. These meetings can be made two-way so that comments staff make are collated and passed back upwards.

- **Question-and-answer sessions.** Managers can host question and answer sessions for staff. These may take the form of informal staff/management meetings, such as breakfast or lunchtime meetings, or more formally organised meetings.

- **External consultants to monitor progress.** External consultants can be engaged to run focus groups or workshops, or conduct staff surveys. Staff may be more prepared to be open and honest about what they say in front of an outsider, particularly if guaranteed some level of anonymity.

- **Staff representatives who collate feedback.** Staff representatives can be nominated to collate feedback. They may be the attendees of the focus groups or workshops.

- **Staff suggestion or commentary schemes** can be used to gather feedback, things that need changing or could be done better. This can be done through e-mail or intranet discussion groups, for example.

- **Confidential 'hot lines'** or internal mail mechanisms.

- **Attitude surveys** and other questionnaires.

does not travel upwards well. This means it requires explicit effort to collate information on how change is progressing from the perspective of the recipients. Various techniques can be used to monitor and evaluate the progress of implementation. See Figure 7.2.

Many organisations use a variety of different mechanisms to obtain feedback. When Bass plc announced in February 2000 that it was putting its brewing operation up for sale, this led to a prolonged period of uncertainty for staff in Bass Breweries, particularly those in the English and Welsh businesses. Finally, on Christmas Eve 2001, it was announced that the US brewers, Coors, had acquired the businesses in England and Wales, and in February 2002, following 24 months of uncertainty for staff, Coors Breweries Limited was formed. A variety of communication channels were used to keep staff informed of progress and maintain morale during the acquisition period. Particular emphasis was placed on feedback from staff. Team briefings were used to generate two-way dialogue between line managers and their teams. A question-and-answers mechanism designed to give instant feedback was provided through the intranet. Focus groups were used to dig deeper into issues. Finally, simple surveys were e-mailed to a random sample of 200 employees every 2 months to check the progress and quality of communications from the perspective of the staff.[7]

Context sensitivity is also an issue for monitoring mechanisms. It is unlikely that people who are feeling unsure about what the future holds, and nervous about 'who's next' for redundancy, will tell an MD on a walkabout what is going badly. To be open about the way they are feeling, and what they see as the obstructions to change, those on the receiving end of the changes may initially need to be afforded some degree of anonymity before they will speak openly. For people to give feedback there also needs to be visible action on feedback, or staff will feel that their managers are not seriously interested in their opinions, so why bother.

7.4 ROLE MANAGEMENT

The nature of the transition state and the impact of change on individuals requires special attention to the nature of change agency, and the roles of middle managers and change recipients during change.

7.4.1 Change agency

Chapter 1 has already discussed a number of skills required of change agents. These skills include the ability to *analyse* the change context, to *judge* the key contextual features of the change context and therefore design an appropriate change approach, to take *action* to achieve implementation, to handle *complexity*, to be *sensitive* about the impact of change, and to be *aware* of the potential impact of one's own preferences on the design choices made. Change agents also require good *influencing* skills because of the political nature of their role. However, change implementation is a complicated and difficult task. Transition management involves:

- Ensuring that what is planned happens, but also anticipating, detecting and dealing with the unexpected.
- Providing continuity between formulation and implementation to ensure consistency in the way plans are turned into practice.
- Overseeing the changes, which includes the co-ordination of the myriad change projects and change-related activities.
- Monitoring change progress against plans.

Whoever is leading the change process may also take responsibility for transition management. However, the more fundamental the transition, the more time consuming transition management is as a task. If change is being led by an individual, such as the MD or CEO, the individual may find that even if all his or her operational responsibilities are delegated, just being visible and championing the change takes up most of the time. Therefore, the bigger and more complex the change, the more likely it is that a transition management team will be needed to support the main change agent(s). Similarly, middle and senior managers with operational responsibilities may also have insufficient time to fully address transition management responsibilities. Therefore, although creating a management team out of the hierarchy, or selecting representatives from the main stakeholder groups within the organisation, or even assigning responsibility for transition management to the line managers, are all possibilities, in large-scale change it is more likely that the transition management team will be most effective if it is staffed with individuals whose sole responsibility is transition management.[8]

The individuals within the transition management team, or for that matter, change agents in general, also need specific skills and training. *Process* skills are more important than *technical* skills.[9] Process skills are to do with managerial and interpersonal skills, including communication, consultation, team building, managing politics and being able to motivate others. Technical skills are more to do with control techniques such as planning, budgeting, resourcing and scheduling, or the techniques and technology required by the change project, such as information systems. This does not mean that planning and scheduling tasks are not necessary, but that transition management involves more than traditional project management. Figure 7.3 lists some of the competencies typically identified for change agents.

Figure 7.3	Change agent competencies

Creativity	To be able to see the big picture and contribute to the visioning process
Courage	To be able to honour the past, yet also to shake things up, speak out, take risks
Perseverance/ motivation	To keep trying and to have personal commitment to the changes and personal enthusiasm
Tolerance of ambiguity	To be able to juggle many changing or unclear priorities
Flexibility	To be able to recognise and seize opportunities as they arise (and let go of avenues not yielding results)
Political judgement	To be able to judge the political landscape and influence others, awareness to manage up
Common touch	To be capable of dealing with people at all levels
Visibility	To be visible as a role model and show how the changes add value
Persuasiveness	To be able to sell and negotiate with others
Networking	To have and be able to leverage multiple strong networks
Team building	To be able to develop a change team
Communication awareness	To be able to communicate the same message through many channels, using a mix of verbal, written and symbolic communications as and when appropriate

Source: Adapted from report *Boundary Spanners: Contexts, Personality, Characteristics and Practices*, Change Management Consortium, Cranfield School of Management, 2002.

7.4.2 Middle managers

Middle managers are often characterised as resistant to change, providing power-ful obstructions to changes that counter their own self-interests.[10] However, more recent research suggests that middle managers may sometimes be the scapegoats, constrained by their organisational settings from making the changes demanded of them by their more senior managers.[11] Furthermore, their role in change is a valuable one, as they act as a conduit for senior management plans and are often responsible for making the outline structures devised by their seniors work.[12]

In fact, most managers fulfil a complex and demanding role in change (see Figure 7.4). They have to:

- undertake personal change themselves.
- implement the needed changes in their departments or teams.
- help and lead their staff through personal change.
- and in the meanwhile, keep the business going.

Thus, for much of the time managers are simultaneously change recipients and change implementers.[13] They fulfil a role more accurately described by the term *change intermediaries* since they are responsible for absorbing change and pass-ing it on. Middle manager interpretation becomes critical. Their interpretation of what is needed underpins the changes they undertake personally, the changes they encourage their staff to undertake, and the changes they put in place in their departments. However, many of the activities they need to engage in to further

Figure 7.4 **Interpretation as the key middle manager task**

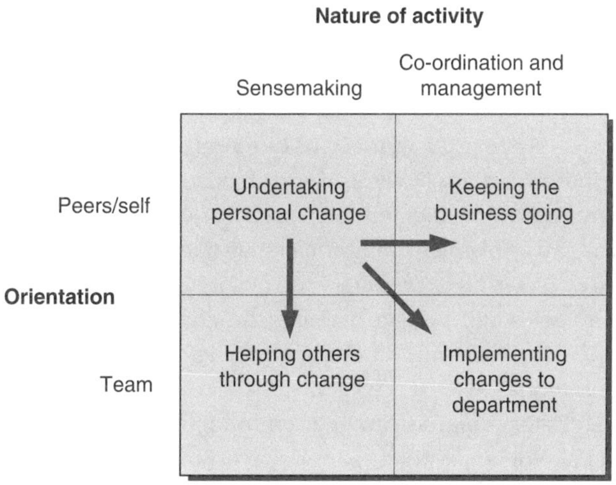

Source: Balogun, J. (2003) From Blaming the Middle to Harnessing its Potential: Creating Change Intermediaries, *British Journal of Management*, 14(1), pp. 69–84.

their own understanding of what is required, such as networking and discussions with senior managers and peers, and the activities they need to engage in to help their staff, such as frequent communication, are invisible and an overhead to the business of keeping their departments going. As a result, middle managers can become overloaded. In turn, this leads to a lack of time for important, although less tangible, change-related activities, such as communication with staff, team building, counselling and coaching.

The notion of middle managers as change intermediaries presents an alternative to the view of middle managers as a source of resistance. It suggests that it is not just getting support from middle managers for change that is important, they also need to have sufficient interpersonal skills and the time to fulfil their intermediary role if they are not to become blockages to change. Designers need to recognise the pivotal role middle managers play in change, and equip them with the necessary skills and support.

7.4.3 Recipients

Change recipients are those individuals on the receiving end of change, those that must adopt and adapt to change. Chapter 5 discusses the transition curve, and makes it clear that change is traumatic for everyone. As such, this text has already discussed some of the issues about recipients and change, and how managers need to help both their staff and themselves through the transition curve. However, three other issues deserve mention – resistance to change, survivor syndrome and organisational justice.

Resistance to change

Resistance to change can develop at all levels of the organisation. Since change is an emotional process, resistance should be expected and seen as natural. The key is to help people through their resistance so that they can move on to accept the changes. There are a number of different models, lists and categories of reasons why individuals are likely to resist change.[14] Figure 7.5 shows one such categorisation. Political implementation games, such as diverting resources, financial or human, away from change projects; using bureaucratic organisational procedures to slow down the acceptance of change proposals; limiting communication of change goals and tasks; damaging the change agent's credibility; or agreeing to change proposals but not doing anything to advance them[15] are also common in organisations.

Stakeholder analysis can be used to identify the various stakeholders or groups of stakeholders, and then consider who might resist change and why during the transition phase. Once potential areas of resistance have been identified, it is necessary to consider the appropriate tactics to overcome the resistance anticipated among the different stakeholders.[16] Tactics include education and com-

Figure 7.5   Resistance to change

Resistance may be due to:

- **Self-interest and politics**: issues to do with personal loss and cost of undertaking personal change, such as loss of turf, loss of status, loss of promotional prospects, separation from long-standing colleagues, or may be even a less convenient journey to work.

- **Psychological reasons**: issues such as fear of the unknown, fear of failure, concern about ability to develop needed skills, or a low ability to cope with change.

- **Emotional reasons**: may include lack of energy and motivation, denial of need for change, or demoralisation. Also uncertainty about impact of change on individuals, such as job security and earnings levels.

- **Change approach**: lack of participation, involvement and communication.

- **Recipient perceptions**: to do with lack of understanding about why change is needed and its implications. May include different assessments about what should be done and the likely outcomes of proposed changes. A lack of trust may result from previous change experiences in which promises were not kept.

- **Cultural bias**: entrenched ways of thinking, (selective perception), and 'we have always done it this way' attitudes and habits. Conflict between proposed changes and existing values and beliefs.

- **Historical organisational factors**: traditional relationships between managers and the unions and the workforce, or traditions of rivalry between functions or departments.

munication to overcome negative recipient perceptions, and emotional and psychological fears of change; participation and involvement to reduce resistance arising from the change approach and reduce concerns about the impact of change and the ability to cope; facilitation and support for those fearful of the impact of change; negotiation and agreement to help overcome self-interest-based resistance; manipulation and co-option; and implicit and explicit coercion.[17] Many of these tactics are similar to the range of change management styles discussed earlier in Chapter 2. The difference here is that the approach taken with one or two individuals to overcome their resistance may need to be different from the general approach taken with other employees.

A lack of readiness for change should not be confused with resistance. If people have been prepared for change, and understand what is expected of them, they are less likely to exhibit resistance. For the majority of staff, therefore, most effort in the early days of change should be devoted to strategies designed to create a readiness for change. However, there may be staff that may never be able to cope with the changes whatever assistance they get. Furthermore, much resistance will not be overt. Some staff will hide their resistance and instead this resistance will manifest itself later in the change process by foot dragging, or poor performance or productivity from the staff concerned. Therefore, some resistance will have to be tackled as and when it is encountered. Those that continue to resist change well into the move phase may be the staff the organisation should choose to let

Illustration 7.2

Survivor syndrome

Survivor syndrome describes the individual reactions to changes happening within organisations, often as a consequence of downsizing, reorganisation and restructuring. The emotional responses of survivors are not unlike those experiencing redundancy, and can range from shock, anger, and anxiety to animosity towards management. Survivors are often concerned and guilty about their colleagues who have been made redundant, but also relieved that they still have a job. Survivors can also experience fear about their future security. The reactions and behaviours of survivors after change are not only potentially detrimental to the individual, but may have a detrimental impact on organisational performance and adverse effects on bottom line results.

Survivor syndrome is also characterised by a variety of behavioural outcomes:

Reaction or emotions	Behaviours
shock	decreased motivation
anger	decreased morale
scepticism	increased stress
guilt	increased work effort
fear	decreased work effort
insecurity	increased loyalty to peers
anxiety	focus on personal goals
excitement	career insecurity

These reactions are often precipitated by increased work pressure. Survivors may be expected to work harder, over longer hours, to fulfil the tasks of departed colleagues. Technological changes and business process re-engineering bring new working practices and different ways of working together. Job security often decreases after layoffs as employees may perceive the threat of additional cuts in the workforce. For many survivors this means a lack of clarity and mission which feeds insecurity and uncertainty about future prospects within the company. Survivors also face the dismay of losing the peers who have formed the social fabric of their work life and often experience a loss of direction in their own career or future with the company. This can result in decreased confidence and commitment, and a lack of trust and loyalty to the organisation, while for others these circumstances may provide an exciting opportunity to forge a new role.

The extent to which remaining employees exhibit the 'symptoms' of survivor syndrome is mediated by both organisational and individual variables. These include the rationale for redundancy espoused by the company, the individual's position and role in the organisation, their attitudes towards work, their self-esteem and personal coping mechanisms. The handling of redundancies is also an important factor. Survivors are concerned with the detail of the layoff procedure, for example how the notice was communicated, what decision rule was used to choose people for redundancy, whether good services were provided for those leaving – including severance pay, counselling and the continuation of benefits. Such factors influence the perceived fairness of the layoffs, the perceived threat of further redundancies and the ability to cope with change, which in turn determine how survivors react when colleagues leave.

Source: Written by Noeleen Doherty. Extracted from Doherty, N. (1997) 'Downsizing In Tysons Ltd', in S. Tyson (ed.) *The Practice of Human Resource Management,* London: Pitman Publishing.

go. It may even be that the persistent resistors are the ones selected for redundancy, since this also sends symbolic messages.

Survivor syndrome

Another issue affecting change recipients that has received far more recognition recently is that of survivor syndrome. Following a change process in which there has been a loss of jobs and a change in working circumstances, those staff left often struggle to cope. Their feelings can lead to lower morale and therefore stress and lower staff performance if this issue is not tackled and managed. Illustration 7.2 discusses survivor syndrome in more detail.

Organisational justice

A related stream of research referenced in Illustration 7.2, which picks up on the emotional aspects of change for recipients, is that on organisational *justice* or *fairness* during change. As organisations change, the extent to which employees perceive what happens during change in terms of, for example, who stays and who goes, who gets what job, how they are rewarded and appraised, as 'fair' and 'just' affects their emotional reactions to the change process and therefore their levels of commitment to and trust of their organisation.[18] There are three factors that affect employees:

- distributive justice: perceptions of the outcomes arrived at.
- procedural justice: perceptions of the processes used to deliver the outcomes.
- interactional justice: perceptions of the actions of the persons delivering the process.

A good example to illustrate these three aspects of justice and fairness is the process of downsizing and reallocation of work roles and responsibilities that accompany many change processes, such as that at mmO2 (see Chapter 5, section 5.8.4). Procedural justice would be about the processes used to decide who stays, who goes, and how roles are reallocated. Are the criteria used to determine who goes and stays transparent and consistently applied? Or is there evidence of bias in the process? Similarly for role reallocation, are the criteria clear with everyone given equal opportunity to apply for the roles they would like, and clear decision processes consistently applied? Is the information used when deciding between candidates accurate? Were personal preferences taken account of? Distributive justice would be about the outcomes achieved. Do the employees believe that what has happened to them is fair in comparison to what has happened to their other colleagues, for example? Finally, interactional justice is about how employees feel they were treated during the process by their line managers, or whoever was making the decisions. These three aspects will then lead into either more positive or negative reactions to the changes.

The overall message from work such as that on survivor syndrome and justice is that unless the human factor in change is recognised, and managed appropriately and sympathetically, the reactions of the employees, on whom the organisation ultimately depends for its performance, can nullify the effects of change, leading to poorer organisational results and profits than anticipated following change. Human process interventions, such as team-building activities to facilitate open communication and rebuild trust, morale and commitment; counselling and support to facilitate the personal change required; and stress management to manage work role conflict, feelings of job insecurity, and role and career confusion; can be critical. So can other interventions which facilitate communication and involve employees in the change process to provide more information to survivors about how the change process has been managed and their future role within the company.[19]

7.5 SUMMARY

This chapter completes the discussion of the design and management of the transition state. Its aim has been to explain how the nature of the transition state places particular demands on those leading change, which in turn has implications for change agency skills, and monitoring and measuring mechanisms. The overall process that a change agent is juggling during the transition looks something like that depicted in Figure 7.6.

Figure 7.6   **Putting it all together**

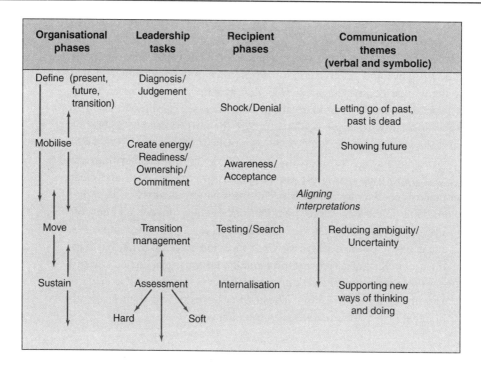

Leadership or change agency requires first of all a diagnosis of the change context and judgement about the best approach to take. Then based on the selected approach, it is necessary to manage both the organisational change path *and* the individual transitions that will ultimately underpin the organisational transformation. The complexity of this process is increased by the need to conduct many additional tasks in parallel with the transition design and management. These tasks include working at all times through various communication mechanisms to keep individual understanding of the need for change and the goals of change aligned with the overall vision.

REFERENCES

1. For a more comprehensive discussion of how to assess progress against change outcomes see Gratton, L., Hope Hailey, V., Stiles, P. and Truss, C. (1999) *Strategic Human Resource Management*, Oxford: Oxford University Press.

2. See Schaffer, R.H. and Thomson, H.A. (1992) 'Successful change programs begin with results', *Harvard Business Review*, 70 (1), pp. 80–9.

3. Sjoblam, L. (1998) BGBank: Creating a Performance Driven Culture, IMD.

4. For more information on the balanced scorecard see three *Harvard Business Review* articles by Kaplan, R.S. and Norton, D.P.: (1992) 'The balanced scorecard: Measures that drive performance', 70 (1), pp. 71–9; (1993) 'Putting the balanced scorecard to work', 71 (5), pp. 134–47; (1996) 'Using the balanced scorecard as a strategic management system', 74 (1), pp. 75–85. For further information on other business performance management techniques see Neely, A.D. (2002) *Measuring Business Performance: Why, What, How*, 2nd edn, London: Economist Books; Neely, A.D., Adams, C. and Kennerley, M. (2002) *The Performance Prism: The Scorecard for Measuring and Managing Business Success*, London: Financial Times/Prentice Hall; and Neely, A.D., Adams, C. and Crow, P. (2001) 'The performance prism in practice', *Measuring Business Excellence*, 5 (2), pp. 6–11.

5. For more information on project management techniques see Reiss, G. (1992) *Project Management Demystified*, London: E&FN Spon, or Turner, R.J. (1993) *The Handbook of Project Based Management*, London: McGraw-Hill.

6. See Harris, L.C. and Ogbonna, E. (2002) 'The unintended consequences of culture interventions: A study of unexpected outcomes', *British Journal of Management*, 13 (1), pp. 31–49.

7. Allman, L. (2002) 'Coors for concern', *Internal Communication*, 77, July/August, pp. 7–9.

8. Some of the issues involved in transition management and putting together a transition management team are discussed by Duck, J.D. (1993) 'Managing change: The art of balancing', *Harvard Business Review*, 71 (6), pp. 109–18.

9. See Buchanan, D. and Boddy, D. (1992) *The Expertise of the Change Agent: Public Performance and Backstage Activity*, London: Prentice Hall.

10. See, for example, Guth, W.D. and MacMillan, I.C. (1986) 'Strategy implementation versus middle management self-interest', *Strategic Management Journal*, 7 (4), pp. 313–27.

11. Fenton-O'Creevy, M. (2001) 'Employee involvement and the middle manager: Saboteur or scapegoat?' *Human Resource Management Journal*, 11 (1), pp. 24–40.

12. The various roles that middle managers can play in change and the implications of this for the middle manager skill set and job roles are discussed briefly in Floyd, S.W. and Wooldridge, B. (1994) 'Dinosaurs or dynamos? Recognizing middle management's strategic role', *Academy of Management Executive*, 8 (4), pp. 47–57. For more detail see Floyd, S.W. and Wooldridge, B. (1986) *The Strategic Middle Manager: How to Create and Sustain Competitive Advantage*, San Francisco: Jossey-Bass.

13. For a description of the three change roles of strategist, implementor and recipient see Kanter, R.M., Stein, B.A. and Jick, T. (1992) *The Challenge of Organizational Change*, New York: The Free Press.

14. For one categorisation of reasons individuals are likely to resist change, and the categorisation of tactics for overcoming resistance used here, see Kotter, J.P. and Schlesinger, L.A. (1979) 'Choosing strategies for change', *Harvard Business Review*, 57 (2), pp. 106–14.

15. See reference 9 above.

16. A simple technique for helping to clarify what resistance management strategies to deploy for which stakeholders is to use the concept of a commitment chart. Beckhard, R. and Harris, R.T. (1987) *Organizational Transitions,* 2nd edn, Reading, MA.: Addison-Wesley.

17. See reference 14 above.

18. For a more extensive discussion on organisational justice and fairness see Gratton, L. and Zaleska, J. (2004) 'Justice and fairness', in Gratton, L., Hope Hailey, V., Stiles, P. and Truss, C. (eds) *Lessons from the Leading Edge*, Oxford: Oxford University Press.

19. There are a range of interventions that can be used to address survivor syndrome, by equipping survivors to cope with personal change, and providing the skills for future survival. See Buch, K. and Aldridge, J. (1990) 'Downsizing challenges and OD interventions: A matching strategy', *Journal of Managerial Psychology*, 5 (4), pp. 32–7.

WORK ASSIGNMENTS

7.1   Draw up a job description/personal specification for the recruitment and selection of a change agent for a major change project.

7.2   Using the Bayer case study, if you were Chris Tobin, what change outcomes would you have identified at the beginning of the change?

7.3   Identify the causes of resistance that may have existed at Lendco among bank staff in the mid-1990s and later in 2002.

7.4   Consider a situation when you have had to undertake change. Why did you feel the process was fair or unfair? How could it have been managed better?

8

Concluding comments

8.1 INTRODUCTION

This text argues that successful change is reliant on the development of a context-sensitive approach to change. A diagnostic framework, the change kaleidoscope, is presented. The kaleidoscope enables change agents to assess the change context in which they are operating, judge which are the key contextual features of this context, and therefore make appropriate design decisions to create a context-sensitive change approach. This chapter summarises the main arguments put forward by revisiting the change flow chart presented in Chapter 1. It also discusses the future challenges of change, with reference to more continuous models of change.

8.2 THE CHANGE FLOW CHART

Chapter 1 presents a change flow chart (see Figure 8.1) to explain the different stages in the development of a context-sensitive approach to change. As Chapter 1 explains, stages 1 to 2, analysing the competitive position, determining the type of change needed and identifying the desired future state, are discussed in detail in this book's sister text *Exploring Corporate Strategy* and are not discussed here. However, we do revisit the future state in Chapter 5 to reinforce the need for a vision, and the need to identify and remove barriers to change.

Stages 3 and 4, analysing the change context, identifying the critical contextual features and determining the appropriate design choices, form the first part of this book and use the change kaleidoscope. Chapter 2 examines the choices that a change agent must make when designing a change process. The choices include the *change path*, the *change start-point*, the *change style*, the *change target*, the range of *change levers* and the *change roles*. However, the key argument in Chapter 2 is that it is impossible to choose from this menu of choices without understanding the context of the organisation. The change context and how to assess it is therefore examined in detail in Chapters 3 and 4.

Chapters 3 and 4 examine the change context through the change kaleidoscope. The concept behind this model is that every organisational change is

Figure 8.1   **The change flow chart**

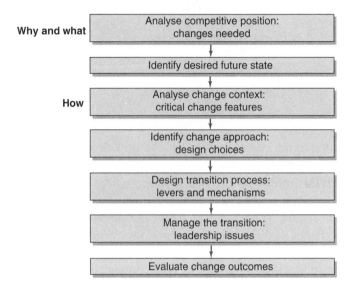

unique. Therefore, in each change situation the configuration of contextual features will also be unique, like an individual's fingerprints. However, there are questions which can be asked about any change context which remain constant. These questions include the amount of *time* available for change, the *scope* of the change required, the degree of *diversity* within the organisation, the staff's *readiness* for change, the change *capability* and *capacity* to undertake change within the organisation, the *power* relations and what needs to be *preserved* within the organisation. Chapter 3 explores each of these contextual features in detail, and examines the implications for the design choices of each feature. Chapter 4 puts the change kaleidoscope into practice. Three case studies of companies undergoing different forms of change are analysed. This chapter also illustrates the criticality of different features in different change situations.

Chapters 5, 6 and 7 consider the design, implementation and management of the transition phase of change – the final stages in the change flow chart. Too often change management stops after the design choices have been made or, worse still, at the point of strategy development. These three chapters reveal the complexity of change management in action. They illustrate to the reader the different stages of transition, and the relationship between organisational transitions and the personal transitions of individuals. They also describe the different levers and interventions that can be used to support each stage of transition, and suggest methods of evaluating change through outcome measures.

8.3 THE COMPLEXITY OF CHANGE

This book has sought to both reveal and address the complexity of change. Some texts either ignore the complexity of the process or reduce its management to ten-step plans. This has not been the purpose of the book. Equally impractical are the texts that reveal the complexity of change management through clever analysis, without seeking to help the practitioner or student through that analytical maze. This book has tried to honour the idea of management as both an intellectual and an analytical pursuit, but simultaneously present it as an activity that is practical and requires action.

The models presented in the book therefore seek to provide universally applicable questions not answers. They ask questions about the features of change contexts that, if ignored by change agents, may become barriers to change in the longer term. Readers may like to see the models as mapping devices which help to hone their judgement in change situations. They are not predictive. They cannot take the place of judgement – but they do seek to inform that judgement. Furthermore, the models have their limitations. They are not dynamic and organisations may need to use them in an iterative way. In addition, they can only capture the complexity of change if the reader grasps the way the contextual features of any change situation interconnect, and the uniqueness of these interconnections within each new change scenario.

8.4 THE FUTURE CHALLENGE OF CHANGE

The complexity of change has been heightened in recent years by a growing number of books and articles that have raised questions about what organisations will be like and how they might be managed as we move through the twenty-first century. Some have proposed radically different approaches to managing: so we should ask if entirely different approaches to managing change might be required.

8.4.1 The future change context

This book has argued that it is very important to take the context of change seriously, how change might be managed in one *context* will and should differ from another context. This is a fundamental lesson if the future challenge of change is to be met.

The idea of stability in terms of competition is beginning to break down. Some have argued that the twenty-first century will give rise to hypercompetition.[1] The search for stable bases of competitive advantage will disappear; and these will be replaced by much more rapid changes in strategy, requiring much more flexible and innovative organisations. So the *time* available to deliver change diminishes as the pace of change increases. Organisations are also becoming more and more complex. The sheer size of global organisations, let alone the increasing move to network organisations, joint ventures, e-businesses and so on, means that there is an increasing dispersion of organisational members widely and, hand in hand with this, increasing *diversity*. To take an example, there are an increasing number of organisations with people working remotely, linked electronically, perhaps meeting occasionally, certainly communicating horizontally rather than hierarchically; and some are doing this on a global scale.

If we just take these two dimensions of context, *time* and *diversity,* some other significant implications arise. It is not conceivable that such rapidity of change can always be masterminded from the top. The *power* dimensions of change shift as does the locus of the *capacity* for change. It is people lower down who are in direct contact with the markets as they are changing; and we know that innovation in organisations often bubbles up from there too.[2] There may need to be a move away from a reliance on the centre to a reliance on the empowerment and activities of those lower down in the organisation. The wellbeing of organisations may come to depend increasingly on the potential dynamism and *readiness* to change from below.

In short, the change context of the organisation of the future may well be different. What then does this say for the management of strategic change? What are the lessons?

8.4.2 Enabling continuous change

In this book's sister text, *Exploring Corporate Strategy*, Johnson and Scholes use three 'lenses' as ways of viewing the subject of strategy. They use the 'design lens', which sees strategic management as a matter of analysis and planning; and the 'experience lens' which, by focusing our attention on the influence of organisational culture and people's experience, helps to explain the sort of inertia that has to be overcome in managing change. However, as managers face the challenges of the twenty-first century the third lens, the 'ideas lens', is also useful, because some of the issues it raises are especially relevant to the new competitive context.

The 'ideas lens' sees strategy as 'the emergence of order and innovation from the variety and diversity which exist in and around organisations'.[3] Here, the emphasis is that organisations consist of very many different people with different ideas, views and propensities; and that this diversity and variety has the *potential* to create newness and therefore change of itself. Change bubbles up from within the organisation, rather than being conceived by the senior managers. It is a similar sort of argument to that made by other authors; that change is a natural phenomenon because all of us, whether in organisations or not, have to continually adapt to the environment we are facing. We have a natural propensity for change. Taking this view, arguably, it may be that traditional forms of organisation and management are, themselves, impediments to change in so far as they embody and preserve hierarchy, order, tight specification of roles and so on. The ideas lens suggests that it may be more important for managers to identify patterns of emerging change than to rely on planned change from the top. This has a number of implications.

The first is that managers need to see themselves as the managers of context in which such changes can occur. For example, rather than trying to define and control the detail of future strategy, this places an emphasis on establishing an overall clarity of vision and then setting the few 'simple rules'[4] required to establish a context and sufficient control through which an organisation can be flexible and adaptive. More rules create inertia; too few (or the wrong ones) can create chaos. So the second task of the manager trying to manage change through diversity is to establish which rules matter most and what their effect would be. Of course this may have to occur through trial and error since it is highly unlikely that it can be predicted upfront. This holds some risks.

Indeed the likelihood is that there will be problems. Hand in hand with the notion of diversity breeding newness, is also that diversity can breed inefficiency, failures, rivalries and so on. The natural tendency in organisations, if such diversity is given reign, is *both* newness and problems. Managers will therefore need to be more tolerant of such inefficiencies and able to manage their way round them.

Managing change in such an organisational context is not about managing one-off big changes in strategy, but more about managing continuous change. There has long been a discussion about the idea of a 'learning organisation', one that is capable of continual regeneration from the variety of knowledge, experience and skills of individuals through a culture which encourages mutual questioning and challenge around a shared purpose or vision. In effect this is what this approach calls for. The idea that the organisation and managers within it need to become more like jazz musicians is another way of looking at this. For jazz musicians playing together, there are central themes, maybe represented by an overall vision and some simple rules, but there is improvisation around those and latitude for such improvisations to emerge from within the orchestra and in the playing. The skill becomes the ability to hang on to the central themes, elaborate them, and continually develop them. No one performance is the same as another; newness becomes the theme. However, should several of the fundamental organisational values or 'rules' that everyone knows and plays by need to change simultaneously for any reason, then there could still be the need for a one-off strategic shift.

8.4.3 The role of design in continuous change

This raises the question of whether such a view is compatible with the design of change and the sort of design choices discussed in this book. If the central theme in *Exploring Strategic Change* is that the management of change needs to take into account the context of change, the additional theme that emerges from the discussion here is that change managers of the future may have to see as necessary the creation and management of an organisational context that will encourage and facilitate continuous change. However, the key issue is still to match the design of change to the context. It may be that the competitive environment of some organisations will not evolve into a context that requires emergent and on-going change, or that the organisational changes required are still best delivered as a series of planned change initiatives.

In organisations where the nature of competition is shifting, requiring more rapid and frequent change, managers of today will need to think about how they might move their organisations to, or at least towards, a future state that facilitates continuous change from within the organisation. Here, the same sort of design choices explained in this book have to be addressed. If the desired *change path* is to be one of continual evolution through the establishment of a 'learning organisation', how will it be achieved?

The *change style* may need to be one of participation or collaboration to gain the benefits of diversity. The *change target* is to release the potential of that diversity throughout the organisation. Different organisations may achieve this through targeting behaviours or values, depending on their analysis of their contextual features. It is probably unrealistic to expect the organisation as a whole to move to such a different way of operating at once; so the *start-point* for such change may need to be pockets of good practice or pilot sites, which can help others to see the benefits of such an approach. The feasibility of these choices will be affected by features of context, such as readiness and capability for change. It also becomes critical that top management recognise the *change role* they play, although other options, such as the use of external consultants and change action teams, can still be considered. There will need to be sufficient clarity of direction from senior managers to achieve necessary coherence, but they will also need to achieve a delicate balance between sufficient control and the facilitation of emergent change. As a result, they will need to pay particular attention to the *change levers* they use to create the context for continual change and to maintain it. However, the precise levers and interventions used will vary from organisation to organisation, as each organisation will have a different starting point and existing culture, with different barriers to overcome. The levers will also need to match the selected change target.

For organisations that need to undergo continuous change, the same questions raised in this book need to be posed. However, the answers to them may be different from those managers may have arrived at in the past.

8.5 IN SUMMARY: CHANGE AGENCY IN THE TWENTY-FIRST CENTURY

The ability to manage change is fast becoming a mainstream competence for managers. It is no longer an optional extra in the managerial toolkit. This is driven by the pace and nature of organisational change, rather than any fashion pushed by business schools or consultancies. The pace and nature of change is also determining the composition of change competence. Change is so rapid and so constant that it is rendering obsolete universalistic formulae to many management problems. As stressed above, best questions become the key tool rather than best practice.

REFERENCES

1. See D'Aveni, R. (with Gunther, R.) (1995) *Hypercompetitive Rivalries*, New York: Free Press.
2. See Johnson, G. and Huff, A. (1997) 'Everyday innovation/everyday strategy', in Hamel, G., Prahalad, C.K., Thomas, H. and O'Neill, D. (eds), *Strategic Flexibility*, Chichester: Wiley; Nonaka, I. and Takeuchi, H. (1995) *The Knowledge Creating Company*, Oxford: Oxford University Press.
3. Johnson, G. and Scholes, K. (2002) *Exploring Corporate Strategy*, 6th edn, Harlow: Financial Times Prentice Hall, p. 50.
4. For a discussion of simple rules see Brown, S.L. and Eisenhardt, K.M. (1998) *Competing on the Edge*, Harvard, MA: Harvard Business School Press.

Clerical Medical: change in the life insurance sector

Gillian Camm • Julia Balogun • Nardine Collier • Veronica Hope Hailey

This case describes the transformation undertaken by Clerical Medical. It can be used to help students and other readers of the book develop a more complete understanding of the issues involved in designing the transition process. Assignment questions are at the end of the case.

Clerical Medical Investment Group (CMIG) is part of the HBOS Group (Halifax Bank of Scotland), and competes in the life insurance sector.[1] Historically, its customers have been professionals, such as lawyers, but the customer base has broadened as the structure of people's careers have changed leading to, for example, more self-employment. The company distributes its products to customers through independent financial advisers (IFAs) rather than selling directly to the public.

This case examines the change process undertaken at CMIG between 1995, when under the direction of a new Chief Executive, Robert Walther, the need for strategic transformation was identified, and 2000. In 1995, there were concerns about the future financial strength of CMIG, the level of sales and the cost base. In 1999 new business reached £325 million, a rise of 36 per cent over the year, profits increased by 20 per cent to £120.5 million, UK retail sales grew by over 30 per cent and international sales by 49 per cent. In the same year, Clerical Medical also received a 5-star award in both the life and pensions and investment categories in the Financial Adviser Survey.[2]

---

1. Life insurance is a general term to describe a variety of personal protection policies, whose main purpose is to pay a sum of money either on death or after a set period.
2. A survey which benchmarks customer service throughout the financial advice industry.

This case was prepared by Gillian Camm, Business Transformation Director of Clerical Medical from 1995 to 2001, and Julia Balogun, Nardine Collier and Veronica Hope Hailey of Cranfield School of Management. It is intended as a basis for class discussion and not as an illustration of either good or bad management practice.

There were three phases of change at CMIG – re-focusing and demutualisation, which included acquisition by the Halifax in 1996, business transformation, and exploitation of core competences. This case study briefly describes these phases, and focuses on the Customer Relationship Management (CRM) initiative. This initiative was part of the business transformation and played a significant role in the revival of CMIG's fortunes. The case looks at the progress of this initiative by mid-2000, and summarises CMIG's position in 2002.

THE PACE OF CHANGE IN THE LIFE INSURANCE INDUSTRY

Until the mid-1980s the life insurance industry was dominated by mutual[3] life offices. In turn, the organisations themselves were dominated by actuaries.[4] Sales to customers, the general public, were conducted through independent financial brokers. Two direct sales life insurance offices were established in the 1970s – Abbey Life and Allied Dunbar. Such companies challenged the histories and traditions of the industry but were not substantial in size. The Financial Services Act 1986 introduced industry deregulation and changed the nature of competition. Technology de-skilled many of the administrative jobs, raising questions about the need for an educated and qualified workforce to carry out what were now routine tasks.

The pace of change for the life insurance industry increased further in the 1990s. New competitors such as Virgin, Direct Line and Sainsbury came into the market, and there were many mergers as the industry entered a phase of consolidation. Competitors sought to build advantage through economies of scale. The government also imposed tighter regulation, pushing for transparent and lower charges. At the same time, working patterns and customer needs were changing. Fewer people work in traditional full-time roles, and therefore there are fewer people receiving large corporate benefits. This has led to less certainty in employment and income, and therefore a greater demand for financial advice.

THE START OF CHANGE AT CLERICAL MEDICAL

In 1995, Clerical Medical was a medium-sized mutual. Consistent with the historical approach of the industry, there were few business measures in place. Profitability, for example, received little attention. Three members of the top team were over 60, and they all had been with Clerical Medical for many years.

---

3. A building society or insurance company is termed a 'mutual' when it is owned by its policyholders. By taking out a policy or contract with one of these organisations the holder not only obtains insurance coverage but also, often without knowing it, becomes an 'owner' of the company. The policyholders then have some or all of its profits divided between them.

4. The directors of most life companies were actuaries by training.

The old Clerical Medical head office was representative of the history and traditions of the company, with stained-glass windows, gilt ceilings and classic paintings. The Clerical Medical advertisements also exemplified tradition, showing clerics and lawyers. An opinion survey at this time revealed that only 14 per cent of staff believed Clerical Medical had a strategy. The survey also revealed uncertainty among staff about the future of the company.

There were three issues that created a burning platform for change. The first was financial strength. Life companies must have sufficient financial strength to cover all of their obligations going forward. Clerical Medical had reasonable financial strength but it was apparent that it was going to come under increasing pressure. The second area was focus. Clerical Medical had branched out into direct sales to the public, and had expanded internationally operating in over one hundred countries. It was not known to what extent these operations were profitable. The third aspect was just performance – *sales were not strong and costs were thought to be high*.

(Senior Manager)

THE NEW STRATEGY: DEMUTUALISATION[5]

Following the appointment of a new Chief Executive, Robert Walther, a new top team was appointed. The new team first tried to establish the business situation of CMIG through a report produced for them by the Boston Consulting Group on potential areas of profitability within the company. The strategic reviews that followed from this report led to a number of critical decisions – first, to demutualise (Clerical Medical were one of the first mutuals to do this), second, in markets outside of the UK, to focus on Europe and exit from less profitable and less strategic markets in the rest of the world; and third, to sell the high net worth direct sales force to create a clear focus for the business. Across the core business overheads also needed to come down by 25 per cent.

The IFA sales force and customer services were restructured to focus on related groups of IFAs. Customer service had been organised around products, such as group pensions, individual pensions and life, even though one IFA might need to deal with all of those groups individually. In 1996, a level of the sales force hierarchy was removed and many of the branches closed. The redundancies in the sales force were painful as many long-serving older employees left the organisation. '*We put an awful lot of effort into actually making sure when people left they were well supported financially and that that process was handled with as*

---

5. Until recently most insurance companies and building societies were mutual societies owned by and run for the benefit of their members, with no shareholders taking profits. Fundamental changes in financial markets, such as deregulation, in the late 1980s and 1990s have led many societies to change from mutual status to gain the benefits of fewer restrictions and better access to financial markets. The process is called demutualisation. Demutualisation converts ownership structure from a mutual insurance company into a share capital insurance company.

Figure 1   Transformation vision

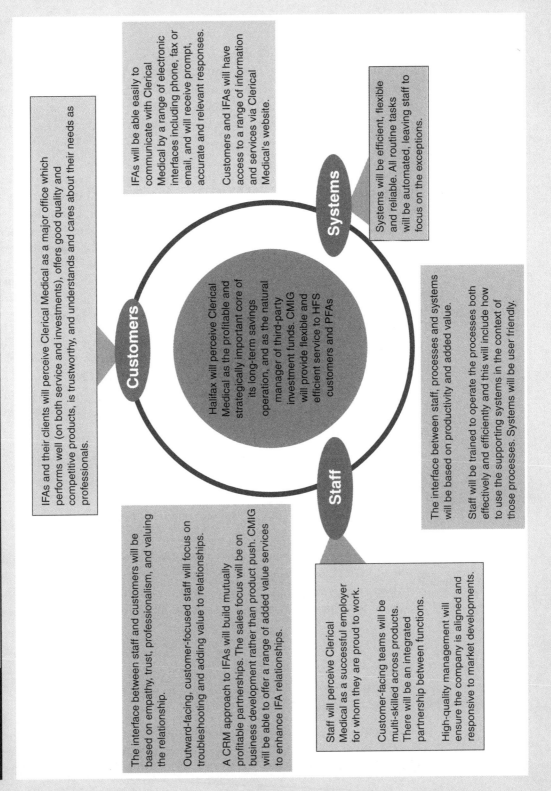

IFAs and their clients will perceive Clerical Medical as a major office which performs well (on both service and investments), offers good quality and competitive products, is trustworthy, and understands and cares about their needs as professionals.

IFAs will be able easily to communicate with Clerical Medical by a range of electronic interfaces including phone, fax or email, and will receive prompt, accurate and relevant responses.

Customers and IFAs will have access to a range of information and services via Clerical Medical's website.

Customers

Systems

Systems will be efficient, flexible and reliable. All routine tasks will be automated, leaving staff to focus on the exceptions.

Halifax will perceive Clerical Medical as the profitable and strategically important core of its long-term savings operation, and as the natural manager of third-party investment funds. CMIG will provide flexible and efficient service to HFS customers and PFAs

The interface between staff, processes and systems will be based on productivity and added value.

Staff will be trained to operate the processes both effectively and efficiently and this will include how to use the supporting systems in the context of those processes. Systems will be user friendly.

Staff

The interface between staff and customers will be based on empathy, trust, professionalism, and valuing the relationship.

Outward-facing, customer-focused staff will focus on troubleshooting and adding value to relationships.

A CRM approach to IFAs will build mutually profitable partnerships. The sales focus will be on business development rather than product push. CMIG will be able to offer a range of added value services to enhance IFA relationships.

Staff will perceive Clerical Medical as a successful employer for whom they are proud to work.

Customer-facing teams will be multi-skilled across products. There will be an integrated partnership between functions.

High-quality management will ensure the company is aligned and responsive to market developments.

much dignity as we could' (Senior Manager). An overhead reduction programme was also put in place.

At the same time, Clerical Medical sought to demutualise and put itself up for sale through a controlled auction. CMIG were acquired by Halifax. The acquisition enabled the retention of the Clerical Medical brand and relative independence of Clerical Medical as a company. In addition, no redundancies were required. The two company cultures were also complementary since Halifax at this time was still a mutual.

BUSINESS TRANSFORMATION

Following a strong first year after the acquisition, CMIG was allowed to retain a significant proportion of the profits to reinvest in business transformation in 1998. A vision was developed for the business (see Figure 1) reflecting the requirements/expectations of customers, staff and systems and the linkages between them. It was recognised that behaviour was likely to be key to the changes, and that change was going to be delivered through people:

> *We needed to take Clerical Medical from A to B and that was about changing Clerical Medical, but we also needed to make sure that we improved our ability to change. We actually needed to change the way we went about changing, because we weren't necessarily the most agile organisation.*
>
> (Senior Manager)

The objectives of the transformation were:

1 *Efficiency* – to reduce unit costs significantly by 2003 in real terms.
2 *Relationships with IFAs* – to shift the sales model from product-push to working in a relationship with the great majority of IFAs.
3 *Customer service* – to improve service standards to a position which is in line with a top-five IFA provider.
4 *IFA market rank* – to achieve a sustainable position as one of the top-five offices in the IFA market.
5 *Top class investment house* – to be perceived as a top-class investment house and be recognised as the Halifax Group's provider of external investment management.
6 *Change capability* – for the management of change to become a point of competitive advantage for Clerical Medical Investment Group.
7 *Communication and involvement* – to have staff and management motivated to make changes work.

A lot of time was spent linking programmes of change to the strategy and the vision of the organisation. The business transformation programme was a series of major change programmes – customer relationship management, operational

| Figure 2 | Structuring the business transformation programme |

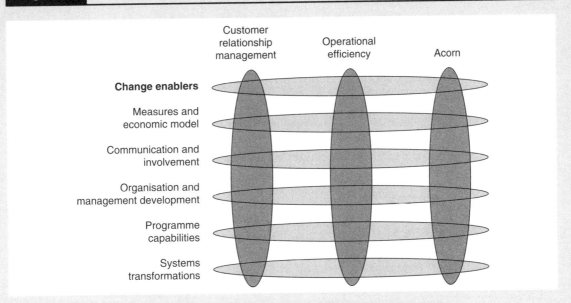

efficiency and a transformation programme (ACORN) for the fund management operation. (See Figure 2.) These programmes were to be delivered through a series of change strategies such as communication and involvement, and organisation and management development.

Extensive communication supported the business transformation programme. CMIG was able to make use of 'Halifax television', the internal Halifax communication system. The business transformation team created Clerical Medical television, and handed it over to the employees, 'we gave them a camcorder and said, you go out, make the programme, tell us how it feels'. There was also a Connect programme, a communication strategy based around five business themes, which were revisited frequently. However, the main emphasis was on employee involvement, so if people felt good about changes in a given area, they could share it.

CUSTOMER RELATIONSHIP MANAGEMENT

Customer Relationship Management (CRM) was the key business transformation programme for the core business. The intent was to build long-term, mutually beneficial, relationships with targeted IFAs, those identified as having the most potential for a profitable relationship, so that CMIG could grow its business by helping the IFAs to grow theirs. Subsequently, new systems would be developed for working with other IFAs. The programme had impact in four areas:

- A new style of operation for the sales force: a shift from product-push to relationship management.

- A new contact approach: a reduction in the points of contact with the organisation for IFAs.

- Value-added services for IFAs: different customers have different needs. Clerical Medical aimed to meet these differing needs through proactively offering value-added services to IFAs such as marketing consultancy, for example.

- Targets and tracking: to develop measurement and monitoring mechanisms to track the successful development of relationships with IFAs.

The aim was to shift the sales force from an internal to an external focus, providing value-added services to IFAs rather than just pushing products, and to break down the functional thinking (sales versus administration) to create linked sales / administration teams providing support to particular IFAs.

Essentially what we were trying to do was to shift our sales force to working with our customers and trying to develop our business and their business in partnership. It meant that the sales people couldn't deliver on their own. They needed to work with the IT department, who then worked with the customer's IT function. They needed to work with customer service and Clerical Medical needed to actually unite everybody around our customers which for an organisation which had worked very much in functional silos was a big issue.
(Senior Manager)

CRM emerged out of discussion within the sales and marketing planning group in May 1997:

We as an organisation, like any other organisation in our market place, were product pushers. We went out to IFAs and said 'use our widget because it's better than someone else's widget because it's got three yellow dots on it.' Looking forward then, with government intervention in our business, we saw reduced margins, then products were starting to become simpler, so the ability to differentiate around products would become more and more difficult.
(Senior Manager)

Clerical Medical was convinced that it had to 'differentiate in a way that was difficult to copy' rather than merely grow based on price. The vision of the CRM initiative itself was simple and clear – to be in the top five of IFA providers. CMIG also identified that some (although not all) of its customers were small to medium-sized IFAs who might welcome the opportunity to grow their business using help from CMIG. The approach taken was to:

1 undertake in-depth market research with IFAs to understand what they wanted from CMIG

2 pull together a task force

3 launch a pilot programme and

4 move to full programme implementation with a full-time project team.

CMIG worked out with IFAs their key business priorities, and then translated these priorities into the way CMIG's systems, processes and people operated. This involved working through the kinds of behavioural change wanted from everybody in the organisation and making that explicit. The pilot scheme in 1998 followed on very quickly from the customer research to create some energy for change. The objective of the pilot was:

> *... a Trojan horse. I wanted to do something that worked and if it worked I didn't have to go and sell it to the sales force that 'This is the way'. Because I was fundamentally telling these very successful guys that that's not the way you sell. I wanted success from the pilot and I wanted the people within the pilot to be the real advocates around the business ... and if it had failed abysmally then we would have killed the thing and moved onto something else ...* (Senior Manager)

The sales and marketing director with senior and middle management colleagues designed a vision of how they would do business in terms of value-added services. The pilot project team was set up and divided into work streams whose job it was to flesh out the vision in terms of the sales process, the customer service, the training needs, and the behavioural change needed. Four sales managers and four sales consultants from four different parts of the country were involved in the pilot, along with five selected IFA organisations in each of the four areas. Team members were chosen on the basis that they were influential within the business – they were either very cynical or very enthusiastic about the idea, but all were 'opinion formers in the sales force'.

The IFAs picked for the pilot as 'CRM IFAs' either had an appalling relationship with CMIG or a very good one, but all had the potential to produce a lot of business. The pilot tried and tested various initiatives with these IFAs over a period of about 9–12 months.

The CRM vision was initially focused on the sales force rather than the rest of the organisation. However, a pilot team was also put into the customer service division to support the aim of creating linked sales/administration teams as part of CRM.

> *So once they've been selected and approached and we've started to build a relationship, the account exec is then becoming very proactive and phoning the IFA and saying 'I'm your representative in customer service, I know you've been dealing with Joe Bloggs our sales consultant, here's my name and telephone number. If there are any customer service queries please contact me' and then we follow it up in a letter.* (Middle Manager)

In addition, the sales division took initiatives such as arranging for head office customer service staff to visit IFA offices to meet the people they were dealing with and put faces to names.

Once the pilot was run, then the programme was rolled out across the whole sales force, and the formal CRM programme was brought in. The formalisation was necessary because of the systems implications, and the behavioural issues across the whole organisation, not just the sales force. For instance, the bonus scheme needed to be aligned, the performance management system upgraded, and the contact systems had to be redesigned. The systems overhaul was necessary because not only did CMIG need to be segmented in order to deal with its policyholder base well, CMIG also wanted to eventually create IFA databases and profile these databases for them so that the IFAs could do more effective marketing. In addition, the telephony service was changed in the customer service area because they had to be able to deliver the personalised service they were marketing to the IFAs, *'we needed a red light to flash if it was Fred on the phone and a blue light to flash if it was Bertie....'*

However, by mid-2000, the changes were viewed as insufficient in terms of the business performance that CMIG was seeking to achieve. As one manager described it:

> *The targets I want to give them next year will be something like 33 per cent above the targets they have this year and I can't squeeze them that hard and so I am looking at how we can operate differently, and as a forerunner to the use of e-commerce, then that is to use the telephone. Some IFAs we deal with face to face, some we deal with over the telephone. What I'm doing is, I don't want to increase the size of the sales force, the people on the road, and salesmen are quite expensive to have on the road, I want to increase the footprint of the sales force....* (Middle Manager)

One important factor in the implementation of CRM was the absolute commitment from all of the top management team. Interviews with staff in mid-2000 revealed a consistent picture of commitment from the top. It was commented that there wasn't a newsletter, or a meeting with managers, where CRM wasn't talked about and given priority:

> *There's a continued momentum with it ... there's a continued pilot scheme, just what lands on your desk, magazines, badges, CRM, commentary about changes within CRM, the way it's going, the success stories. It just gives it that feeling of it's here to stay and it's working.* (Sales Consultant)

REACTIONS TO THE CHANGES

All levels of staff agreed that one very positive outcome from the CRM was the bringing together of the sales and marketing division and the customer service division. This was mirrored by the senior managers uniting together to present CRM as a business change, not just a sales initiative:

> *Previously Clerical Medical would have consisted of two organisations. One was the sales force whose task it was to sell targeted levels of business,*

and behind that was the other organisation who administered that busi-
ness and I think one of the things that has come out of this was there was
not much collusion between those two parts of the organisation ... from
a sales point of view they were not interested in administration and from
an administrative point of view they weren't really interested in how the
business was transacted. I think if CRM did anything it highlighted that
two parts of the organisation were not working from the same hymn
sheet. ...   (Middle Manager)

Customer reaction was also important – the customers loved it. However, a staff
opinion survey in 2000 showed that although 91 per cent of staff agreed that CRM
was the right way forward, only 50 per cent of people understood that CRM was
meant to change the way they did their job. A further piece of work, 'Bringing
CRM to Life', aimed to address that. The role of the individual was no longer to
push paper through the system and key in data, but to add value to the process.

Senior managers also felt that the majority of the focus in CRM had been on
measurement and structure, rather than understanding in detail the implications
for changing roles. One admitted to finding the changes threatening to himself at
a very personal level – would he be able to respond to the new demands of this
cross-functional working? Sales staff also identified the mindset change that CRM
required in both sales and customer services:

In the past it would have been a case of 'I'm going to see this organisation
and I'm going to talk to them about a "with-profit" bond whether they like
it or not because I've got a target to sell this and that's what I'm going to
go and do'. That was the old sales mentality but now it's a case of 'from a
previous discussion with the IFA I've discovered that he has a major prob-
lem regarding recruitment and retention of quality staff, how can I help
him?' and people are having to think a whole lot more before they go back
to people whereas in the past it would have been 'I'll just take this bundle
of literature on with profit bond and go and talk to him about it'.

Other change outcomes

One consequence of the recent change activity was that middle and lower levels of
staff perceived a different relationship between themselves and senior managers:

You could ask every employee of Clerical what the aims and objectives
are, what we're trying to achieve and a significant percentage could
answer that correctly. 5 years ago they wouldn't have had a clue.
                                                               (Middle Manager)

Those middle managers who were involved in the pilot project honestly felt
that they had communicated well with staff. However, front-line staff in customer
service saw things differently:

I mean a change for us . . . you can be completely unaware of the need for that change and you can come into work on Monday and be told that, you know, in 3 weeks' time a change is going to occur. Although sometimes, you can think things through yourself . . . but there is a lot of guesswork there. . . .

There was also a complaint from the head office staff, rather than the sales consultants, that there were inadequate resources to actually deploy the change. Staff felt that any resistance was not necessarily a reaction to the nature of the change itself but instead a reaction to trying to incorporate the changes at the same time as managing with reducing resources. There were also some sales consultants who had not incorporated the changes yet:

I personally think that there is a part of the sales force that will never change. 'This is the way I've always done business and that's the way I'm going to continue to do it irrespective of whether somebody tells me this new idea works or not'. And no amount of training or any initiatives is going to change them, that's just the way those people are.

(Sales Consultant)

Change interventions

Training

Concern was expressed about the move from pilot scheme into 'roll-out', and in particular about the design of training. Those who had been involved in the pilot scheme felt that the first cohort's experience of training had been far removed in content and style from the pilot scheme recommendations. The training was seen as too theoretical and '*a major disappointment within the sales force*'. Practical details about the services Clerical Medical could offer to IFAs were left to the end and rushed through with '*too much textbook stuff about customer relationship management*'. Sales consultants were left with few ideas as to what they could offer customers. The course was redesigned and the second cohort was more positive.

The performance management system

The system had been overhauled but was not seen as successful by all levels. Senior managers identified the problem as the use of the system by line managers rather than the design of the system itself. They said that line managers remained reluctant to differentiate between poor and good performers. The operating core appeared rather negative about the scheme. However, sales staff could see linkages from CRM to their performance:

Your CRM IFAs are clearly identified and your performance is gauged on how we are progressing the business with those CRM IFAs. There's what we call our value model which just takes a picture of what we did last year with them, what we're doing this year to progress the business and what is ultimately the projection of business towards the end of the year. Senior management have access to that and middle management.

(Middle Manager)

360-degree feedback was also introduced through the organisation. This feedback was part of the development process and separate to appraisal.

Communications strategy

A sophisticated internal communications strategy had been developed by the Head of Corporate Affairs who noted in its presentation that staff had felt they were 'drowning' in pieces of information. The aim of the strategy was to 'contribute to behavioural change' and help staff to become information seekers rather than receivers. In addition managers were to take on communication responsibilities as part of their leadership roles. Communication was to become two-way, and there would be an increase in sensory 'feel good' communication. In addition to the use of CMTV, communication initiatives included in-house magazines, team briefings processes, and the use of the intranet.

The company has also set great store by putting in several measurement tools that enable the change to be constantly evaluated. These range from traffic-light systems reporting changes within specific change programmes to more numerical indices. One senior manager commented that they had moved from measuring nothing to measuring everything!

In customer services, workshops were needed to translate the CRM vision into specifics for staff. Surveys revealed that managers felt they could not bring CRM alive for their teams and other staff felt that CRM would not change the way they did their jobs. The aim was to enable team leaders to define how they needed to change locally rather than imposing change.

Symbolic change

Senior staff who did not agree with the direction the company was taking were asked to go, but these departures were handled in a transparent and honest way that sent powerful messages to the staff:

It wasn't early retirement or anything like that, it was 'we do not agree with the way forward' and therefore he had to go and it was handled very simply like that. There was a view that they applied the rules to themselves and they don't beat around the bush and that would never have been dealt with in the past. The individual wouldn't have gone and if he had eventually gone he would have retired early. So that went down very well that there weren't different rules....　　　　(Senior Manager)

Senior managers also tried to walk the talk:

I still go out myself a lot to see IFAs and there was one case in point where I was out with a consultant in London who really didn't think that CRM would work for his IFAs because these guys were a very successful firm, what would they need us for? We went and had lunch with this guy and you know by the end of it the guy was saying you know more or less 'where do I sign?' and the consultant is going 'wow, you know, never thought he would be interested'. So we are trying to demonstrate, you know consistently through sales that this is the way we go about things.

POSTSCRIPT: CLERICAL MEDICAL AT THE START OF THE NEW MILLENNIUM

CRM led to big increases in income for CMIG, and at the same time the cost-reduction programmes led to a 50 per cent reduction in unit costs. It also led to substantial changes in the way business was done. Many of the staff had been with Clerical Medical a long time and had been used to a paternalistic, caring organisation that was also very tolerant. Now staff were being asked to produce more, be more flexible, be prepared to accept change. Some roles had been de-skilled through systems improvements and e-commerce would lead to more changes. There were many changes in the people processes to support this shift. It was not only the performance management process that needed to change, but also recruitment, selection, and staff development.

However, Clerical Medical was still a very much stand-alone business within Halifax, and next decided to exploit the opportunities within the Halifax Group. Identified core competencies included the long-term savings product development, long-term savings administration and fund and asset management. Halifax was also changing rapidly. They acquired J Rothschild and built an 'Intelligent Finance' proposition. Clerical Medical won contracts to provide product development and administration for those different parts of Halifax. CMIG also took over Halifax's whole external fund management, and acquired Equitable Life and their operating systems, customer service systems and the IT function, providing opportunities for savings through economies of scale.

Today Clerical Medical is in a new head office. The modern building of glass and steel is a very different building from the old head office. For example, when the move was made to the new office, as a break with the past, it was decided not to hang the portraits of all the former Chief Executives as in the old offices. Robert Walther is the first Chief Executive not to have a portrait. The vision for 2002 is for CMIG to become a billion-pound company. The top team are now in their 40s, and attitude surveys show 80 per cent of staff believe in the strategy. Robert Walther retired in 2001. The new CEO is the sales and marketing director. The company is enjoying strong business results. The strength of CMIG as a group is demonstrated in many ways. The new Chief Executive of Clerical Medical effectively now runs HBOS's life and pensions function, which supports a series of business brands, of which Clerical Medical is only one. CMIG provides an in-house servicing capability to all of those brands, and there are a series of corporate functions which are largely the old Clerical Medical corporate functions, which now support a much wider group.

ASSIGNMENT QUESTIONS

1 In 1995, at the start of the transformation process, what was the change context at Clerical Medical?

2 What were the design choices taken by the new Top Management Team and were they appropriate?

3 Map out the CMIG change process between 1995 and 2000 in terms of the Mobilise, Move and Sustain framework and the different interventions in the different four subsystems (technical, political, cultural and interpersonal).

4 What are the strengths and weaknesses of the change approach adopted? What has been achieved?

5 What recommendations would you make for mid-2000 to embed the CRM initiative and take business transformation forward?

The cultural web

A1.1 Introduction

The cultural web shown in Figure A1.1 provides organisations with a way of auditing their organisation's culture, and the barriers to change presented by the existing culture. All of this is discussed in some detail in *Exploring Corporate Strategy*, Chapters 2, 5 and 11, to which the reader should refer if they require a more detailed understanding of these issues. It is also possible to use the web to build an outline vision for a desired new organisation. This is referred to as re-webbing.[1] A comparison of the new and old webs gives managers a good feel for the extent of change to be undertaken.

The purpose of this appendix is to provide a reminder of the principles of the cultural web for those who have read *Exploring Corporate Strategy* and an introduction to the web for those who have not done so.

Figure A1.1 **The cultural web of an organisation**

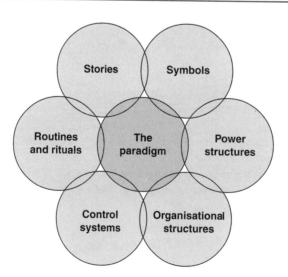

Source: Adapted from G. Johnson, 'Mapping and re-mapping organisational culture', in V. Ambrosini, G. Johnson and K. Scholes (eds) (1998) *Exploring Techniques of Analysis and Evaluation in Strategic Management*, Hemel Hempstead: Prentice Hall.

A1.2 A definition of culture

Culture is often defined as 'the way we do things around here'. However, this definition implies that the visible action and behaviour of an organisation's members *is* the organisation's culture. Behaviours are certainly part of culture, but not the only aspect of it. They represent the tip of the iceberg, the visible manifestation of culture. Beneath the day-to-day language, behaviour and actions of the members of an organisation lie a set of basic assumptions and beliefs that are driving the behaviour. Therefore, culture here is defined as 'the deeper level of basic assumptions and beliefs that are shared by members of an organisation, that operate unconsciously and define in a basic 'taken for granted' fashion an organisation's view of itself and its environment'.[2]

Figure A1.2 **Elements of the cultural web**

- The *paradigm* is the set of assumptions about an organisation which is held in common and taken for granted in the organisation.
- The *routine* ways that members of the organisation behave towards each other, and that link different parts of the organisation. These are the 'way we do things around here' which at their best lubricate the working of the organisation, and may provide a distinctive and beneficial organisational competency. However, they can also represent a taken-for-grantedness about how things should happen which is extremely difficult to change and highly protective or core assumptions in the paradigm.
- The *rituals* of organisational life, such as training programmes, promotion and assessment point to what is important in the organisation, reinforce 'the way we do things around here' and signal what is especially valued.
- The *stories* told by members of the organisation to each other, to outsiders, to new recruits and so on, embed the present in its organisational history and flag up important events and personalities, as well as mavericks who 'deviate from the norm'.
- Other *symbolic* aspects of organisations, such as logos, offices, cars and titles; or the type of language and terminology commonly used: these symbols become a short-hand representation of the nature of the organisation.
- The formalised *control systems*, measurements and reward systems that monitor and therefore emphasise what is important in the organisation, and focus attention and activity.
- *Power structures* are also likely to be associated with the key constructs of the paradigm. The most powerful managerial groupings in the organisation are likely to be the ones most associated with core assumptions and beliefs about what is important.
- In turn the formal *organisational structure*, or the more informal ways in which the organisations work are likely to reflect power structures and, again, delineate important relationships and emphasise what is important in the organisation.

Source: Adapted from G. Johnson, 'Mapping and re-mapping organisational culture', in V. Ambrosini, G. Johnson and K. Scholes (eds) (1998), *Exploring Techniques of Analysis and Evaluation in Strategic Management*, Hemel Hempstead: Prentice Hall.

A1.3　The cultural web

The cultural web reflects this cultural definition in the way it is constructed. The assumptions and beliefs are held in the paradigm, and are hedged around and connected to everyday visible behaviour by the other aspects of the web surrounding the paradigm, namely tangible aspects of the organisation such as structures and control systems, but also harder to define aspects such as formal and informal power structures, symbols, stories and myths, and routines and rituals. Figure A1.2 provides an explanation for all the elements of the web.

Figure A1.3 shows a completed web for Pentagram, the design partnership. The assumptions in the *paradigm* are to do with 'generosity' for all partners, which means respecting one another's work, sharing ideas and giving each other the financial freedom needed to do creative work. The organisation provides free-

---

Figure A1.3　A cultural web for Pentagram

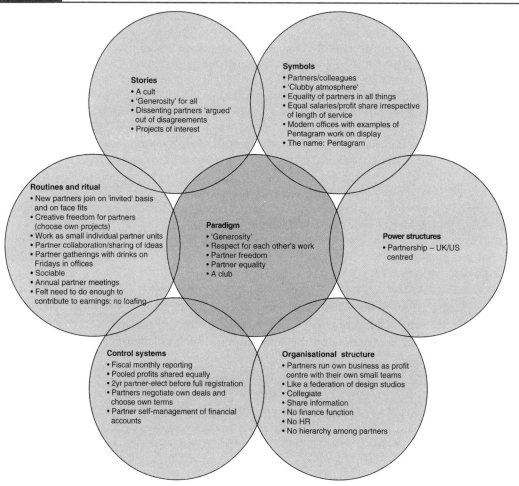

Source: Based on 'Equals to the task', *Financial Times*, 8 January 2002, Creative Business, pp. 8–9.

dom and equality for all partners – length of service affords no rights of seniority. There are no junior and senior partners. The organisation resembles a club in the way it operates more than a formal organisation. The other aspects of the web supporting the paradigm include:

- Many *routines* support the club-like nature of the partnership and the equality of all partners. New partners join on an invited basis only. Partners are allowed creative freedom – they can undertake jobs that offer little profitability, but are of interest to them. However, there is a felt need among all the partners to do enough to contribute to earnings, so that no loafing occurs. The organisation is generally sociable with, for example, partner drinks in the offices on Fridays, although there are few formal partner meetings.

- *Symbols* emphasise the equality in the partnership, such as equality in decision making (for example, choosing who can join as a new partner), the equal salary and profit share irrespective of time with the organisation, and the club-like nature of the organisation.

- The *structure* is a grouping of small partner-run profit centres, or studios, with no central support functions, and no partner hierarchy as would be found in traditional partnerships.

- *Control systems* are noticeable more for their absence. There is fiscal monthly reporting, but no performance management or appraisal systems, or bonus systems, as partners receive equal salaries and an equal share of the pooled profits irrespective of length of time with the organisation (see *Symbols*).

- The *power* resides with the partners.

- The key *stories* reflect the cult nature of the organisation, with even outsiders viewing them as a little like a cult, and the concept of generosity for all (see Figure A1.3).

A1.4 Completing a cultural web

When completing a cultural web, fill in the outside circles first. Remember to consider not just the formal structures, but also the informal structures and power networks. In particular concentrate on the softer aspects, such as language and ritual. Once the outside circles are complete, consider what these circles say about the organisation. Try to work out what the organisation cares about most. Customers? Costs? Staff? Consider how the organisation functions. Is it complacent, arrogant, entrepreneurial, bureaucratic, fast to respond, slow to respond and so on? Use these thoughts to complete the paradigm.

To complete a desired web for the future organisation, fill in the paradigm first, then think about what is needed in each of the outer circles to support this. For instance, it is no good putting 'market-led' into the paradigm if there is then nothing about customers or understanding markets in the outer circles.

A1.5   Conclusion

This appendix is intended only to provide a brief review of the key aspects of the cultural web. However, once the cultural web has been completed, it is possible to use it to address a number of questions. These include issues such as:

- To what extent does the existing culture support or hinder the desired changes that need to be made?

- To what extent does the existing culture need to be changed if the desired changes are to be implemented?

- To what extent does the existing culture underpin existing organisational competencies that need to be retained?

The main text of this book builds on this list of questions. In Chapters 3 and 4, it discusses how to use the cultural web to help identify the scope of change to be undertaken, the degree to which existing aspects of the culture need to be preserved or destroyed, and the degree of cultural homogeneity across the organisation. In Chapters 5 and 6, the text discusses how to use the web to diagnose barriers to change, and how to use the new web to develop some of the levers and mechanisms that can be used to help deliver the needed changes.

References

1. For more information on webbing and re-webbing, also refer to Johnson, G. (1998) 'Mapping and re-mapping organisational culture', in Ambrosini, V., Johnson, G. and Scholes, K. (eds) *Exploring Techniques of Analysis and Evaluation in Strategic Management*, Harlow: Prentice Hall.
2. Edgar Schein gives this definition of culture in *Organisational Culture and Leadership,* San Francisco: Jossey-Bass, 1985, p. 6.

The people process model

A2.1 Introduction

The people process model[1] has been developed by Lynda Gratton and assesses the strength of strategic linkage between human resource management processes and business strategy. Therefore, since the model can assess the links between strategy and employee behaviour it is also useful for measuring *change capability*. If an organisation has a visible ability in narrowing the gap between what an intended business strategy wants to achieve and how employees direct their everyday behaviour, then strategic implementation is more likely to become a reality and not just a rhetoric. Correspondingly, if that strategic linkage is strong, then an organisation's capability in implementing strategic change processes will

Figure A2.1 **The people process model**

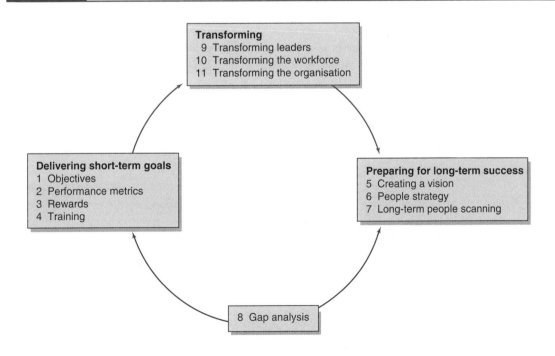

be greater than in companies where there is no apparent link between employee behaviour and business strategy.

A2.2 The people process model

The model works by grouping human resource management processes into three clusters: achieving *short-term business objectives*; assessing the *long term*; and embedding *transformational processes* (see Figure A2.1). The model argues that by being constantly attentive to both short- and long-term people management requirements, an organisation can:

- Assess what its human resource needs are for the future.
- Assess these needs against its current short-term abilities.
- Implement a series of transformational interventions to narrow the gap between future requirements and present capabilities.

The *transformation cluster* examines the activities of *leadership development*, *transformation of the workforce* and *organisational transformation*. These measures alone assess *change capability* within an organisation. However, a further indication of change capability is gained by assessing the extent to which these three change activities are also linked to the activities in the short-term and long-term clusters. If they are linked then the organisation is capable of constantly realigning employee behaviour on an incremental basis.

The cluster of human resource processes concerned with achieving *short-term business objectives* are standard activities within a performance management system. They include objectives, performance criteria or the measures against which performance is assessed, identification and delivery of training and development and determination of rewards. The key question that the model poses is the extent to which these activities are strongly aligned with business objectives. Can an individual link his or her individual performance objectives with the objectives of the organisation's overall business strategy? Do reward, training and development appear to reinforce behaviour that is consistent with business objectives? Are the measures used within the performance appraisal scheme reflective of business objectives?

The *long-term processes* are concerned with the creation of a long-term human resources strategy and the amount of external labour market scanning that is carried out. This cluster of activities are similar to the activity of scenario planning within general business strategy. This model asks how much equivalent scenario planning is carried out for people management issues.

The model also allows for organisations to be rated in each of these activities along a scale of 1–5, where 1 = low linkage and 5 = high linkage.

A2.3 Summary

This text uses the people process model to help assess the contextual feature of change capability within the change kaleidoscope. The purpose of this appendix has been to explain how to complete the model. Chapters 3 and 4 give more detail on how it can help organisations to assess change capability.

Reference

1. For more detail on the people process model see Gratton, L., Hope Hailey, V., Stiles, P. and Truss, C. (1999) *Strategic Human Resource Management*, Oxford: Oxford University Press.

Stakeholder analysis

3.1 Introduction

Stakeholder analysis is covered in detail in Chapter 5 of *Exploring Corporate Strategy*. The purpose of stakeholder analysis is to identify those key individuals or groups of individuals who have an interest in an organisation's performance and may be able to influence it in some way. As such, stakeholders include not only employees, managers, shareholders, and unions, but also bankers, customers, suppliers and, potentially, the wider community.

When undertaking change, it is important to understand how much power these different stakeholders have to either facilitate or hinder change and whether or not they view the proposed changes favourably. Those that have power and support change need to be encouraged to support and back the changes. Those who have power but do not view change favourably either need to be convinced of the wisdom of the changes or worked round in some way. In particular, any change agent needs to understand the relative position of the most powerful people in the organisation to the proposed changes, and how much power they have in comparison to the change agent, as the degree of support and opposition will affect the approach the change agent needs to take. This is discussed in some detail in Chapters 3 and 4. The purpose of this appendix is to explain how to conduct a stakeholder analysis.

A3.2 Stakeholder analysis

The technique presented in this chapter is the one proposed by Grundy,[1] which is an adaptation of Piercy.[2] It builds on the approach presented in *Exploring Corporate Strategy*. *Exploring Corporate Strategy* proposes the use of the power/interest matrix, in which the stakeholders are plotted on a grid in terms of their level of power to influence and their level of interest in the particular event or change under consideration. Here instead the matrix used is an influence/attitude matrix (see Figure A3.1). Stakeholders are plotted on the grid in terms of their attitude to the proposed changes, and the degree of influence they have on the organisation. The degree of influence involves both a stakeholder's level of power and their degree of interest in the organisation and what it does. For

| Figure A3.1 | Stakeholder analysis |

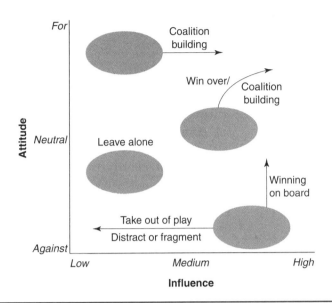

Source: Reprinted from *Journal of Project Management*, 16, 1, Tony Grundy, 'Strategy Implementation and Project Management', pp. 34–50, copyright (1998), with permission from Elsevier Science.

example, a stakeholder may be potentially powerful, but if he or she is also disinterested in the particular changes, then he or she will exercise a low influence. Just as with the power/interest matrix, once stakeholders are positioned on the matrix it is then possible to consider how to reposition them to gain the support needed for the proposed changes.

A3.3 Constructing a stakeholder analysis

Stakeholder analysis is best carried out by following a process. The steps in stakeholder analysis include the following:[1]

1 Identify the key stakeholders given the current stage of implementation. Internal stakeholders are often the most influential and important during change and should therefore be considered first. However, this is not always the case as some strategic changes can impact greatly on customers and therefore make shareholders nervous. The stakeholder identification also needs to be as broad as possible, encompassing not only those who have decision-making power, but also those who will be affected in some way by the changes.

2 Decide if the stakeholders have high, medium or low influence on the issue in question.

3 Decide if, at the time the assessment is being made, the stakeholders are for the proposed changes, against them, or neutral.

4 Position the stakeholders on the grid to assess the extent to which the change agent can exercise his or her power to direct change.

5 If the change agent cannot direct change, or directing change would be inappropriate for some reason, maybe because it would risk alienating key stakeholders, or possibly losing key members of staff, then it is necessary to consider a different change style and approach.

Various strategies can be considered for tackling obstructive stakeholders. As shown in Figure A3.1, obstructive stakeholders can be won over or removed from the game in some way. Obstructive stakeholders may be converted into supporters of the changes if they are involved in a more collaborative or participative change approach, and are able to contribute their ideas. Alternatively, it may be necessary to use more manipulative or coercive means on powerful and obstructive stakeholders. This may involve ensuring they do not lose out as a result of the changes in a way they fear they might. If the change agent has enough power, very antagonistic stakeholders could be allowed to leave the organisation, or moved to a position where they have less power to obstruct the changes.

A parallel approach may be to build the power and influence of those who do favour the changes. Those who are for the changes, but weak in power, can possibly be brought together into a coalition to make them more powerful. It may also be possible to use stakeholders who are in favour of the changes to win over those who are antagonistic.

A3.4 Conclusion

The main purpose of stakeholder analysis, as it is presented in this text, is to enable change agents to determine the relative position of key stakeholders to the proposed changes, and therefore how this affects the approach to change they need to take. The analysis can also be used to identify what barriers to change are presented by the stakeholders. It therefore provides a starting point to enable any change agent to develop a strategy for tackling those stakeholders who have the power to exert a negative influence on the change process.

REFERENCES

1. See Grundy, T. (1997) 'Accelerating strategy change: The internal stakeholder dimension', *Strategic Change*, 6, pp. 49–56.
2. See Piercy, N. (1989) 'Diagnosing and solving implementation problems in strategic planning', *Journal of General Management*, 15 (1).

Index